Anthony Asquith

MANCHESTER
1824

Manchester University Press

BRIAN MCFARLANE, NEIL SINYARD *series editors*

ALLEN EYLES, PHILIP FRENCH, SUE HARPER,
TIM PULLEINE, JEFFREY RICHARDS, TOM RYALL
series advisers

already published

Roy Ward Baker   GEOFF MAYER

Jack Clayton   NEIL SINYARD

Lance Comfort   BRIAN MCFARLANE

Terence Davies   WENDY EVERETT

Terence Fisher   PETER HUTCHINGS

Launder and Gilliat   BRUCE BABINGTON

Derek Jarman   ROWLAND WYMER

Joseph Losey   COLIN GARDNER

Carol Reed   PETER WILLIAM EVANS

Michael Reeves   BENJAMIN HALLIGAN

J. Lee Thompson   STEVE CHIBNALL

Anthony Asquith

TOM RYALL

Manchester University Press

MANCHESTER AND NEW YORK

distributed exclusively in the USA by Palgrave

Published by Manchester University Press
Oxford Road, Manchester M13 9NR, UK
and Room 400, 175 Fifth Avenue, New York, NY 10010, USA
www.manchesteruniversitypress.co.uk

Distributed exclusively in the USA by
Palgrave, 175 Fifth Avenue, New York NY 10010, USA

Distributed exclusively in Canada by
UBC Press, University of British Columbia, 2029 West Mall,
Vancouver, BC, Canada V6T 1Z2

British Library Cataloguing-in-Publication Data
A catalogue record for this book is available from the British Library

Library of Congress Cataloging-in-Publication Data
A catalog record for this book is available from the Library of Congress

ISBN 13: 978 0 7190 6453 1

First published by Manchester University Press 2005

First digital paperback edition published 2011

Printed by Lightning Source

Contents

Series editors' foreword

The aim of this series is to present in lively, authoritative volumes a guide to those film-makers who have made British cinema a rewarding but still under-researched branch of world cinema. The intention is to provide books which are up-to-date in terms of information and critical approach, but not bound to any one theoretical methodology. Though all books in the series will have certain elements in common – comprehensive filmographies, annotated bibliographies, appropriate illustration – the actual critical tools employed will be the responsibility of the individual authors.

Nevertheless, an important recurring element will be a concern for how the oeuvre of each film-maker does or does not fit certain critical and industrial contexts, as well as for the wider social contexts which helped to shape not just that particular film-maker but the course of British cinema at large.

Although the series is director-orientated, the editors believe that reference to a variety of stances and contexts is more likely to reconceptualise and reappraise the phenomenon of British cinema as a complex, shifting field of production. All the texts in the series will engage in detailed discussion of major works of the film-makers involved, but they all consider as well the importance of other key collaborators, of studio organisation, of audience reception, of recurring themes and structures: all those other aspects which go towards the construction of a national cinema.

The series explores and charts a field which is more than ripe for serious excavation. The acknowledged leaders of the field will be reappraised; just as important, though, will be the bringing to light of those who have not so far received any serious attention. They are all part of the very rich texture of British cinema, and it will be the work of this series to give them all their due.

Acknowledgements

I should like to thank Chas Critcher and the Film, Media and Communications Research Centre at Sheffield Hallam University, and Sylvia Harvey and the Humanities Research Board Centre for British Film and Television Studies for financing the periods of study leave during which this book was written. Thanks are also due to the British Academy for awarding me a research grant for travel. I would also like to thank my Film Studies colleagues at Sheffield Hallam University (Gerry Coubro, Catherine Constable, Sheldon Hall, Frank Krutnik, Angela Martin, Chi-Yun Shin, Suzanne Speidel) who tolerated my lengthy period of absence from the university. Thanks also to the library staff at Sheffield Hallam University and the British Film Institute (Reading Room and Special Collections), and the viewing staff at the National Film Archive; all were invariably courteous and helpful.

I am very grateful to Brian McFarlane who read the manuscript and made a number of helpful comments and suggestions. Thanks are also due to the editorial staff at Manchester University Press.

Thanks to Sheldon Hall, Paul Ryall, and David Williams who provided me with material on Asquith otherwise difficult to obtain, and to Paul Marris for drawing my attention to an article on *The V.I.P.s* in *Vanity Fair*. On a sadder note I would also like to thank the late Tessa Perkins who loaned me material relating to her father, John Pudney, who worked with Asquith on two films. Tessa died just before this book was finished and is greatly missed by friends and colleagues at Sheffield Hallam University. The final thanks are to Helen for everything.

The cover illustration is reproduced courtesy of the British Film Institute's Stills, Posters and Designs section. Every effort has been made to obtain permission to reproduce the illustration but if any proper acknowledgement has not been made, copyright holders are invited to contact the publisher.

Introduction

It is impossible to think of the history of British cinema without thinking
of Anthony Asquith. (Dilys Powell)[1]

Dilys Powell's acknowledgement of Asquith's significance to the British
cinema was written as part of a tribute to the director and published in
1968 by the British Film Institute shortly after his death. The tribute,
understandably effusive in the context of a commemorative publication,
has not quite been echoed by those who have written about the history
of British cinema in the years since Asquith's death in 1968. One film
historian has suggested that he is 'perhaps the most underrated director
in British film history';[2] yet it may be closer to the mark to suggest that
Asquith has not really received the critical attention that would enable a
rating of his work in terms of the British cinema as yet. Although not
ignored by scholars and critics, his work has certainly not had anything
like the attention enjoyed by his most distinguished contemporary,
Alfred Hitchcock, and neither has it had the consideration devoted to
figures such as Michael Powell and David Lean. The riposte to that, of
course, may be that his achievement is not as great as Hitchcock, Powell,
and others, and, indeed, with a handful of exceptions, his work has not
been highly regarded in the context of modern Film Studies. At best, his
films have inspired local admiration for specific titles as in Raymond
Durgnat's comment that Asquith's 'best films aren't vaporized by the
sternest comparison – with Ophuls'.[3] At worst he has been dismissed in
somewhat harsh terms as in David Thomson's caustic entry in his
biographical dictionary of cinema, where Asquith is characterised as 'a
dull journeyman supervisor of the transfer to the screen of proven
theatrical properties'.[4] In the context of critical neglect, one of the aims
of this study is simply to fill a gap, to provide an account of Asquith's
films – thirty-five features and a handful of shorter films – and to draw
attention to the varied body of work with which he is associated. The

study also aims to position the work in relation to the various directions taken by the British film during the period of his career. Asquith was a film director in the British cinema for almost forty years, serving his apprenticeship in the last years of the silent period and making his final film, *The Yellow Rolls-Royce* (1964), during the 'swinging sixties'. The remainder of this chapter is devoted to a career overview as a preparation for the subsequent more detailed attention to the various phases in his career.

Early years

Asquith entered the film industry in the mid-1920s, towards the end of the troubled silent period when the production industry in Britain was in decline in the face of competition from the American film. Hollywood dominated the British screen and its films were highly popular with the British public but the domestic industry struggled to find a position in the market and seemed to many on the brink of extinction. There was considerable pressure for government action to halt the decline and this resulted in the quota legislation of the late 1920s. The 1928 Cinematograph Films Act effectively laid the foundations for a British production industry by, amongst other provisions, requiring exhibitors to screen a number of British films as part of their annual schedules. Asquith's early films were made during a period of optimism generated by the quota arrangements; new companies were starting up, new studios were being built, and British films had an assured place on the nation's cinema screens. It was also a period marked by 'a lively engagement with issues of film criticism and aesthetics'.[5] This engagement was stimulated in part by the new adventurous films from Germany, France, the Scandinavian countries, and the Soviet Union, and it formed the basis for the development of a thriving intellectual film culture in Britain manifested in the formation of film societies and specialist cinemas, and the development of serious reflection on the medium in journals such as *Close Up*.

Asquith was one of what Rachael Low refers to as 'the new generation of well-connected, well-educated young men, who, unlike their parents, were prepared to take films seriously'.[6] He was eminently well-connected as the son of the former Liberal Prime Minister, Herbert Asquith, and his mother, Margot, was a 'writer and brilliant society figure',[7] a prominent member of the metropolitan social and cultural circles. Asquith had a traditional upper-middle-class education at Winchester public school and Oxford University, which was where he began to take an interest in the cinema. After graduating he spent a short time in Hollywood 'as a guest of Douglas Fairbanks and Mary Pickford, and watched some of the great directors of the American silent cinema at work'.[8] His American experience left its mark; in particular, he met and befriended Charles Chaplin who provided him with a potent and influential sounding board for his developing views on the art of cinema. Writing about his experiences some years later he was to recollect: 'I realise now, far more than I did at the time, what a tremendous experience it was for me – a green, filmstruck undergraduate – to be able to talk for hours on end with the greatest artist the cinema has produced.'[9]

In 1926 he joined Harry Bruce Woolfe's British Instructional Films, then part of the Stoll organisation, the largest British producer of the early 1920s. This began his practical apprenticeship, providing him with a varied experience of film production. For example, on Sinclair Hill's *Boadicea* (1926), in addition to contributing to the scenario, he also acted as 'Property Master, Assistant make-up Man, Assistant Cutter and Stunt Man'.[10] He was also involved in a film called *Thou Fool* (1928), mainly as an editor. However, in Asquith's own words, 'I even directed a shot for it, taken from Chelsea Bridge. It was of Lotts Road Power Station, shot on a misty November afternoon.'[11] In a sense this was a minor rehearsal of sorts for a subsequent film – *Underground* (1928) – which featured more extensive location shooting at the power station as the backdrop for its dramatic denouement.

Asquith had joined British Instructional at a time when the company was rethinking its production strategies and responding, no doubt, to the new opportunities for British films anticipated as a consequence of the forthcoming quota legislation. The company was best known for its documentary reconstructions of the First World War battles with films such as *The Battle of Jutland* (1921) and *Zeebrugge* (1924), and had also developed the celebrated *Secrets of Nature* natural history series. However, the firm was reorganised and relaunched as a public company in 1927 and fiction films were to be central to its future plans. In fact, the first film announced in this change of direction was an adaptation of *Tell England*, a best-selling novel set in the First World War, written by Ernest Raymond and published in 1921.[12] In the event, the *Tell England* project was delayed, and the first venture into fiction film by the company was to be *Shooting Stars* (1928). The film, based upon an original Asquith scenario, is usually regarded as his first picture as director, though it is credited to A. V. Bramble, an experienced director brought in by British Instructional to work with the novice film-maker. Asquith was then promoted to sole directing credit on his next films – *Underground* (1928) and *The Runaway Princess* (1928). Both had romantic themes though in somewhat contrasting social settings. *Underground* is a story of romance set in a working-class milieu whereas in *The Runaway Princess*, an Anglo-German co-production shot mainly in Berlin, the romance is set in a royal milieu. Both films, however, used London-based location sequences and those in *The Runaway Princess* prompted one reviewer to suggest that 'the London settings are used to much more advantage than most British directors have yet put them'.[13] Asquith's final silent film was *A Cottage on Dartmoor* (1930) though, as with many films in production in 1929, a sound-on-disc musical component was provided together with some dialogue sequences. Indeed, its importance as a film on the boundary between the silent and sound eras has been compared to Hitchcock's much-venerated *Blackmail* (1929).[14] Though an Anglo-Swedish co-production, the film was made at British Instructional's newly completed Welwyn studios.

Tell England (1931), the much-delayed project about the Gallipoli campaign during the First World War, was to be Asquith's first sound film proper, though, as with *Shooting Stars*, he was to work in collaboration with another experienced figure. His co-director, Geoffrey Barkas, was brought in for his specialist expertise in location shooting as a good deal of the film was to be shot abroad with Malta standing in for the Dardanelles. Inevitably, its status as a sound film was somewhat compromised by its long gestation from the initial silent project. British Instructional had acquired the screen rights to the novel in 1925 and, according to Asquith:

> It was bought as a picture subject for Walter Summers who made the 'Battles of Coronel and Falkland Islands.' When he was due to commence turning the Raymond story into a picture the powers that be felt that war films were no longer doing well at the box office. So the project was shelved for the time being.[15]

In fact, the film had been advertised in the trade press late in 1927 with a release date of September 1928, and the project 'launched' at a dinner at the Savoy addressed by the novelist John Buchan, a member of the British Instructional board.[16] The film betrayed its silent roots; the location work in particular was filmed silent with sound added later, and it also retained the use of intertitles from the silent period. Yet the film which finally emerged prompted comparisons with distinguished war pictures such as Pudovkin's *The End of St. Petersburg* (1926) and Milestone's *All Quiet on the Western Front* (1930). Paul Rotha selected the landing and battle sequences shot by Barkas and edited by Asquith for special praise though he was critical of the fictional story element of the film;[17] the *Evening News* critic judged the film to be 'one of the two or three outstanding British talkies made so far';[18] and, in a much later assessment, Peter Cowie suggests that 'the massacre on the Gallipoli beaches has taken its place as one of the most compelling and cinematic war sequences ever made'.[19] In one sense *Tell England* marked the end of Asquith's apprenticeship; he had established a reputation as an inventive silent film-maker with two films from his own screenplays and he had also adapted the work of others; he had worked abroad on a co-production and he had made the transition to the sound film. The subject matter of his first five films was diverse – the world of film-making, working-class life, middle-European royalty, the First World War – and the tone of the films varied from the gravity of *Tell England* to the frivolous world of *The Runaway Princess*, and from the reflexiveness of *Shooting Stars* to the realism of *Underground*. Though the films were made in the context of the commercial film industry, Asquith's keen interest in the art and aesthetics of the film, and his involvement with the Film Society, meant that he brought to his work a knowledge of the various directions taken by the international cinema in the 1920s, from the classical narrative of the American film to the experimental cinemas from Germany, France, and the Soviet Union. In addition, he had achieved a degree of public recognition; as Charles Drazin has suggested, his critical standing was such that, 'by the last days of the silent cinema he would be mentioned with Hitchcock as one of Britain's two leading film directors'.[20]

Asquith was to make one more film for British Instructional, an adaptation of the Compton Mackenzie novel *Carnival* (1912), the story of a ballet dancer set in Edwardian times and featuring dance sequences performed by the Marie Rambert company. The film – *Dance Pretty Lady* (1931) – did not perform well at the box office though it impressed both John Grierson and Robert Flaherty.[21] There were press reports of a further project entitled *The Window Cleaner* based on an original story by Asquith,[22] but he was to leave British Instructional early in 1932. *Dance Pretty Lady* was his last film for the company which was shortly to be absorbed by the rather more commercially orientated British International Pictures. British Instructional had proved to be a congenial context for the start of a career in film-making; the next phase of Asquith's career was to prove somewhat more problematic.

The 1930s: the barren years

On the face of it, the prospects for Asquith should have been good as he left a small, though enterprising, company for a much larger one. He joined Gainsborough Pictures, which had merged with the Gaumont-

British company in the late 1920s to become one of the most powerful of the British vertically integrated combines. In addition to this, Asquith was joining the company during an expansionary production phase, and was to be working under the supervision of Michael Balcon, 'the only producer in Britain of Hollywood calibre apart from Korda'.[23] Gaumont-British was an ambitious studio which during the decade was to recruit an impressive array of stars, directors and technicians drawn from both indigenous talent (Jessie Matthews, Alfred Hitchcock, Victor Saville) and from the increasing flow of émigrés from Europe (Conrad Veidt, Alfred Junge), supplemented from time to time with American directors such as Tim Whelan and Raoul Walsh. However, things did not quite work out for the director and Asquith effectively got lost in such a context, as a letter written by studio boss Balcon some years later indicates:

> When Asquith joined us at Gaumont-British we already employed several well-known directors, among them Walter Forde, Alfred Hitchcock, Anatole Litvak, Victor Saville, William Thiele, Berthold Viertel, etc., and I suppose they had the first choice of subjects ... it must be remembered that our policy was somewhat different then. I was called upon to make a large number of specialised comedies with well-known comedians, and these films would hardly have been in Asquith's line. Also there was a period when we were carried away by the possibility of the Anglo-American type of subject, with American stars, and I do not think that these were suitable for Asquith, either.[24]

Asquith spent around two years at Gaumont-British and directed just one film – *The Lucky Number* (1933) – a 'Cockney romance' in the words of *Kine Weekly*,[25] and, like *Underground* and *A Cottage on Dartmoor*, another foray into the 'lower depths' for the aristocratic director. Critics such as John Grierson had previously noted some affinities between his work and that of the French director, René Clair, and *The Lucky Number*, which revolved around a lost lottery ticket, prompted direct comparisons with the French film-maker's similarly themed *Le Million* (1931).[26]

Asquith's other work during this period was confined to working for or with other directors: he wrote the screenplay for a musical comedy, *Marry Me* (1932), a remake of a German film directed by William Thiele; he acted as co-director on the English version of a bilingual film, *The Unfinished Symphony* (1934), based on the life of Schubert and shot partly in Vienna; and he was also responsible for supervising the second unit work on *Forever England* (1934), which was directed by one of Gaumont-British's top film-makers, Walter Forde. It was a mixed and largely unsatisfying experience. He was reluctant to engage fully with *Marry Me* and wrote to Balcon expressing his willingness to help on the script and the preparation for the film but also saying that he would prefer not to go 'onto the floor'.[27] As a lover of classical music, he was more interested in *The Unfinished Symphony*, due, no doubt, to its subject matter – the life of Schubert – Asquith's favourite composer.[28] His second unit work on *Forever England* was subsequently praised by the *Observer*'s film critic though it was a somewhat back-handed compliment included as part of a critical dismissal of his film *Moscow Nights*:

> Much against my will, I promised Mr Asquith at the time that I would not mention his share in 'Forever England.' He was anxious you see, not to destroy one jot of Walter Forde's credit for the film. Now, in view of 'Moscow Nights,' I have no compunction in breaking my promise. There are pretty things in 'Moscow Nights,' but it is obviously unfair to judge Mr Asquith's work by this derivative French melodrama, when some of his best original work in 'Forever England' is going the rounds of the country this week.[29]

Moscow Nights (1936), the ostensible subject of the review, was made for Alexander Korda's ambitious internationally-orientated London Films to which Asquith had moved following his disappointing stint at Gaumont-British. Initially, he had been assigned to another Korda project – a feature-length film to mark the Silver Jubilee of King George V in 1936 from a script to be written by Winston Churchill. Indeed, it has been suggested that Asquith's appeal to Korda, though partly professional – he was a relatively experienced film director – was also to do with his superior social status and connections which made him ideal for enterprises such as the Jubilee project.[30] Korda had planned to make a series of short educational films with Churchill but, after an unfavourable exhibitor response to the idea, he suggested the Jubilee film as an alternative.[31] Churchill was to provide the scenario – dramatic reconstructions of the key events of the King's reign – and Asquith was to direct. However, the project was abandoned and Asquith was assigned to direct *Moscow Nights*, a remake of a French film released in 1934. Press reception of the film was mixed with *Sunday Times* critic Sidney Carroll suggesting that Asquith's direction of the picture 'denotes a master director of films'.[32] In stark contrast to this, Graham Greene, writing in *The Spectator*, dismissed the film as 'completely bogus' and commented that Asquith's 'direction is puerile'.[33] Asquith's time with Korda was brief and in addition to the abandoned Jubilee film there was also a project based upon the life of Queen Elizabeth I which failed to materialise.[34] Asquith had not managed to make a significant mark in a large combine, Gaumont-British, and he now failed to make a mark in the smaller but still high-profile and prestigious London Films run by the flamboyant Hungarian-born Korda. Although his standing had been high at the beginning of the sound period, this was not reflected in the way his career developed, or failed to develop, as the British film industry moved into a prolific production phase towards the middle of the 1930s. As a *Picturegoer* feature was to put it, 'British film production was enjoying a boom, but producers forgot to employ Asquith ... No British producer ... had yet troubled to avail himself of Asquith's full talent.'[35]

Asquith's next move was to prove even less successful than his association with Balcon and Korda. He signed a contract with Max Schach, a Hungarian-born film entrepreneur who had worked in Germany before setting up business in Britain. Schach formed a string of small production companies and was at the heart of the financial scandals which precipitated the production crisis in the British cinema in the late 1930s.[36] In fact, Asquith did not make any films during this period and it is not clear what he actually did during his time with Schach. Daphne Bennett, in her biography of Asquith's mother, suggests that he was filming in Germany in 1937,[37] and Kevin Brownlow claims that Asquith 'was about to abandon the cinema and join the newly-formed BBC Television drama department'.[38] The one clear feature of his professional life at this time was his appointment as President of the ACT, the film technicians' union. In some respects, with his social background, Asquith appears as an unlikely candidate for such a post; yet, in another sense, it was precisely his elevated social position which probably made him an attractive candidate. The high social and political connections of an ex-Prime Minister's son would undoubtedly prove useful for what was a lobbying role on behalf of the industry's technical workers. In addition, despite his background, his attitude towards his fellow workers was admirably egalitarian. George Elvin, then General Secretary of the union, later wrote of his recollections of Asquith in the early 1930s:

> I well remember when Anthony joined ACT, as it then was. He enquired through Harry Kratz, then a sound technician, if film directors could join. I said we had none but why not, and, as he replied, he was a technician like the rest of the crew, so he became the first British film director to become a Trade Unionist.[39]

Asquith's renaissance

In the early 1930s Asquith had written, 'I have always written my own screenplays, and it seems to me to be an absolute necessity for a director to do so.'[40] His first two films – *Shooting Stars* and *Underground* – had been based on his own original scenarios but his 1930s films were mainly adaptations of novels. Ironically, in the light of his assertion, the two films which rehabilitated his career towards the end of the decade were adaptations of theatrical works by major writers both of whom were closely involved in the process of adapting their own work for the screen. Yet *Pygmalion* (1938) and *French Without Tears* (1939), based on plays by George Bernard Shaw and Terence Rattigan respectively, re-established Asquith as a leading film-maker and, perhaps more importantly, were effectively to define the 'middlebrow' Asquith, the accomplished adapter of mainstream theatre for the screen, perhaps the dominant strand in his eventual directorial image. He became something of a specialist in theatrical adaptation with thirteen out of the twenty-five features made after these two films adapted from plays. Yet it was a move in a direction supposed by many to be inimical to the development of film as an independent art form, a form of cultural dependence and subordination which has been seen as inhibiting the development of a truly 'cinematic' British cinema. For many critics 'the oft-iterated conviction that British cinema with its persistent link to theatrical and literary culture, has never attained cinematic maturity at all'[41] was to be borne out by the direction that Asquith's career had taken in the late 1930s. The encounter with Shaw was especially crucial as the distinguished playwright had rather firm views on the relationship between the two mediums, and on the licence that film-makers should enjoy in respect of the adaptation of a Shaw play. Indeed, the production of *Pygmalion* found Asquith surrounded by a formidable array of cultural personalities – Shaw himself, the enterprising Hungarian producer Gabriel Pascal, who had persuaded Shaw to sanction the adaptation of his work for the screen, and Leslie Howard, by then a major Hollywood star. There had been several attempts, including many in Hollywood, to bring Shaw's plays to the screen even in the silent period, and the dramatist himself had been involved in the adaptation of two of his plays filmed at British International Pictures in the early 1930s. In addition, *Pygmalion* had appeared in German and Dutch versions in 1935 and 1937 respectively before Shaw entered into his agreement with Pascal to make the 'authorised' version. The film was made at the recently opened Pinewood Studios and once again Asquith was obliged to work with a co-director – Leslie Howard – who was also to play the leading role of Professor Higgins. Shaw himself was closely involved with the screenplay, rewriting material and even creating new scenes for the film. It was a major success with critics and the public, both in Britain and in America where the version released differed slightly from the British one in order to meet censorship demands.[42] The film was nominated in the best picture category for the 1938 annual Academy Awards, and its stars, Howard and Wendy Hiller, were nominated for best actor and best actress respectively. Shaw won the Oscar in the Writing (Screenplay) category, and Cecil Lewis, W. P. Lipscomb, and Ian Dalrymple, who also worked on the adaptation at various stages, won the Oscar for the separate Writing (Adaptation) category.

Critic Franz Hoellering, writing in American journal *The Nation*, commented, 'The direction (Anthony Asquith and Leslie Howard) and the production (Gabriel Pascal, who must have the credit for con- quering Shaw's antagonism to the movies) compete successfully with Hollywood's best works of this kind.'[43] Asquith's previous films had been released in America though none had made much of an impact. His contribution to *Pygmalion*, though overshadowed in terms of the film's publicity by Shaw and Pascal, nevertheless provided a platform from which he was to progress to the position of one of the leading directors in the British cinema, a position which his silent films had promised almost ten years before the Shaw adaptation. Following *Pygmalion*, according to Peter Noble, Leslie Howard had plans to make further films with both Asquith and Pascal; he had also announced a new project about the world of the newspaper tycoon with Asquith as director, but nothing seems to have come of it.[44]

Shaw was an intellectual playwright and his work focused on ideas, on social and political problems; Asquith's next film – *French Without Tears* – was an altogether lighter proposition, a comedy of manners, adapted from a highly successful West End play written by Terence Rattigan. It was produced by Two Cities, a company formed in 1937 by two Italians, Filippo Del Giudice and Mario Zampi, and was designed as a quota picture for Paramount. The American major had acquired the rights to the play in 1937 and it was originally envisaged as a vehicle for Marlene Dietrich. The decision to make it in Britain was prompted by the new 'Quota Act' of 1938 and its 'triple quota' clause which encour- aged American companies to produce or commission more expensive pictures than the 'quota quickies' used to fulfil the majors' quota obligations earlier in the decade. In the summer of 1938 Paramount announced that 'the company would concentrate on the production of triple Quota pictures suitable for world distribution',[45] and *French Without Tears*, an early reflection of the new policy, was described in the trade press as the company's 'first big British production'.[46] The film consolidated Asquith's reputation and even prompted the glowing comment from the previously sceptical Graham Greene that '*French Without Tears* is a triumph for Mr Anthony Asquith'.[47] Others saw key aspects of Asquith's directorial qualities in the film. For example,

William Whitebait, writing in the *New Statesman and Nation* when the film was re-released in 1944, echoed earlier comments by Grierson, suggesting that Asquith was 'one director who has sensibility and can poke fun, who enjoys being English and making jokes about it, as Clair did once for France and Preston Sturges does for America'.[48] The film was also significant in so far as it brought together Asquith, Terence Rattigan and Anatole de Grunwald, who were to work together on a number of occasions over the next twenty-five years or so. Rattigan's play had opened in London's West End in 1936 where it ran for just over two years; it opened on Broadway in 1937, and its enormous success established Rattigan as one of Britain's leading playwrights. Though he did not receive a credit, Rattigan worked on the screenplay, drawing perhaps on the limited experience of writing for film that he had acquired as a staff writer at the Warner Bros.' Teddington studio.[49] De Grunwald, one of the two credited writers on the film (the other is Ian Dalrymple), was at the beginning of his film career as a scriptwriter with Two Cities and was soon to become a producer as well. Indeed, in an interview some years later, de Grunwald claims a central role in the success of Two Cities based on his crucial role in *French Without Tears*:

> It was I who launched them into their first big international film when I brought them American interests ... I found an American company which had a subject and part of the finance and bought them together with this small English company. The only thing I wanted was to write the script, which I did.[50]

Rattigan's biographer, Geoffrey Wansell, has written that the film of *French Without Tears* was achieved 'in partnership with two men who were to become central to his working life over the next two decades: Anatole de Grunwald and Anthony Asquith.'[51] By the same token, Rattigan and de Grunwald were to become central to Asquith's working life during the same period.

Wartime

French Without Tears, a light comic concoction about the impact of a young woman on a group of young men attending a language 'crammer' in France, was released late in 1939, a few months after the outbreak of the war. A comedy of manners and romance, the film showed no trace of the turbulent context into which it was released. However, it was not long before Asquith threw himself into the war effort and started making films which drew directly on the drama of the global conflict. *Freedom Radio* (1940), Asquith's first war-related film, was a large-scale production made for the Two Cities company though, despite its fervent anti-Nazi theme, both Mario Zampi (its producer) and his associate Filippo Del Giudice were interned in 1940 as aliens when Italy, the country of their birth, entered the war. The film was part of an early though short-lived propaganda strand which included *Pastor Hall* (John Boulting, 1940) and *Pimpernel Smith* (Leslie Howard, 1941), in which distinctions were made between the German people and the Nazis.[52] As with *French Without Tears* the film was made under quota arrangements for an American company – Columbia-British. Asquith's next film – *Quiet Wedding* (1940) – was also a quota picture, for the Paramount company. It was a romantic comedy adapted from a play by Esther McCracken with a script by Terence Rattigan and Anatole de Grunwald, and was produced by Paul Soskin. The film was a box-office success and when Soskin announced a war subject for his next film, Asquith was named as director along with a scriptwriting team of Rattigan and de Grunwald. However, though trade-press stories suggest that Asquith was involved in the preliminary work on the film, scouting locations and choosing music, the film – *The Day Will Dawn* (1942) – was eventually directed by Harold French.[53]

Though his experiences at Gaumont-British in the early 1930s had not been successful, in 1941 Asquith returned to the large company context when he re-joined the Gaumont-British combine signing a four-picture contract with Gainsborough Pictures. The combine had recently become part of the expanding Rank Organization and Asquith was to direct three war films and a costume picture for the company. The first was *Cottage to Let* (1941), a comedy-thriller with archetypal war hero John Mills improbably cast as a Nazi fifth columnist in RAF uniform. The film was an adaptation of a West End stage success written by Geoffrey Kerr, and de Grunwald wrote the script with John Orton, who had worked with Asquith previously on *Shooting Stars*. Orton had established himself as a top comedy writer in the 1930s working with stars such as Will Hay and Jack Hulbert, and the comic mode was reflected in the film. Asquith directed two further war pictures and a costume film for the studio, all filmed at the Shepherd's Bush Studios where he had spent a somewhat unhappy time almost a decade earlier. Like *Freedom Radio*, *Uncensored* (1942), with a script co-written by Terence Rattigan and Rodney Ackland, was another resistance film but set this time in wartime Belgium rather than the Germany of the late 1930s. *We Dive at Dawn* (1943) was a more orthodox war picture combining naval adventure – the pursuit of a battleship by a British submarine – with domestic scenes on the home front. It was praised for its documentary authenticity though its release a few months after *In Which We Serve* (1942) prompted critics to compare it somewhat unfavourably to the Noël Coward/David Lean picture which became the most popular of British wartime films.[54] The costume film, *Fanny by Gaslight* (1944), was the final film of his Gainsborough contract and a contribution to the studio's costume melodrama cycle. It was the second film in the cycle and the studio were aiming to repeat the success of *The Man in Grey* (1943) using a number of that film's stars including James Mason, Stewart Granger, and Phyllis Calvert.

In between *We Dive at Dawn* and *Fanny by Gaslight*, Asquith had returned to Two Cities, where he was to direct two war pictures. Though Mario Zampi had been interned for the duration of the war, Filippo Del Giudice had been released after a few months and had returned to revive the company with the production of *In Which We Serve*. The first film, *The Demi-Paradise* (1943), was somewhat overtly propagandist, uniting the theme of national identity and character with a story about an engineer from the Soviet Union. Its stars, Laurence Olivier and Penelope Dudley Ward, had appeared in *Moscow Nights* and the producer was Russian-born Anatole de Grunwald, who had lived in England since childhood. The second, *The Way to the Stars* (1945), is regarded by many critics as Asquith's best film and also as one of the major British films from the wartime period. It reunited Asquith with both Rattigan and de Grunwald with the latter producing as well as collaborating on the script. The story was by Rattigan and it is loosely based on his play, *Flare Path*, which Asquith had directed on the West End stage in 1942.[55] While the propaganda aims of *The Demi-Paradise* had included the promotion of good Anglo–Soviet relationships, *The Way to the Stars* dealt with Anglo–American relationships and was set in an air force base which played host to US airmen from 1942 onwards. Though it was a moving story marked by the emotional understatement, its propaganda relevance was endangered by a protracted production schedule which meant that the war was almost over when the film was ready for release in the middle of 1945. At Rattigan's suggestion the film opened with a sequence set in 1945 and then moved into flashback for the narrative, transforming it into an exercise in nostalgia appropriate to its release date so late in the war.[56]

In common with many directors of the time, Asquith also made a number of propaganda drama-documentaries for the Ministry of Information including *Channel Incident* (1940), about Dunkirk, *Rush Hour* (1941), about travel to work, and *Two Fathers* (1944), a brief poignant tale with a mild hint of feminist sentiment. There was also a longer film, *A Welcome to Britain* (1943), designed to present the character of British social life and customs to the visiting American troops, and a kind of prelude to *The Way to the Stars*. In addition to the busy production schedule, Asquith was also active in other ways. He was a member of the 'ideas committee', a liaison body between the government and the film industry, set up in 1941 by the Films Division of the Ministry of Information. He was also involved in organisations formed to protect and foster cultural activities both highbrow and lowbrow such as the Committee for the Encouragement of Music and the Arts (forerunner of the Arts Council of Great Britain) and the Art and Entertainment Emergency Council with a committee which included other film-makers such as Paul Rotha alongside figures from the world of music and drama such as Sir Thomas Beecham and Asquith's erstwhile professional colleague, George Bernard Shaw.

Post-war

Asquith was now well established as one of the British cinema's leading directors on the basis of a diverse output – the middlebrow drama adaptations of Shaw and Rattigan, lowbrow genre films including a comedy thriller and a costume melodrama, patriotic war pictures, and documentary dramas. In 1947, after a two-year gap possibly explicable in terms of personal crises – the death of his sister, Elizabeth, and their mother within months of each other in 1945, the alcoholism which had dogged his life for many years – Asquith resumed his directing career. *While the Sun Shines* (1947) was based on another Rattigan play which Asquith had directed on the stage in 1943 with considerable success as it enjoyed a slightly longer run in the West End than *French Without Tears*.[57] The play was a comedy and whereas *Flare Path*, Asquith's previous stage work for Rattigan, was a drama of wartime tensions which had paved the way for the seriousness of *The Way to the Stars*, *While the Sun Shines* represented the lighter comic side of Rattigan. As he himself commented later: 'I suppose it would be fair to say that I tried to recreate *French Without Tears*; I certainly set out to try to create some purely escapist laughter for those dark days of the war.'[58] The film, which was produced by de Grunwald, reflected the tone though not the success of its stage predecessor. Asquith's next film, *The Winslow Boy* (1948), was also a Rattigan adaptation. The playwright had envisaged the project as a film script for de Grunwald and Asquith but their initial lukewarm response prompted him to write it as a play. However, they did eventually agree to collaborate with Rattigan and the film adaptation of the play was made for Korda's revived London Films and British Lion. It was the first of three somewhat austere films Asquith was to make which centred on a trial – the others were *Carrington VC* (1955) and *Libel* (1959). With *The Woman in Question* (1950), Asquith returned to genre cinema. There had been other possible projects since *The Winslow Boy*, including a screen version of Rattigan's *Love in Idleness* on which, according to Peter Noble, Asquith worked on for more than a year,[59] and an adaptation of Graham Greene's 1938 novel, *Brighton Rock*. Rattigan and de Grunwald had acquired the film rights to the novel and, though they had been sold to the Boulting Brothers' Charter Films, Rattigan was to write the script with Asquith scheduled to direct. In the event, Rattigan was to work with Greene himself on the screenplay with John Boulting directing instead of Asquith.[60] *The Woman in Question* was produced by Teddy Baird, a long standing colleague of Asquith's from his British Instructional days. Baird had been Assistant Director on a number of Asquith's 1930s films including *Pygmalion* and *French Without Tears* and Associate Producer on both *While the Sun Shines* and *The Winslow Boy*. *The Woman in Question*, a thriller centred on the murder of a young woman, has been seen as part of a British *film noir* cycle along with films such as *Odd Man Out* (Carol Reed, 1947) and *Brighton Rock* (John Boulting, 1949).[61] Like *Brighton Rock* it has a seaside setting including a fairground, and it also shares a complex narrational strategy with the American *noir* cycle and, indeed, with *Citizen Kane* (Orson Welles, 1941). It begins with the discovery of the murder then unravels the events leading to it through a series of flashbacks representing different perspectives on the murder victim, a feature highlighted in the pressbook for the film:

> Another interesting aspect of the treatment is the presentation of the events themselves, for we do not see any of them in chronological order, but just as they are told to Lodge by the witnesses he is examining. Thus the audience is able to follow the evidence step by step with Lodge just as it is presented to him. And, as there is no cheating, they should arrive at the solution of the murder at the very moment that Lodge discloses his theory.[62]

Jean Kent played the central character, the murdered woman, and though she drew upon her 'bad girl' image established in the Gainsborough costume pictures and in crime films such as *Good Time Girl* (David MacDonald, 1948), the nature of her role in *The Woman in Question* also meant playing against that type in some sections of the film.

Asquith returned to theatrical adaptation for his next two pictures – *The Browning Version* (1950) and *The Importance of Being Earnest* (1951). *The Browning Version* was based on what was to become one of Rattigan's best-known and most admired plays which had opened in London in 1948 as one half of a double bill under the title *Playbill*.[63] It was a one-act single-set play and had been well-received by the critics; in addition, in Geoffrey Wansell's words, the play – effectively a character sketch of a somewhat downtrodden schoolmaster – 'marked Rattigan's arrival as a British dramatist of serious consequence'.[64] The film version was adapted by Rattigan himself and it won him the Best Screenplay prize at the Cannes Film Festival in 1951. The gravitas of *The Browning Version* contrasted greatly with the light, witty qualities of Asquith's next film. *The Importance of Being Earnest*, a version of Oscar Wilde's famous play from the 1890s, was Asquith's first film in colour. It had a formidable cast including Michael Redgrave (who had played the central character in *The Browning Version*) and Edith Evans, who gave her now famous exaggerated performance as Lady Bracknell. The film emphasised its stage origins by opening with a couple taking their places in a theatre to watch a performance of the play. In a witty transition, however, Asquith uses a glance through opera glasses to move into Wilde's fictional world. The film also ends with a shot of the theatre curtains closing. Critics perceived a problem in the incompatible acting registers of the cast and, in particular, with the striking discrepancy between the naturalistic performance of Michael Redgrave and the mannered exaggeration of Edith Evans.[65]

The Importance of Being Earnest consolidated Asquith's reputation as a director of 'photographed stage plays',[66] but the features which followed it had no connections with the theatre. *The Net* (1952) and *The Young Lovers* (1954) are genre films, and *The Final Test* (1952) was an adaptation of a Terence Rattigan television play. *The Net* was made for Javelin Films and Two Cities though the producer was Anthony Darnborough, and *The Young Lovers* was made for Rank's Group Film Producers with Anthony Havelock-Allan producing. *The Final Test* was made by the ACT – the film technicians union – which had an agreement with the National Film Finance Film Corporation for the production of low-budget second features. In fact Asquith's film was an exception, as the 'only first feature for which the NFFC did agree a loan.'[67] Though most of his films between 1950 and 1954 were made for independent producers such as Baird and Havelock-Allan, and companies such as Two Cities and Javelin Films, they were dependent in part on the Rank Organisation which provided studio facilities at Pinewood and handled the distribution of the films.

The Net, a Cold War thriller combining a story of supersonic air travel and espionage, tends to be regarded as second best to David Lean's highly successful *The Sound Barrier* (1952), a film with comparable subject matter, which was released some six months or so before Asquith's film. Rattigan had written an original script for Lean's picture and Asquith, according to his biographer, disappointed not to be asked to direct it, turned to a not dissimilar subject with *The Net*.[68] The film was based on a novel by John Pudney whose poetry Asquith had used to great effect in *The Way to the Stars*. The Cold War also provided a background to *The Young Lovers*, a romantic drama based on an intense love affair between an American working in London in the code department of the US Embassy and a young woman working in an 'Iron Curtain legation' as *Variety* diplomatically put it.[69] The lovers were played by the relatively unknown American actor David Knight and Odile Versois, a French actress who appeared in a handful of British films in the 1950s. David Knight also appeared subsequently in Asquith's short film about opera at Glyndebourne. The film, *On Such a Night* (1955), was one of a number of musical projects directed by Asquith during this period; many were for television but he was involved also in a stage production of Bizet's *Carmen* at Covent Garden.[70] *The Final Test* had been written for the BBC for the Festival of Britain celebrations and was broadcast in 1951.[71] It was produced by R. J. Minney, Asquith's biographer, and it featured members of the England cricket team playing themselves in story about a father/son relationship which counterposed a love of cricket with a love of poetry. The film included a US senator on a fact-finding mission, and there is an echo of Asquith's previous Anglo-American preoccupations in wartime films such as *A Welcome to Britain* and *The Way to the Stars*. Jack Warner played the lead role of the aging England cricketer playing in his last test match, but Robert Morley, dressed in an Asquithian boiler suit, provided the film's main energy as a cricket-loving poet.

After a number of films made at Rank's Pinewood studios, Asquith moved back to Shepperton where he had made *French Without Tears* and *The Winslow Boy*. *Carrington VC* also reunited him with producer Teddy Baird, and with the theatre, as it was an adaptation of a popular play by Dorothy and Campbell Christie about the court martial of an army officer accused of embezzling regimental funds. Apart from a minor change to the ending, the film was a close adaptation of the West End stage success and was dominated by a series of courtroom scenes. David Niven played the accused officer and Margaret Leighton his estranged wife. The film was well-received and, for Dilys Powell, it embodied a distinct approach to cinema which differentiated British cinema from the Hollywood film. 'Some film directors', she suggested, 'are interested in the cinema primarily as visual narrative, some use it as a means of drawing character.' She continued:

if you compare a film by Asquith with an American film by John Huston, the difference in emphasis is clear. The American tells a story in which people are concerned; the Englishman tells a story about people. As a matter of fact I am inclined to think that the difference is one between American and English film in general. America with her expansive history, her chances for outdoor movement, her instinct for speed, has developed the cinema of action. England, like France, has turned to the cinema of examination.[72]

Asquith belonged to the character-drawing trend and *Carrington VC*, though drawing upon the tension inherent in a trial story, was basically a study of a number of characters including Carrington himself, his wife, and the younger female officer with whom he has had a brief affair.

Orders to Kill (1958), a Second World War picture, was made for British Lion and produced by Anthony Havelock-Allan. Unlike many war films of the time, it eschewed collective heroics and dealt with an individual undercover mission – the assassination of a suspected French double agent by an American air force officer in occupied France. The twist in the story – the assassination victim proves to be an innocent man – turns the film into an agonising moral tale about killing in wartime. The film was Britain's official entry in the Cannes Film Festival and caused something of a furore. Charles Vidor, the American representative on the festival jury, attacked the film as 'being offensive to the United States' in its portrayal of the Americans who planned and executed the mistaken operation, though the film was based on an actual wartime incident.[73] Paul Massie, the Canadian actor who played the assassin, was to write in glowing terms about his experience on the film praising Asquith's sensitivity and professionalism as a director. 'It was my introduction to film-making', he wrote, 'and I couldn't have hoped for a better one'.[74]

After *Orders to Kill* Asquith returned to Rattigan and de Grunwald to work on a film based on the life of T. E. Lawrence. *Kine Weekly* carried reports towards the end of 1957 that 'Dirk Bogarde is to play the title role in "Lawrence of Arabia" for producer Anatole de Grunwald. Anthony Asquith directs.'[75] It was to be a big-budget picture, made for the Rank Organisation, forming the centrepiece of their 1958 production programme, and providing a vehicle for one of their biggest stars. It was then the latest in a long line of attempts to make a film about Lawrence's exploits in the desert, stretching back possibly to Herbert Wilcox and Rex Ingram in the 1920s, Korda in the 1930s, and to Columbia Studios in the early 1950s.[76] The project was Rattigan's; he had completed the first draft of a script based on Lawrence's autobiography, *Seven Pillars of Wisdom*, early in 1956.[77] Also, de Grunwald and Asquith had already visited the Middle East in search of potential locations. However, it joined the long list of unrealised 'Lawrences' when Rank withdrew from the project early in 1958, possibly, according to Geoffrey Wansell, after learning of the version planned by the independent American producer, Sam Spiegel and director, David Lean.[78] Lean had been approached by Columbia about such a project in the early 1950s and, ironically, the director had also been contacted by Rattigan at around the same time with an alternative Lawrence proposal.[79] The trade paper comment couched the matter in terms of 'postponement' but, of course, the Lawrence baton had now been taken up by Spiegel, though David Lean's film was still a number of years away from production.[80] Rattigan salvaged the screenplay material and used it as the basis for his play – *Ross* – which opened in London in 1960.

The Doctor's Dilemma (1959) was yet another foray into 'respectable' theatre, an adaptation of George Bernard Shaw's satire on the medical profession first performed in 1906. The film was made in conjunction with MGM's British production arm, the first of a number of titles from the de Grunwald/Asquith team to be made at Elstree studios for the American major. *Variety* thought the film a 'risky prestige venture' oddly out of tune with the times and suitable for art house circulation rather than for a popular audience though it was a success in America.[81] In Britain it was less successful; Dirk Bogarde was a popular star based on his appearances in films such as *Doctor in the House* (1954) and he suggested that, 'nobody went to see it. They all thought it was a *Doctor in the House* sequel, sat through the first ten minutes with all that discussion going on then they walked out'.[82] Roger Manvell, writing in *Films and Filming*, saw the film as evidence of Asquith's skill as an adapter though he pinpointed some problems arising from the differences between stage and screen:

> One of Asquith's particular skills lies in the meticulous and elegant transfer of highly theatrical plays to the screen. Since the essence of such plays as *The Importance of being Earnest* and *The Doctor's Dilemma* lies in the verbal exchange of unusually articulate characters whose personalities depend on their tongues, it is no good expecting in the films derived from them the conventions of mobility, suspense and the active pursuit of actuality that are regarded as normal for the screen. These become films of people talking.[83]

Prompted by the American success of *The Doctor's Dilemma*, MGM agreed financing for a second de Grunwald film, *Libel* (1959), an adaptation of a 1930s play by Edward Wool, the film rights to which MGM had bought some years earlier.[84] It was another Asquith film based on a trial, and featured Bogarde alongside the Hollywood star, Olivia de Havilland, and Paul Massie from *Orders to Kill*.

International Asquith

The final phase of Asquith's career is marked by a certain internationalising of the scope of his films – his 'polished Rolls-Royce period', as Kevin Brownlow has described it.[85] Since the late 1940s, the major Hollywood companies and the new breed of independent American producers had been making films in Britain and other European countries, generating a more international approach to the business of film-making. It was a trend that was to become more marked in the 1960s leaving its imprint on the kinds of films made. *The Doctor's Dilemma* and *Libel*, though British in character, were made as part of MGM's British production strand and, as a consequence, featured stars – Leslie Caron and Olivia de Havilland – well-known to American audiences. Asquith's third Shaw adaptation, *The Millionairess* (1960), made for Anatole de Grunwald's company and produced by his brother, Dimitri, was also made under American auspices, as a contribution to an expanded British-based schedule of 'runaway' productions planned by Twentieth Century Fox. It featured an international cast including Italians Sophia Loren, by 1960 an established Hollywood star, and Vittorio de Sica, together with Peter Sellers, well-established in Britain, and on the brink of international stardom.

Asquith's next film, *Two Living, One Dead* (1961), was international in another, somewhat different, way. *Kine Weekly* described the film as the 'first Anglo-Swedish co-production',[86] though *A Cottage on Dartmoor*, made by Asquith in the late 1920s, had been a collaboration between British Instructional and the Swedish Biograph company.[87] Unlike the earlier film, however, *Two Living, One Dead* was shot entirely in a Swedish studio and on location in Stockholm. Teddy Baird was the producer and the film had a predominantly British cast including Virginia McKenna, Bill Travers, and Patrick McGoohan. The subject matter, however, was drawn from a Norwegian Nobel Prize-winning novel though the setting was changed to Sweden for the film. Asquith's follow-up film was *Guns of Darkness* (1962), produced for the Associated British Picture Corporation as a Warner Bros. release. It had a foreign setting, a story of revolution in a Latin America republic, and much of the film was shot on location in Spain. The international cast included David Niven and Leslie Caron. Niven, though Scottish-born, was a major Hollywood star and had only appeared in a small number of British

films. Both films indicated the 'international trend' in some respects –
non-British settings, filmed wholly or partly overseas, 'international
Hollywood stars' and US distribution links in the case of *Guns of
Darkness*. However, it was Asquith's two final films which embodied what
most critics thought of as the vices of 'international' film production in
the 1960s. It was a trend which embraced other leading British film-
makers with well-established reputations. As Robert Murphy has put it:

> Asquith spent his last years making increasingly banal prestige pro-
> ductions like *The V.I.P.s* (1963) and *The Yellow Rolls-Royce* (1964). Carol
> Reed fell even more deeply into the pit of vacuous internationalism,
> following up *Our Man in Havana* (1959) with *The Running Man* (1963).[88]

Like *The Millionairess*, *The V.I.P.s* and *The Yellow Rolls-Royce* were made
with American backing though, in this case, from the MGM-British
company, and their somewhat old-fashioned qualities fitted in well with
the conservative cast of the parent American studio. Indeed, it has been
suggested that *The V.I.P.s* grew out of a plan to remake *Grand Hotel*
(1932), an MGM hit from the early 1930s also featuring an all-star cast
and a portmanteau narrative pattern.[89] Both films were produced by
Anatole de Grunwald with screenplays written by Terence Rattigan; the
list of stars involved included Elizabeth Taylor and Richard Burton, with
Orson Welles in *The V.I.P.s* and Rex Harrison, Omar Sharif, and Ingrid
Bergman in *The Yellow Rolls-Royce*. The films were highly expensive –
both topped the million-pound budget mark – and both were mightily
successful at the box office even if subsequent critical judgement dismissed them as 'banal celebrations of the rich and empty-headed ... which
perfectly suited MGM's taste for overblown escapism'.[90] Together, the
films have somewhat blighted Asquith's subsequent standing with
critics and historians; Roy Armes, for example, writing in the late 1970s,
suggested that 'his reputation is coloured by the inanities of *The V.I.P.s*
and *The Yellow Rolls-Royce*'.[91] *The Yellow Rolls-Royce* proved to be Asquith's
final film. There were other projects following the film including a
ballet film to be made as an 'Anglo-Soviet or Soviet-American production'.[92] Asquith had a longstanding interest in ballet and had contributed to *An Evening with the Royal Ballet* (1963), a film produced by
Anthony Havelock-Allan for British Home Entertainment, a pay-TV
company.[93] Asquith was also scheduled to direct *The Shoes of the Fisher-
man*, based on the best-selling novel by Maurice West, and had actually
begun the preparatory work on the Roman locations for the film before
his premature death from cancer early in 1968.

As indicated in this survey of his career, Asquith was involved in the
British cinema for a long time, forty years or so, entering it towards the

end of the silent era as the industry struggled to establish itself in the face of Hollywood's power. Ironically, Asquith's final films were made in the British cinema of the 1960s which was basically financed by the Hollywood companies. During his career, the industry went through numerous changes, responding to the challenge of Hollywood, to the example of European cinema, to major events such as the Second World War, constructing a body of films which prompted both despair and enthusiastic endorsement by critics at various times. The subsequent chapters will take a closer look at a selection of titles from Asquith's career, identifying their general qualities as British films as well as the qualities which derive from the more immediate circumstances of their production. The twenty or so titles chosen from the thirty-five features that Asquith directed reflect a number of things, not least of which is ease of availability. However, the selection represents a diverse career in which art cinema, middlebrow culture, and popular art are reflected, although the films chosen are not intended to indicate any particular ranking in Asquith's career as a whole.

Notes

1 G. Elvin, *Anthony Asquith a tribute* (London: British Film Institute, 1968), n. p.
2 G. Macnab, *J. Arthur Rank and the British Film Industry* (London: Routledge, 1993), p. 169.
3 R. Durgnat, *A Mirror for England. British Movies from Austerity to Affluence* (London: Faber and Faber, 1970), p. 191.
4 D. Thomson, *The New Biographical Dictionary of Cinema* Fourth Edition (London: Little, Brown, 2003), p. 35.
5 C. Barr, *All Our Yesterdays* (London: BFI Publishing, 1986), p. 7.
6 R. Low, *The History of the British Film 1928–1929* (London: George Allen & Unwin Ltd., 1971), p. 182.
7 O. Baldwin, 'These People Make British Pictures', *Picturegoer* (29.7.39), p. 12.
8 C. Drazin, *The Finest Years. British Cinema of the 1940s* (London: Andre Deutsch, 1998), p. 187.
9 A. Asquith, 'Days with Chaplin. Hollywood Memories of the Nineteen Twenties', *The Cine-technician*, Nov.–Dec. (1952), p. 125.
10 R. J. Minney, *Puffin Asquith* (London: Leslie Frewin, 1973), p. 49.
11 C. Belfrage, *All is Grist* (London: Parallax Press, 1988), p. 31.
12 *Kine Weekly* (8.9.27), p. 59.
13 L. Collier, 'Trade Shows Surveyed', *Kine Weekly* (21.3.29), p. 51.
14 M. Smith, 'Technological Determination, Aesthetic Resistance or A Cottage on Dartmoor. Goat-Gland Talkie or Masterpiece', *Wide Angle*, 12:3 (1990), pp. 80–97.
15 'Anthony Asquith's Defence!', *The Film Weekly* (7.11.31), p. 9.
16 *Kine Weekly* (22.9.27), pp. 16–17.
17 Rotha is quoted in P. Noble, *Anthony Asquith* (London: BFI, 1951), p. 16.
18 *Evening News* (3.4.31).
19 P. Cowie, 'This England', *Films and Filming*, October (1963), p. 13.

20 Drazin, *The Finest Years*, p. 187.
21 See F. Hardy (ed.), *Grierson on Documentary* (London: Faber and Faber, 1966), pp. 79-80.
22 *Kine Weekly* (7.1.32), p. 84.
23 Low, *The History of the British Film 1928-1929*, p. 133.
24 Noble, *Anthony Asquith*, p. 20-1. Noble quotes from the letter, which was written around 1950.
25 *Kine Weekly* (1.6.33), p. 18.
26 *Ibid.*
27 Balcon Collection, British Film Institute Special Collections, B 92. Letter from Asquith to Balcon dated 21.4.32.
28 Minney, *Puffin Asquith*, p. 84.
29 *Observer* (10.11.35) – BFI cuttings collection: *Moscow Nights*.
30 See K. Kulik, *Alexander Korda. The Man Who Could Work Miracles* (London: Virgin Books, 1990), p. 145.
31 See C. Drazin, *Korda. Britain's Only Movie Mogul* (London: Sidgwick & Jackson, 2002), pp. 112–18.
32 *The Sunday Times* (10.11.35) – BFI cuttings collection: *Moscow Nights*.
33 G. Greene, *The Pleasure Dome* (London: Secker & Warburg, 1972), p. 36.
34 See P. Tabori, *Alexander Korda* (London: Oldbourne, 1959), p. 187.
35 *Picturegoer* (21.3.42), p. 7.
36 See R. Low, *Film-making in 1930s Britain* (London: George Allen & Unwin, 1985), pp. 198–208.
37 D. Bennett, *Margot. A Life of the Countess of Oxford and Asquith* (London: Victor Gollancz Ltd., 1984), p. 384.
38 K. Brownlow, *David Lean* (London: Faber and Faber, 1996), p. 121. The BBC post is also mentioned in P. Cowie, 'This England', *Films and Filming*, October (1963), p. 14.
39 Elvin, *Anthony Asquith a tribute*. n. p.
40 Quoted in Noble, *Anthony Asquith*, p. 20.
41 C. Gledhill, 'Taking it Forward: theatricality and British cinema style in the 1920s', in L. Fitzsimmons and S. Street (eds), *Moving Performance. British Stage and Screen, 1890s–1920s* (Wiltshire: Flicks Books, 2000), p. 7.
42 A. Slide, 'Banned in the USA'. *British Films in the United States and their Censorship, 1933-1960* (London: I. B. Tauris Publishers, 1998), pp. 122–3.
43 S. Kauffmann (ed.), *American Film Criticism* (New York: Liveright, 1972), p. 364.
44 Noble, *Anthony Asquith*, p. 25. The newspaper tycoon project is mentioned in Brownlow, *David Lean*, pp. 127–8.
45 *Kine Weekly* (11.8.38), p. 19.
46 *Kine Weekly* (19.10.39), p. 19.
47 Greene, *The Pleasure Dome*, p. 248.
48 *New Statesman and Nation* (22.4.44) – BFI cuttings collection: *French Without Tears*.
49 G. Wansell, *Terence Rattigan. A Biography* (London: Fourth Estate, 1996), p. 96.
50 'The Champagne Set', *Films and Filming*, February (1965), p. 8.
51 Wansell, *Terence Rattigan*, p. 96.
52 J. Chapman, 'Why We Fight. *Pastor Hall* and *Thunder Rock*', in A. Burton, T. O'Sullivan, and P. Wells (eds), *The Family Way. The Boulting Brothers and British Film Culture* (Trowbridge, Wiltshire: Flicks Books, 2000), p. 86.
53 *Kine Weekly* (26.6.41), p. 25 and (10.7.41), p. 28. An early title for the film was *Fate Knocking at the Door*, a reference to the opening notes of Beethoven's Fifth Symphony.
54 See S. P. Mackenzie, *British War Films, 1939-1945* (London: Hambledon and London Ltd., 2001), p. 85-6.

55 *Flare Path* opened on 13 August 1942 at the Apollo Theatre, London.

56 Wansell, *Terence Rattigan*, p. 139.

57 *While the Sun Shines* opened on 24 December 1943 at the Globe Theatre, London.

58 Quoted in Wansell, *Terence Rattigan*, p. 133.

59 Noble, *Anthony Asquith*, p. 41. Noble also mentions 'a film of *Beau Brummell*' and 'a remake of *Shooting Stars*'.

60 See S. Chibnall, 'Purgatory at the End of the Pier: Imprinting a Sense of Place through Brighton Rock', in Burton *et al.* (eds), *The Family Way*, pp. 135–6, and Wansell, *Terence Rattigan*, p. 163.

61 J. Petley, 'The Lost Continent', in C. Barr (ed.), *All Our Yesterdays* (London: BFI Publishing, 1986), p. 111.

62 *The Woman in Question* Pressbook, in BFI Special Collections – Teddy Baird, Item 34.

63 The other play is *Harlequinade*.

64 Wansell, *Terence Rattigan*, p. 180.

65 See R. Findlater, *Michael Redgrave. Actor* (London: William Heinemann Ltd., 1956), p. 111 ff.

66 Jympson Harman, *Evening News* 26.5.52 – BFI cuttings collection: *The Importance of Being Earnest*.

67 S. Harper and V. Porter, *British Cinema of the 1950s. The Decline of Deference* (Oxford: Oxford University Press, 2003), pp. 13–14.

68 Minney, *Puffin Asquith*, pp. 152–3.

69 *Variety* (1.9.54), p. 22.

70 Minney, *Puffin Asquith*, p. 155.

71 Wansell, *Terence Rattigan*, p. 213.

72 *The Sunday Times* (12.12.54) – BFI cuttings collection: *Carrington VC*.

73 'Fury Inside Cannes Jury', *Kine Weekly* (21.5.58), pp. 3–4.

74 P. Massie, 'What Asquith Did For Me', *Films and Filming*, February (1958), 28.

75 'British Production Scene', *Kine Weekly* (12.12.57), p. 93.

76 Brownlow, *David Lean*, pp. 405–7.

77 Wansell, *Terence Rattigan*, p. 267.

78 *Ibid.*, p. 299.

79 Brownlow, *David Lean*, p. 407.

80 P. Evans, 'Studio Round-Up', *Kine Weekly* (27.3.58), p. 19.

81 *Variety* (3.12.58), p. 6.

82 B. McFarlane, *An Autobiography of British Cinema* (London: Methuen, 1997), p. 68.

83 R. Manvell, *Films and Filming*, April (1959), 21.

84 *Kine Weekly* (15.10.59), p. 17.

85 In an interview in McFarlane, *An Autobiography of British Cinema*, p. 99.

86 *Kine Weekly* (10.11.60), p. 24.

87 *Kine Weekly* (14.2.29), p. 45.

88 R. Murphy, *Sixties British Cinema* (London: BFI Publishing, 1992), p. 91.

89 *Kine Weekly* (28.3.63), Production Review Supplement, p. iii.

90 Murphy, *Sixties British Cinema*, p. 265.

91 R. Armes, *A Critical History of British Cinema* (London: Secker and Warburg, 1978), p. 98.

92 Minney, *Puffin Asquith*, p. 216.

93 *Kine Weekly* (22.11.62), p. 19.

The formative years

Asquith began his film career in 1926 at a point when the British film industry was moving through a production crisis. The First World War, of course, had disrupted the European cinemas in particular but, in terms of the volume of production, the British cinema had recovered well and, for example, well over a hundred films were produced annually from 1919 until 1922. Thereafter production began to decline and a pattern of 'boom and bust' became discernible, one which was to become familiar to British film-makers as a recurrent feature of the British film industry at various times in its history. It was also a time in which the nature of cinema, its specific character as a form of art, its relationship with the more traditional forms of cultural expression, its presence in the relatively new but burgeoning world of mass communication, and its social and political significance, were topics urgently debated and discussed by the intelligentsias of various countries including Britain. It was also an era in which a plurality of film forms and styles emerged, a period of film experimentation especially in Europe. It was a period of flux, of instability, with questions raised about the very survival of the indigenous European film industries in the face of Hollywood's power and influence; it was also a period when the nature and identity of cinema was the subject of intense debate: Was it an art form? Was it 'merely' entertainment? What was the social and artistic role of this relatively new medium?

British cinema in the 1920s

In 1926 the British film production industry was famously threatened with extinction. Although British cinemas were thriving, it was on the basis of screening films from America – the westerns, the comedies and the melodramas, the Chaplin films, the Mary Pickford films – rather

than British films. Audiences flocked to see the latest Hollywood offer-
ings apparently untroubled by the absence of the indigenous product.
By 1926 the number of British films actually produced had dwindled
from well over one hundred in the early post-war years to the calamitous
figure of thirty-four, which reflected the production crisis that had
befallen the industry a year of so previously.[1] The domestic industry's
decline has been explained in various ways. The obvious explanation
was the power of the Hollywood film industry with its aggressive
marketing through British-based distribution arms acting on behalf of
major companies such as Paramount and First National. The block- and
blind-booking policies pursued by such firms required British cinema
owners to purchase exhibition rights to packages of films leaving little
screen time available for the indigenous product. Rachael Low has
suggested that it was a period of difficult transition for the British film
industry. The American film industry was changing the basis of cinema,
moving towards a high-investment, mass-production industry, using a
range of marketing strategies to ensure that their films enjoyed the
widest international circulation. Pioneer British film-makers such as
Cecil Hepworth and George Pearson and the large British companies
such as Stoll and Ideal failed to respond to the challenges posed by
Hollywood and stuck with the practices that had served them well in
earlier times:

> In general, the picture is one of unfounded optimism after the war when
> the old guard of producer expected to return to much the same sort of
> production as before 1914, and a gradual decline from 1920 to 1924 or
> 1925 during which they were almost all forced out of business and a new,
> more modern, type of producer began to appear.[2]

The new producers – Michael Balcon, Victor Saville, Harry Bruce
Woolfe, Herbert Wilcox – were around fifteen to twenty years younger
than pioneers such as Hepworth and Pearson, when they began their
careers in the early 1920s. Though their first films were produced in a
piecemeal fashion in the unpromising context of production decline,
they were well placed to take advantage of the stabilisation of the
industry that came with the introduction of quota legislation in 1928.
For example, Balcon had formed Gainsborough Pictures in 1924 which
merged with Gaumont-British in 1928 to form a strong and powerful
combine with interests in production and distribution as well as
exhibition; Wilcox was involved with the American entrepreneur J. D.
Williams in the setting up of the large modern studio complex at Elstree
which became known as the 'British Hollywood', where he based his
British and Dominions company set up in 1928. Both companies were

to become important forces in the British cinema of the 1930s in a context in which British films were guaranteed some sort of screening in British cinemas following the quota legislation of 1928.

Asquith's entry to the industry was at a time of transition; the industry, it is true, was moving through a crisis but with the impending quota legislation expected to be in place by the late 1920s, production prospects appeared to be healthy and investment in British films, in studios, in cinemas, was increasing. However, the question of the kinds of films to be made remained. Hollywood's production hegemony was not a simple matter of economics and business. The films that emerged in considerable volume from the developing complex of 'film factories' in Los Angeles, had also set a path for the formal and stylistic development of the medium. The cinema of stars and genres, of fast-paced narration, of romance and violence, had effectively established itself as 'cinema' *per se* in the minds of audiences in a range of countries, and especially in Britain. As Victoria de Grazia has suggested, by the 1920s 'the sway of America's cultural industries was so powerful that some Europeans questioned whether old-world states still exercised sovereignty over their citizens' leisure'.[3] Its substantial presence in British film culture had certainly prompted ideological concerns among the intelligentsia and fears of cultural colonisation. One press article suggested that the British film audience was 'Americanized to an extent that makes them regard the British film as a foreign film ... they talk America, think America, dream America; we have several million people, mostly women, who, to all intents and purposes, are temporary American citizens'.[4] In a letter published in the *Telegraph* newspaper a group of concerned figures from literature and the arts including Robert Bridges, Thomas Hardy, and Edward Elgar referred to the 'high national and patriotic interests' involved in Hollywood's domination of the British screen, the 'non-British atmosphere' of such films, and a fear that 'the psychological influences which they convey may have far-reaching consequences'.[5] The British film industry, a British cinema, meant far more than economics and business, and was deeply implicated in issues of cultural and national identity.

The British silent film

Alongside the concern about the effects of the American cinema dominating the British screen, there were also concerns – artistic, cultural, ideological – about the perceived absence of an authentic British cinema, a cinema which could be seen as interacting in a positive fashion with the culture from which it sprang. British films were being made despite the hegemonic position of the American industry, albeit in reduced numbers, yet a distinctive national cinema had not emerged from either the endeavours of the pioneers nor from the initial efforts of the younger entrants to the industry. Despite the odd individual success, such as the early films of Alfred Hitchcock, for example, British film-makers were not producing films which could compare either with those of their European counterparts or with the American films which dominated the British screen. The British silent film – a body of several hundred films – was dismissed during its time; as Oswell Blakeston wrote in the journal *Close Up* in 1927, 'Where in the history of British pictures are to be found films with the aesthetic merits of "Caligari"; "Warning Shadows"; or "The Last Laugh"?'[6] The decade also has attracted little attention from subsequent critics and historians; it has remained invisible. Charles Barr has suggested that:

> To most people other than specialist academics and historians, British silent cinema is an unknown country. No British feature films from the silent era belong to an internationally known repertoire, or to a national tradition that is absorbed by, or at least known to, later generations of film-makers and cinephiles. Our film culture has no roots in, and no memory of, the formative silent period. For a country which was to become a major producer in the sound period, this is extraordinary.[7]

The British cinema, it is suggested, failed to contribute to the 'internationally known repertoire' of films of the period despite the fact that it did possess an industry with a history comparable to its European neighbours. But Barr's comment is also about perceptions of British silent cinema, the fact that it is an 'unknown country' – a body of films only now beginning to be explored in detail.[8] On a more positive note, the decade did see the beginnings of a substantial film culture in Britain – the development of a network of exhibition venues, discursive forums, journals, and books such as Rotha's *The Film Till Now* written at the end of the decade. The interest, however, was focused primarily upon the new cinemas of Europe and the Soviet Union, as the Blakeston comment quoted above indicates. The Film Society that was founded in London in 1925 aimed at bringing the new European films to a somewhat select metropolitan audience of artists, intellectuals and film-makers. The Society's aims were partly to enrich the film culture by arranging screenings for films which would not have obtained commercial distribution; but, as Jamie Sexton has written, 'whilst it was primarily a site in which international "advances" could be consumed, it hoped that these could feed back into native production and therefore rejuvenate British film-making'.[9] The film intelligentsia – Ivor Montagu, Adrian Brunel, Iris Barry – who set up the society implicitly identified shortcomings in the indigenous cinema which might be corrected through exposure to a more varied diet of film viewing. The 1920s also saw the beginnings of serious commentary on cinema in the broadsheet newspapers and the intellectual weeklies, and the introduction of specialist journals such as *Close Up* which published its first issue in 1927. The various currents of British thought about cinema, its cultural and artistic significance, were encapsulated in 1930 in the publication of Paul Rotha's *The Film Till Now*, an ambitious book which merged history and aesthetics, political and cultural judgement in a detailed account of the first thirty years or so of the medium. It was fiercely anti-Hollywood, and militantly pro-European 'art' cinema, reflecting the cultural stance taken by many at the time; it was also sceptical about British cinema with, at best, a degree of grudging praise for the endeavours of promising young film-makers such as Alfred Hitchcock and Anthony Asquith.

European film

In stark contrast to the perceived inadequacies of British cinema, and despite the fact that all film-producing countries had the problems of coping with the power of Hollywood, the films coming from elsewhere in Europe, from France, Germany, the Soviet Union, and from the Scandinavian countries, did constitute viable national cinemas, offering distinctive experiences which engaged positively with the cultures from which they emerged. As in Britain, the Hollywood film constituted the typical film fare in many of these countries as well, but the artistic responses – the great films from directors such as Murnau, Lang, Clair, Eisenstein, Gance, Dreyer – indicated other avenues of cinematic exploration which challenged the American film at least on the aesthetic front if not in terms of mass international circulation. Such films also signalled the emergence of what would subsequently be called an 'art' cinema of distinctive forms and styles recognised at the time by intellectuals and artists in the metropolitan centres of culture – Berlin, Paris, New York and, indeed, London.

In the course of reconstructing their film industries following the First World War, Germany, France, and the Soviet Union in particular, created a diverse range of cinemas making films that differed in key respects from their Hollywood counterparts that were filling European screens. These countries did have domestic equivalents to the American entertainment films but the art strands represented alternative approaches to film-making which were aligned with the modernist and avant-garde artistic currents of the time – Expressionism, Surrealism, Dadaism, and Constructivism. In France films such as *La Souriante Madame Beudet* (1923), *Ménilmontant* (1926), and *La Coquille et le clergyman* (1928) deployed a range of techniques to represent the inner psychological life of their protagonists, while film-makers such as René Clair, with *Entr'acte* (1924), and Salvador Dali and Luis Buñuel with *Un Chien andalou* defied the narrative logic of the mainstream Hollywood films. The German film acquired an international prominence with the appearance of *The Cabinet of Dr. Caligari* (1919), a self-consciously artistic film which combined the psychological qualities associated subsequently with the French cinema, with an approach to *mise-en-scène* influenced by Expressionist drama and painting. Most German films during the period were commercial genre pieces, historical spectaculars and thrillers. Yet, it is the handful of Expressionist films which followed *The Cabinet of Dr. Caligari* which have imprinted themselves on film history as founding examples of art cinema both through their eccentric style and their international circulation through specialised cinema clubs and societies. The other important art cinema of the 1920s came from the Soviet Union and the films of Eisenstein and Pudovkin with their formal and narrative innovations, particularly in terms of 'montage'. Films such as *Battleship Potemkin* (1925), *October* (1928), and *Mother* (1926) also injected a political edge into the art film. In economic terms, art films were financed from a mixture of sources including the state itself in the case of the Soviet film, large commercial concerns such as Germany's UFA, smaller specialist firms, and private financing by the film-makers themselves or by wealthy patrons. In 1920 the German government instituted financial incentives for exhibitors screening films with artistic and cultural value – a move which many governments would emulate in the future in order to protect and foster an indigenous cultural cinema.

The 1920s established a number of the parameters for the cinema, setting the art film, in particular, as a challenge – artistic, cultural, financial – to the Hollywood film which had established itself as the exemplar of cinema in most countries of the world. The art film presented a parallel but contrasting experience – complex artistic films instead of entertainment narratives, intimate screening venues instead of picture palaces, intellectual journals instead of fan magazines – addressed to audiences familiar with modernist developments in literature, music, and painting. Asquith entered the film industry during a time of industrial ferment – the formation of new companies each devising ambitious production plans in the wake of the anticipated quota legislation, new studios being built to accommodate such plans. But it was also a period of intellectual ferment and, in Britain, a period of social and political reservations about the increasingly influential Hollywood film running alongside considerable excitement and interest in the new 'art' cinemas coming from Europe. Asquith's early films emerged from this context of challenge and opportunity.

Shooting Stars (1928)

Shooting Stars was made by British Instructional Films whose founder, Bruce Woolfe, was one of the new, younger producers to emerge in the 1920s. It was a small company which was best known for its documentary reconstruction films based on episodes from the First World War – *Zeebrugge* (1924) and *The Battles of the Coronel and Falkland Islands* (1927) – and its *Secrets of Nature* series documenting natural history. The company was reorganised in the late 1920s and though the documentary films had been successful, its relaunch was based on a move into the fiction film, a strategy which undoubtedly reflected the new opportunities promised by the impending government legislation on film quotas. However, the company's initial announcements in 1927, following its flotation as a public company, indicated that something of its commitment to war subject matter would be retained. Initial publicity for the change of direction focused on a film about the Gallipoli campaign that would blend wartime preoccupations with fictional elements:

> It has been decided to adopt the well-known novel, 'Tell England', by Mr Ernest Raymond, as the subject into which the Gallipoli campaign will be woven. Your directors felt that the entertainment value of a film of the Gallipoli campaign would be greatly enhanced by securing continuity by introducing a story of human interest.[10]

Asquith was to be involved in some capacity on the project but it actually took some years to materialise and his debut film was *Shooting Stars*, a subject far removed from the war or from the natural history traditions of the company, reflecting a substantial change of direction for British Instructional Films.

The film's title card reads: 'Shooting Stars by Anthony Asquith' and though the film is usually credited to Asquith and regarded as his first film, the director listed on the credits is A. V. Bramble. Bramble was an experienced film-maker who had begun his directing career in 1914 and had made a number of films for the Ideal company before joining British Instructional. Asquith, in contrast, had limited production experience consisting of the various roles in Sinclair Hill's *Boadicea* (1926), and some editing and second unit work on Fred Paul's *Thou Fool* (1926).[11] The supervision of a more experienced film-maker such as Bramble was thought to be necessary in such a context. However, as Charles Barr has commented, it is possible that Bramble's contribution has been overlooked and that he may be 'a candidate for rediscovery' in the still hazy world of 1920s British cinema:

> He is remembered by history mainly for his director's credit on Anthony Asquith's highly accomplished and inventive first film, *Shooting Stars*, and we take it for granted that he was simply an experienced professional who had a consultative role and allowed his name to be foregrounded in order to satisfy the money-men, while Asquith really did it all; but maybe it is more complex than that.[12]

The film, though, was based on a story written by Asquith and when it was mentioned in the trade press during production, it was invariably referred to as an Asquith film. For example, late in 1927 P. L. Mannock, studio correspondent of *Kine Weekly*, wrote, 'A. V. Bramble has just finished the footage of Anthony Asquith's "Shooting Stars" for British Instructional';[13] and a short news piece under the heading, 'Anthony Asquith's First', announced the film in the following terms:

> The Anthony Asquith film, 'Shooting Stars', was completed last week and the date of the premier presentation is likely to be made at an early date by New Era.
> Made entirely in England, 'Shooting Stars' is likely to create something of a sensation in the film industry – not only in this country, but all over the world, says a representative of New Era.[14]

Subsequently Asquith was to establish a reputation as an adapter of the work of others, to become, in the critical terms of the 1950s and 1960s, a *metteur-en-scène* rather than an *auteur*. In contrast, his entry into the industry was by way of his original story though the screenplay was co-written with John Orton. The other key members of the production team were cinematographer Stanley Rodwell and German lighting expert Karl Fischer. On the latter, Rachael Low commented that the 'first important lighting credits in this country were those of the German technician Karl Fischer on *Shooting Stars* and *Underground* in 1928 for British Instructional, and from now on the key importance of lighting was inescapable'.[15] The leading actors were Annette Benson, Brian Aherne, and Donald Calthrop. Calthrop was the most experienced with acting roles dating from the 1910s whereas Benson and Aherne had both began their careers in the early 1920s. Annette Benson had worked with major British directors such as George Pearson, Graham Cutts, and Alfred Hitchcock, and took top billing in the film's advertising.[16] Aherne was younger and slightly less experienced but was referred to as 'one of our most promising juvenile actors'.[17] They played a husband and wife film star team with Calthrop, a character actor who became familiar in slightly seedy, mildly villainous roles, playing a Chaplinesque film comedian who was having an affair with the Benson character.

Setting the simple love triangle story in a film studio provided the film with a reflexive quality, playing the tale of romantic betrayal against the mores and morality of the film world; in addition, it offered a series of observations on the process of film-making itself, and provided the audience with a glimpse behind the scenes of the most familiar of cultural experiences. The revelatory aspects of the film – its depiction of the various processes of production, its dissection of backstage scandal – proved too much for one exhibitor who wrote to *Kine Weekly* in protest:

> This brings me to a consideration of 'Shooting Stars', which will shortly be offered to exhibitors. Someone with a name writes a story. The author, being the author, has a scenario written for him by a professional writer, and the film is produced by a professional director. The result appears to be an attempt to poke fun at production (at a time when we all trying to take it very seriously), and to present to *our* public the very aspect of our business which we desire should remain a mystery.[18]

Shooting Stars is reflexive both in terms of its 'behind the scenes' subject matter, the world of film stars and film-making, and in its self-consciously artful realisation as a film. Its reflexivity is announced in the opening moments. The film begins with a close-up of Mae Feather (Annette Benson) and Julian Gordon (Brian Aherne) kissing in what looks more like the closing shot of a romantic film than its opening. Aherne's stetson and check shirt, however, clearly indicates that it is a western. Aherne rides away and the camera remains on Benson who has a dove in her hands. The dove pecks her and flies off; she delivers a diatribe in the direction of the camera; then a cut to a film crew reveals the fictional reality – a film is being made. The tone is parodic, the play with the dove perhaps an echo of Griffith's frequent association of animals and birds with his heroines, while a subsequent shot shows Aherne riding away somewhat precariously on a wooden horse being pulled by one of the crew. The choice of genre is interesting, reflecting perhaps the popularity of the western with British audiences, or even the realities of British film-making in the early years when a number of westerns were made including one by Cecil Hepworth.[19] Indeed,

Asquith was a great admirer of the western genre, and in a 1928 issue of *The Picturegoer* he argued that such films 'exhibit the art of the kinema in its simplest and purest terms because they express the drama solely by movement'.[20] Despite his immersion in the artistic currents of cinema coming from France and Germany, conventional Hollywood films also played an important role in his thinking about cinema.

Yet the early moments of the film also incorporate the kind of virtuoso camera movements associated with the more overtly artistic cinemas of Europe and with 'Europeanised' Hollywood films such as *Sunrise* (F. W. Murnau, 1927). A low-angle shot looking up at the fugitive dove is followed by a shot from high above the studio floor; the camera begins to move surveying the people below, picking up and following Mae as she walks from the stage on which the western is being shot to an adjacent stage where another film is in progress. The shot lasts for about one and a half minutes and, although it lacks the fluidity and steadiness of the German masters, it is nonetheless a striking shot and, of course, one carried out under the supervision of a German cinematographer.

The film's opening shots then play with audience perspectives delineating an initial reality (the kiss) which is the shown to be fictional, a film within a film, the first of several sequences in which the film-making process is depicted. The lengthy crane shot which moves between the studio's two shooting stages is the first of a number of technically ambitious and imaginative approaches to narration and style which mark the film out as an accomplished if somewhat raw contribution to film form in the late silent period.

The dissection of the world of film continues with Mae interviewed for a fan magazine but her saccharine answers to questions about her private life, her interests and desires, are juxtaposed with images which undercut them. It defines Mae's character as self-deluding and duplicitous. She has already been constructed as a rather temperamental star, sharp with her colleagues on the set yet she claims to love 'all her fellow workers'. She tells the journalist that she has found her 'ideal mate' – the title follows an image of her and Julian sitting together; but, in a bold and unexpected link the subsequent image is of Andy Wilkes (Donald Calthrop), the slapstick comedian, the star of the film being shot on the adjacent stage, with whom she is having an affair. In addition to the 'behind the scenes' material, the film also contains a sequence in a cinema – another variant on the 'film within a film' strand. Julian, alone for the evening while his wife is with Andy, goes to see *My Man*, Mae's latest release. Shots from the film, an old-fashioned melodrama with highly ornate intertitles, are intercut with shots of the audience responding to the cliff-hanger ending as Julian rushes to rescue Mae from the clutches of the villain. The film's final image has Mae and Julian in an embrace following her rescue; 'The End' appears on the screen and, in another inventive link, a dissolve replaces it with Mae and Andy embracing in his flat during their illicit evening together.

Examples of directorial ingenuity could be multiplied. Roger Manvell has noted the allusion to Eisenstein in the 'impressionistic accident to the stuntman on the bicycle (which is similar in treatment to the shots of the man who falls near the beginning of the Odessa Steps sequence in *Potemkin*)'.[21] The bravura shots from Andy's point of view from the swinging chandelier recall the shots from the trapeze artist in Dupont's *Variety*. The finale – Mae in a studio church set which is being dismantled around her – is a skilful illustration of the ways in which *mise-en-scène* and theme can work together without recourse to overt expressionism. The film embodies the range of stylistic currents discernible in mid-1920s cinema though in a 'contrived' manner, according to Manvell;[22] it also effectively documents British film-making towards the end of the silent era and is a satire on popular film magazines and fan culture. Contemporary comment ranged from the abusive to the congratulatory. *Variety*, in one of its three reviews of the film, described it as 'a disgrace to the film industry of any country',[23] while Lionel Collier, review editor of *Kine Weekly*, wrote that it 'is a remarkably good British picture and one that with "The Ring," sets a higher standard, technically, histrionically and constructively than we are accustomed to on this side'.[24] Although *Kine Weekly* called it a 'brilliant British production which should appeal to all markets',[25] one of the *Variety* reviews suggested that 'the picture is too modern for the average moving picture patron'.[26] The reflexive qualities of the film, its stylistic virtuosity, merged with its accessible melodramatic romantic triangle theme, places it in a category of films which sit somewhat precariously in between the popular conventions of the Hollywood film and the more arcane demands of the art film. In this respect, the comparison with Hitchcock and *The Ring* (1927) in Collier's article is apposite.

Underground (1928)

Asquith's next film, *Underground*, was also based on one of his original stories and, in addition, his apprenticeship under Bramble deemed to be complete, he received sole director credit. It was also British Instructional's second feature film and, though the company had embarked on the building of a new studio at Welwyn, it was not to be completed until late in 1928, and the studio sequences were shot on rented stages at the modern British International Picture studios at Elstree.[27] However, though the interiors did attract comment partly for Karl Fischer's lighting, it was the location work that distinguished the film. *Shooting Stars* had included one lengthy location sequence – a beach on which scenes for the comedy film were being shot – but most of the film was shot in the studio although the studio interior itself was effectively a location for the 'behind the scenes' dimension of the film. *Underground*, in contrast, made extensive use of locations in London including notably the London Underground, its trains, track, and stations including Waterloo and Warren Street, but also the Lots Road power station (the source of electricity for the tube system at the time), the department store, Selfridges and the Thames embankment. For some critics, this solid iconographic anchor presented the director with an opportunity for a truly indigenous film. Paul Rotha, for example, wrote that, 'Britain is the most fertile country imaginable for pure filmic material. Our railways, our industries, our towns, and our countryside are waiting for incorporation into narrative films.' He also suggested that London was 'probably the richest city in the world for cinematic treatment'.[28] However, his judgement on Asquith's film was negative; Asquith had missed the opportunities presented by the subject matter – London, the underground railway system – and had subordinated reality to melodrama. He suggested that, 'Anthony Asquith made *Underground*, but became lost in the Victorian conception of a lift-boy, in place of the soul of London's greatest organisation.'[29] Despite the solidity of the settings, the detailed attention to a range of familiar metropolitan locations, the picture that emerged – a 'story of ordinary work-a-day people' in the words of the film's opening intertitle – was centred on the romantic relationships of four individuals and no better, in Rotha's view, than the routine escapist entertainment coming from Hollywood. In a related fashion, the American critic Harry Alan Potamkin also saw a missed opportunity for a realist depiction of ordinary people. The film was as 'unreal as the revelation of the people it purported to represent. There was no indication of their Underground existence in their lives.' 'Just to have had', he continued, 'certain adventures occur in the Underground does not allow you to offer your film as a document of the Underground people.'[30]

The core of the film is the interlocking series of romantic relationships which bring the four leading characters – Bert (Cyril McLaglen), Nell (Elissa Landi), Bill (Brian Aherne), and Kate (Norah Baring) – together. Though the opening intertitle presents them as 'ordinary people' preparing the viewer for a 'document of Underground people', the film establishes them according to the conventions of screen melodrama. Bert is first seen sitting on the underground train behaving in a somewhat boorish fashion towards his fellow passengers; Kate boards the train and sits next to him, he flirts with her in a somewhat aggressive fashion though she rebuffs him in a spirited and confident manner. He follows her from the train to the escalator where Bill, a railway employee, trips him up and ends his pursuit. The romantic triangle is complete though somewhat overdetermined in terms of outcome given the ways in which the characters have been delineated. The fourth 'ordinary' person – Kate – is introduced in the wake of the other three as Bert's somewhat nervous girlfriend whom he is in the process of discarding in a callous manner in keeping with his rather unpleasant character. When his aggressive pursuit of Nell fails he attempts revenge on Bill, persuading Kate to accuse him of assaulting her. This fails and when Kate goes to the power station to confront Bert, threatening to expose him, he kills her, pushing her against a live power box. The film concludes with a chase – Bill pursuing Bert through the power station and subsequently through the underground itself. Bert is apprehended and the film's coda confirms the melodramatic destiny of Nell and Bill – now a married couple.

The extensive location shooting, the focus on a familiar British institution – the London underground railway system – pushes the film in the direction of realism and there are several sequences which exploit the open air spaces of London: Bill and Nell on an open-top bus journey, their picnic in a park, and the imposing exterior of the Lots Road power station, the naturalistic backdrop for Bill's pursuit of Bert after he has killed Kate. The realism is carried into some of the interior footage of the film with some of the store sequences shot in the Selfridges department store. Yet, the film also moves in other directions drawing upon Asquith's knowledge of European cinema and on his collabora-tion with the lighting expertise of Karl Fischer. When Nell meets Bill in the underground for the second time, they sit together at the bottom of the emergency staircase enjoying a somewhat chaste exchange while arranging a date. During the course of this, the camera moves away from them to reveal the shadows of another couple embracing and finally kissing. The style of presentation, the shadows, evoke the German cinema though the juxtaposition with the muted exchange between Nell and Bill is more in the spirit of contrastive montage. In subsequent sequences there is much play with light and shadow; the introduction of Kate traps her restless and nervous behaviour in low-angled shots through staircase bars and shadows and the expressionist presentation is repeated later in the film when Nell visits her. The film opens with a point of view shot from a camera mounted in the driver's cab of an underground train as it enters a station, a shot that is repeated firstly at the beginning of the film's finale and then in an inverted fashion as the closing shot of the film. The shot is inventive in terms of mobile framing: at the beginning of the film it starts with a black screen, then a speck of light representing the station enlarging gradually to reveal the platform crowded with passengers as the train emerges from the tunnel. The bookending of the entire film with an inverted version of the shot beginning in the station then moving into the blackness of the tunnel is innovative in terms of narrative construction, providing a formally satisfying conclusion to the film. There is also a bow to the French 'Impressionist' film-makers and their strategies for representing inner subjective life. Bert, after a fight with Bill in the pub, is shown in close-up with the shot of the punch superimposed a number of times on his brooding features as he plans his revenge. As with *Shooting Stars*, the film demonstrates a range of cinematic techniques and styles, shifting from the realism of the opening sequence with its 'range of recognizable English social types'[31] travelling on the underground to the melodrama of the murder and chase towards the end of the film.

A Cottage on Dartmoor (1929)

A Cottage on Dartmoor was a British Instructional international co-production with the Swedish Biograph company. It was Asquith's second international co-production; his previous film, *The Runaway Princess*, had been made in conjunction with a German firm, Laenderfilm, and had been filmed largely at their studios in Berlin. *A Cottage on Dartmoor*, however, was filmed entirely in Britain at the new British Instructional Welwyn Garden City Studios which opened towards the end of 1928. The film's international background was reflected in the casting with the leading male characters played by Swedish actor, Uno Henning, and German actor, Hans Schlettow, though the lead female part was played by Norah Baring, the English actress, who had appeared in *Underground*. The film was released in Sweden as *Fången 53* in what Geoff Brown refers to as a 'straightened out' version which eliminated the flashback structure of the British version.[32] Though scripted by Asquith, the film was an adaptation of a story by Herbert C. Price.

The film was begun early in 1929 during the period of transition from silent to sound cinema in Britain. Like a number of British titles from that year it incorporated some synchronised sound, '6% dialog' according to its review in *Variety*,[33] and is sometimes regarded as British

Instructional's first sound film.[34] It was made during an uncertain period for the British industry with some commentators forecasting the shift to all-sound production that was to come whilst others considered the sound film to be a novelty or, less dismissively, as a form best suited to the short subjects – comedies, music hall acts and brief dramas – which it had been used for earlier in the 1920s. Sidney Bernstein, founder of the Granada cinema chain, conducted the first of his famous questionnaires early in 1929 and the results revealed a great deal of public scepticism about the future of the sound film. Leading producer Michael Balcon, in his autobiography, comments 'how thoroughly we deceived ourselves into believing that sound in relation to films was but a passing phase'[35] and like other prominent producers of the time he anticipated continued demand for silent films. However, by 1929 Balcon was busy on a sound version of the successful play *Journey's End* although he had to go to America to make the picture in the absence of sound facilities in his own studios. In May 1928 *Kine Weekly*, whilst recognising that 'the sound film has achieved a widespread vogue in America', offered the prediction of separate development for the two types of film in Britain with 'our kinemas divided into halls specialising some in the silent screen, others in the "talkies"'.[36] Rachael Low indicates that both British Instructional and Asquith himself were interested in the new possibilities presented by sound technology making plans for sound production with the recently formed British Phototone:

> The firm was from the first connected with both Blattner and British Instructional. Asquith was rumoured to be 'musical consultant and adviser' and it was announced that British Instructional might make weekly one-reelers, and also that British Phototone would provide the musical and effects background for three British Instructional Films including Asquith's *Underground*.[37]

It is not difficult to envisage *Underground* with a specifically designed effects and music track. One sequence in particular seems almost planned for its sound possibilities. After Bill's entrapment by Kate in the underground he goes to see Nell and waits outside the store for her. Early in the sequence there is a shot of a man outside a pub playing a tin whistle to a group of children. On its own it may be regarded simply as residual realist detail but the sequence ends with another shot of the whistle player, suggesting, perhaps, that a specific musical motif could have been used to underscore the pathos of the dramatic situation in which Bill and Nell fear the consequences of Bert and Kate's conspiracy. A number of Hollywood companies had adopted this 'interim' sound strategy with films such as *Don Juan* (Alan Crosland, 1926), *Sunrise* (F.

W. Murnau, 1927) and *Seventh Heaven* (Frank Borzage, 1927), basically silent films with specially designed musical scores and sound effects, a stage in the transition to the dialogue film which became the Hollywood norm by 1930. Even *The Jazz Singer* (Alan Crosland, 1927), the film most closely associated with the advent of the sound picture, was largely a silent film with music and effects; however, its two synchronised speech sequences, which included Al Jolson's famous emblematic line 'You Aint Heard Nothing Yet', marked it out from the other sound films of the time. The British cinema had followed a similar pattern to Hollywood in relation to the development of the sound film, producing a number of shorts – comedies, music hall acts, brief dramas – during 1926 and 1927, but there do not appear to be any British equivalents to the Hollywood early sound features with integral music and sound effects.

By the beginning of 1929, when Asquith began work on *A Cottage on Dartmoor*, the momentum for the dialogue picture was building up and during that year British producers released a number of silent productions which had been hastily converted into sound pictures with the addition of dialogue scenes, music, and sound effects, together with a smaller number of pictures conceived for sound. However, many films from that year remained silent, which was hardly surprising as few theatres in Britain were actually converted to project sound films until the early 1930s. Only one in five theatres had been converted by the end of 1929 and almost two in five theatres still remained unwired for sound at the end of 1930.[38] *A Cottage on Dartmoor*, described in trade advertising as 'Anthony Asquith's first dialogue production',[39] incorporated synchronised sound using German Klangfilm Tobis equipment and recorded in Berlin.[40] The film was almost certainly released in both sound and silent versions with the sound version having a continuous musical score, a song, and some dialogue from the film being watched by the main characters during the cinema scene.[41]

For Asquith the film marks a return to the inventive, experimental impulses of *Shooting Stars* and *Underground* after the somewhat conventional assignment of *The Runaway Princess*. It has a relatively bold narrative structure built around a flashback as well as demonstrating a degree of experimentalism in relation to the emergent sound film, and like *Shooting Stars* and *Underground* it has numerous directorial touches which reflect Asquith's immersion in European cinema, his interests in Expressionist film and montage cinema. Yet the film can also be linked to the narrative drive and movement of the American film and the opening sequence in particular is built on the basis of an alternating montage strategy traceable to Griffith.

The film's dramatic opening has been well-described by Geoff Brown: 'The opening moments (mostly static shots, beautifully composed) establish the spiritual milieu – the escaped prisoner making his way with difficulty across the bleak moors, silhouetted against a vast expanse of sky, with swirling mist and gnarled leafless trees.'[42] The escaped prisoner stops by a pool and there is a shot of his reflection on its surface which dissolves into a shot of a bath in which a child is being bathed by his mother Sally (Norah Baring). From that point the film intercuts images of the child and mother, the escaped convict's flight, and the discovery of his escape at the prison, until eventually he arrives at the cottage and confronts the mother. There is a series of close-ups of the mother, the convict, then back to the mother, and then the first intertitle – 'JOE!' – when she recognises him. At this point, some ten minutes into the film, the narrative shifts back to the past with a shot of Joe (Uno Henning) in his barber's uniform turning to the camera followed by the intertitle – 'Yes, Sally?' This is followed in turn by a shot of Sally – the mother – and a shot locating them both in the hairdressing salon at which they work. It is an abrupt and inventive transition and from that point the film traces the series of events which lead to the confrontation in the lonely cottage on the moor. Eventually the narrative folds back on itself, returning to the cottage for the film's tragic finale. It is a narrative structure not dissimilar to that of a 1930s film such as *Le Jour se lève* (Marcel Carné, 1939) or a Hollywood *film noir* of the 1940s, with a dramatic and heavily charged but enigmatic opening inviting a rollback in time. The other striking aspect of the opening sequence is its fluidity – it is a consummately achieved piece of silent narrative exposition in which the various images – the escaped convict, the woman, the prison cell – are interwoven without recourse to explanatory intertitles; indeed, this is a characteristic of the film as a whole which relies predominantly on image and editing to convey its meanings and uses intertitles very sparingly for a small number of very brief dialogue exchanges.

The film is a simple romantic melodrama and, like *Shooting Stars* and *Underground*, mixes together love, jealousy, and violence. Joe and Sally begin a brief romance which ends when Harry (Hans Schlettow), a customer at the hairdressers, starts courting Sally. It is a courtship conducted in full view of Joe at the hairdressers and his humiliation and jealousy build up in the course of the film to a crescendo which culminates in an attack on his rival. Joe is shaving Harry while Sally is giving him a manicure; tension is already there, established previously, and it is built up through a series of close shots of Joe, razor in hand, and Sally and Harry exchanging intimate glances. At one point in the sequence there is a brief array of non-diegetic images – a piece of string breaking, guns firing – a Soviet-style symbolic montage metaphorically depicting Joe's breaking point. Joe threatens Harry, an intertitle reads: 'You've tortured me long enough – now it's my turn', then the attack takes place. Although there is one full shot of Harry staggering after the attack, the episode is largely presented in a flurry of brief images – close shots of the other characters' responses, a shower hose spraying water, a scent bottle spilling onto the floor, 'metonymic images', to use Murray Smith's term, in place of actual images of the attack and its aftermath.[43]

The film bears the imprint of its time – the cusp of the sound revolution – in various ways and, in Smith's view, despite being over-shadowed by its near-contemporary *Blackmail* (1929), *A Cottage on Dartmoor* deserves as much attention as Hitchcock's film as 'an early sound film noted for the inventiveness and precocity of its sound technique'.[44] The inventiveness, he suggests, lies in its attempt 'to forge an alternative "sight-sound aesthetic"' to the 'synchronous sound aesthetic which has become the basis of mainstream cinema'.[45] In some respects the attempts are cumbersome. For example, conversations between Joe and his customers are represented by montages of news-reel extracts – cricket and tennis matches, a speedway race, a political speech (by Lloyd George, successor as Prime Minister to Asquith's father), rather than represented directly through synchronised dialogue. However, the cinema sequence in which dialogue from *My Woman* – the talkie being screened – is used in counterpoint to the images represents a more imaginative move in the context of the rush to synchro-nous sound. In the sequence Joe has followed Sally and Harry to the cinema and is seated near them, watching them intensely. In some respects it is a reprise of the sequence in *Shooting Stars* in which the central character, Julian, goes to the cinema to watch himself on the screen; even the film's title – *My Man* – is similar to the one in the later film. However, in *Shooting Stars* extracts from *My Man* are shown intercut with the audience's responses; in *A Cottage on Dartmoor* neither of the films being screened is shown, only images of the audience's responses. The other difference is that the dialogue from the second film (a talkie) was included in the sound version of the film. The sequence also contains two brief series of images linked to Joe and presented as his thoughts. The first composed of images from earlier in the film is mainly a résumé of Joe and Sally's brief romance and Harry's arrival on the scene but it also includes a new image of Joe kissing Sally somewhat roughly. The second contains shots yet to come in the film, flashforwards to Joe's attack on Harry. It is an impressive piece of film-making, as Murray Smith has suggested: 'The scene displays a very sophisticated treatment of time, space and narrative, notably in the confusion between "real" and "imaginary" events. This is especially striking in that the film was made in the British industry, widely regarded as a slavish but inept imitator of Hollywood.'[46] The sequence even contains a Hitchcock-like cameo from Asquith which is combined with a cinematic in-joke. The first film on the programme is a Harold Lloyd comedy; Asquith, playing a member of the audience, is wearing a pair of Lloyd's trademark spectacles, and the point is underlined by two boys staring at him, then at the screen, then back again.

On the basis of his early films, Asquith had demonstrated a degree of mastery of the medium with Rotha regarding him as 'the most fortunately situated of British directors'.[47] As he began his film career British cinema was in the process of redefining itself in a popular film culture dominated by the Hollywood entertainment film with its hold on the imagination of the British audience, and in an intellectual film culture which was responding to the experimental and 'art' cinemas coming from Germany, France, and the Soviet Union, with its hold on the imagination of the cultural intelligentsia and the artistic communities. Like Hitchcock, with whom he was frequently compared, Asquith found himself in between these currents with both a feeling for the vigour and power of the American cinema, and an interest in the innovative forms of the European cinemas. His debut film, *Shooting Stars*, seems to draw them together. It is both a film about popular cinema with its stars and genres, its westerns and slapstick comedians, and a reflexive 'art' film, an example of 'meta-cinema: films which embody a reflection on the processes and functions of making, and watching, films', as Charles Barr has suggested.[48] The highly sophisticated formal processes of the art film, and the ordinary excitements of popular cinema – romance, action, violence, passion – are embodied in tandem in the early films. Both *Underground* and *A Cottage on Dartmoor* have 'metacinematic' film-viewing sequences, as well as sustained passages of subjective cinematography, expressionist *mise-en-scène*, and Soviet-style montage; both films are also simple and uncomplicated romantic tales involving crimes of passion.

Notes

1 PEP,*The British Film Industry* (London: Political and Economic Planning, 1952), p. 41.
2 R. Low, *The History of the British Film 1918-1929* (London: Faber and Faber, 1971), p. 107.
3 V. de Grazia, 'Mass Culture and Sovereignty. The American Challenge to European Cinemas, 1920-1960', *Journal of Modern History*, 61 (March 1989), p. 53.

4 Quoted in *ibid*.
5 *Kine Weekly* (25.8.25), p. 40.
6 O. Blakeston, 'British Solecisms', in J. Donald, A. Friedberg, and L. Marcus (eds), *Close Up 1927–1933. Cinema and Modernism* (London: Cassell, 1998), p. 41.
7 C. Barr, 'Before *Blackmail*. Silent British Cinema', in R. Murphy (ed.), *The British Cinema Book* (London: BFI Publishing, second edition, 2001), p. 11.
8 See, particularly, A. Higson (ed.), *Young and Innocent? The cinema in Britain 1896–1930* (Exeter: University of Exeter Press, 2002) and C. Gledhill, *Framing British Cinema 1918–1928* (London: BFI Publishing, 2003).
9 J. Sexton, 'The Film Society and the Creation of an Alternative Film Culture in Britain in the 1920s', in Higson (ed.), *Young and Innocent?*, p. 292.
10 *Kine Weekly* (8.9.27), p. 59.
11 C. Belfrage, *All is Grist* (London: Parallax Press, n.d.), p. 31.
12 C. Barr, 'Writing Screen Plays Stannard and Hitchcock', in Higson (ed.), *Young and Innocent?*, p. 235.
13 *Kine Weekly* (1.9.27), p. 50.
14 *Ibid*. (17.11.27), p. 45.
15 Low, *The History of the British Film 1918–1929*, p. 252.
16 *Kine Weekly* (26.1.28), pp. 6–7.
17 *Ibid*. (8.9.27), p. 70.
18 *Ibid*. (16.2.28), p. 29 (emphasis in original).
19 See B. McFarlane, *The Encyclopedia of British Film* (London: BFI/Methuen, 2003), p. 717.
20 A. Asquith, 'In Praise of Westerns', *The Picturegoer*, June (1928), p. 13.
21 R. Manvell, 'Revaluations – 3. Shooting Stars, 1928', *Sight and Sound*, 19:4 (1950), p. 174.
22 *Ibid*.
23 *Variety* (13.6.28), p. 12.
24 *Kine Weekly* (9.2.28), p. 59.
25 *Ibid*., p. 61.
26 *Variety* (29.2.28), p. 23.
27 *Ibid*. (1.3.28), p. 25.
28 P. Rotha, *The Film Till Now* (Middlesex: Spring Books, 1967), p. 315.
29 *Ibid*.
30 Quoted in Low, *The History of the British Film 1918-1929*, p. 183.
31 Gledhill, 'Between Melodrama and Realism', p. 145.
32 G. Brown, 'A Cottage on Dartmoor', *Monthly Film Bulletin*, 47:504 (1976), p. 14.
33 *Variety* (16.4.30), p. 49
34 Low, *The History of the British Film 1918–1929*, p. 204.
35 M. Balcon, *My Life in Films* (London: Hutchinson, 1971), p. 34.
36 *Kine Weekly* (5.7.28), p. 21.
37 Low, *The History of the British Film 1918–1929*, p. 204.
38 Gomery, D., 'Economic Struggle and Hollywood Imperialism. Europe Converts to Sound', *Yale French Studies*, 60 (1980), p. 82.
39 *Kine Weekly* (2.1.30), p. 110.
40 R. Low, *Film-making in 1930s Britain* (London: George Allen & Unwin, 1985), p. 78.
41 The sound elements of the film are described in the review in *Kine Weekly* (23.1.30), p. 44. There is also a description of the sound for the cinema sequence in *Close Up*, V:I (1929), pp. 70–1.
42 G. Brown, 'Review. A Cottage on Dartmoor', *Monthly Film Bulletin*, 43:504, January (1976), p. 14.
43 M. Smith, 'Technological Determination, Aesthetic Resistance or *A Cottage on Dartmoor*. Goat-Gland Talkie or Masterpiece', *Wide Angle* 12:3 (1990), p. 91.

44 *Ibid.*, p. 81.
45 *Ibid.*, p. 82.
46 *Ibid.*, p. 89.
47 Rotha, *The Film Till Now*, p. 320.
48 C. Barr, 'Introduction: Amnesia and Schizophrenia', in Barr (ed.), *All Our Yester-days. 90 Years of British Cinema* (London: BFI Publishing, 1986), p. 19.

The 1930s

Although Asquith had established something of a reputation by the end of the silent period, his career in the 1930s wavered somewhat. He had directed (or co-directed) four features in two years in the late 1920s, but was only to direct six films between 1930 and 1939 (or seven if the English version of the multiple language film *The Unfinished Symphony* is included). Yet, in general terms, under the stimulus of the 1928 Quota Act and the protected market for British films, it was a decade of opportunity for film-makers. Based on one set of statistics, from 1932 until 1938 the annual production figure never fell below a hundred, and in 1936 almost two hundred films were released;[1] indeed other analyses have produced higher annual production figures of more than two hundred films for the boom years 1936 and 1937.[2] Whatever the exact statistic, the British film industry of the 1930s was prolific, producing, according to one participant, 'the second highest national output in the world'.[3] Yet it was an industry through which Asquith meandered in the 1930s, working first for a large concern, Gaumont-British, then moving to a small-scale, high-quality studio, London Films, and finally linking up with independent producers Max Schach and Gabriel Pascal.

The British cinema of the 1930s

The British film industry of the 1930s resembled, to an extent, its American counterpart. It was made up of large companies operating in all branches of the industry, along with more specialised independent producers and small firms concentrating upon production; each company, big or small, positioned itself in various ways in relation to the powerful American industry which supplied the bulk of the films for British cinemas. Many of the principal companies formed in the silent period – production concerns such as Gaumont, Gainsborough, British

National Pictures; distributors including Ideal, Wardour Films, and the W & F Film Service; major exhibitors such as Provincial Cinematograph Theatres – had been merged into two large firms by the end of the decade. The two large combines – Gaumont-British and British International Pictures (renamed the Associated British Picture Corporation in 1933) – became the integrated giants of the British cinema. There was, however, space for a range of other smaller concerns to develop and prosper at least until the production crises which occurred late in the decade. Alexander Korda's London Films, for which Asquith was to work, Basil Dean's Associated Talking Pictures, and Herbert Wilcox's British and Dominions Film Corporation, each made important contributions to the profile of British cinema in the 1930s despite operating in the shadow of the majors. Aside from them, a number of companies, such as Butcher's Film Service, British Lion and Nettlefold Productions, concentrated on the cheap 'quota quickie' films made for the American majors, although it is important to note that most companies, apart from Korda's prestige operation, also had space on their schedules for quota films. British Instructional Films, where Asquith worked when it operated as an independent, was absorbed into British International Pictures in the early 1930s, around the time that Asquith was completing *Tell England*.

The films produced by this array of very different companies varied in scope and ambition from large-budget epics and costume pictures with potential international appeal to small-scale comedies drawing upon the indigenous working-class culture of the music hall. Both London Films and Gaumont-British invested heavily in productions aimed at the American market, producing historical costume pictures such as *The Private Life of Henry VIII* (Alexander Korda, 1933) and *Tudor Rose* (Robert Stevenson, 1936). The Associated British Picture Corporation concentrated on more modest programme pictures to supply its expanding cinema chain, while a company such as Associated Talking Pictures made its reputation on the basis of the films of music-hall stars such as Gracie Fields and George Formby. The conventional wisdom about the British cinema of the period, however, is that the films produced rarely matched the quality of their Hollywood counterparts. The British cinema of the 1930s is often dismissed as trivial and escapist, class-bound, dominated by an ethos associated with the middle-class West End theatre, oblivious to the social realities of the time, tarnished by the low quality of the American-sponsored 'quota quickies', and, when ambition was reflected in larger budgets, a pale imitation of Hollywood. Many reasons have been put forward for this state of affairs – the strict conditions of censorship, the poor level of skills possessed by

British producers compared with the drive and flair of their Hollywood competitors, even the preponderance of foreigners in key positions in the industry. Yet it was a period in which film-makers had many advantages compared with the previous decade, including modern, purpose-built studios, a high level of production funding, and an opportunity for their films to be screened in the nation's cinemas guaranteed by the quota system. In such a context Asquith's promising credentials, established by his silent films, should have meant a thriving career in the 1930s, although it was not until late in the decade that he really re-established himself as a director of importance.

Tell England (1931)

Tell England, as noted previously, was originally envisaged as British Instructional Films' first fiction film following its reorganisation in 1927. Though the novel 'was abused, despised, and dismissed by virtually every reviewer', according to Samuel Hynes, it was a popular success 'reprinted fourteen times in 1922, and six times in 1923'.[4] A double-page advert in *Kine Weekly* in September 1927 announced the planned film adaptation with something of a fanfare – 'It is confidently believed that "Tell England" will be the greatest British Motion Picture yet made' – and a release date of 17 September 1928 was specified.[5] This was followed by a dinner organised at the Savoy in October 1927 to celebrate the starting of the film, an event attended by various public figures including some who had served at Gallipoli, the First World War event on which the film was based.[6] Asquith also attended the gathering but his role in the production at this point was unclear; as late as November 1929 *Kine Weekly* reported that a 'talking version' of the novel was now planned and that the 'scenario is in the hands of Anthony Asquith, who has been working at it for the last four or five weeks'.[7] The article went on to state that '(n)o definite arrangements have yet been made as to the director or the cast' although Walter Summers, who had directed the wartime reconstructions *Ypres* (1925) and *Mons* (1926) for British Instructional earlier in the decade, had been mentioned as the scheduled director in a previous report.[8]

As it transpired the direction of the film was shared between Asquith and Geoffrey Barkas. Barkas, a specialist in location shooting, had previously directed *Palaver* (1926), one of the earliest of British Instructional's dramatic films, as well as working on the First World War reconstruction film, *The Somme* (M. A. Wetherell, 1927), for New Era. *Tell England* reflects, to an extent, its origins as a silent project dating back to 1927, in features such as the use of a handful of intertitles; yet it does have significant amounts of dialogue, music and sound effects and can be regarded as Asquith's first sound picture following the limited use of sound in his previous film, *A Cottage on Dartmoor*. It also marks a thematic departure. Asquith's first four films were romances of one sort or another, slight stories in one sense though with dark elements, domestic melodramas, and in many ways the stuff of popular cinema. *Tell England* is a story of the First World War, and a real historical episode – the Gallipoli campaign – which involved British, French, Australian, and New Zealand troops.

In some respects Asquith's silent films had disappointed the high-brow critics. Paul Rotha, while acknowledging his cinematic expertise, questioned the use to which he was putting his technical abilities in a summary comment on his first four films:

> His technique still remains, after four productions, primitively on the surface. In his last picture, for example, there are several instances of quick cutting and symbolic reference, but they were employed because of themselves and not as a contributory factor to the film composition. For this reason, Asquith's work appears that of a virtuoso.[9]

Rotha admired some aspects of *Tell England*, and in particular he singled out the beach landing sequences and the final dramatic episode when one of the central characters takes out a Turkish trench mortar. He had misgivings, however, about the narrative framework of the film, the story of the two young officers barely out of public school trans-ported to the heat of battle. He lamented the fact that the documentary-style sequences had been 'intermixed with a story of such poorness, in fact a story of any kind'. 'Yet again', he continued, 'we who care for cinema have to submit to the sight of splendid material being pulled down to the depths of bathos by the introduction of story-interest.'[10] John Grierson echoed this in his review for *The Clarion*: 'The difficulty has been to separate the intelligence of Asquith as a technician and his great ambition as an artist, from the thoroughly false importances which either the story of Raymond's or Asquith's own mind has imposed on the fabric of the film.'[11] Ironically, in later years – most notably during the Second World War – the fusion of documentary and fiction anticipated in *Tell England* was to be regarded as a distinctive British contribution to the development of cinema, and an important ingredient in the most successful British films of the 1940s.

In some respects the first half of the film does fall into distinctive sections separating out the fictional and documentary elements some-what starkly. A long opening section introduces the central characters,

Edgar Doe (Carl Harbord) and Rupert Ray (Tony Bruce), public schoolboys in their final days before leaving school – they swim in a river, they sail in a punt, they joke around, and Edgar competes in the school's swimming contest. A poster carefully dates the contest where Edgar wins the relay for his team against the odds. It is 15 July 1914, i.e. about three weeks before Britain declared war on Germany. The victorious Edgar is borne aloft by his supporters but there is a fade to black and the sound of a bell tolling. In the next scene Edgar's mother says ominously, 'I suppose this means war', and there is a cut to a soldier bayoneting what turns out to be a dummy – it is a training exercise rather than a combat situation. However, the tolling bell, the resigned comment about the impending war, and the abrupt cut to a violent image shifts the tone of the film substantially. Edgar and Rupert are now being trained for war and are far removed from their carefree final days at school. This section of the film ends with a shot of Rupert looking out of a window; there is a familiar martial tune on the soundtrack and he says, 'Wonder where they're going?' There is an abrupt cut to an intertitle – 'To Gallipoli ...'

The film then shifts from the fictional mode to that of the documentary-reconstruction about troops en route by boat to the Dardanelles, and their attempted landings on the beaches of Gallipoli. Indeed, for around twenty-five minutes, Edgar and Rupert disappear from the film, along with the fictional thread established in the opening section. It is these sequences that Geoffrey Barkas was closely involved with and, as a veteran of Gallipoli, he brought personal experience as well as location-shooting expertise to the enterprise. Asquith, however, according to his own testimony, was present at the shooting which was done with coastal Malta standing in for Gallipoli. As he later wrote, 'We turned Malta into a tremendous film studio camp. Barkas and myself were the "Field-Marshals" in charge of operations.'[12] Rotha had singled out this section for specific praise:

> From the moment we see the great black battleships belching their smoke across a clouded sky, surrounded by launches and pinnaces, the film grips our imagination. Shot succeeds shot with the rapidity of rifle-fire. No war film yet produced has been more convincing than these scenes of the landings, not even the often-mentioned sequence in Pudovkin's *End of St. Petersburg* or the long tracking shots of the French attack in Milestone's *All Quiet on the Western Front.*[13]

The power of the landing sequences in particular is enhanced by the inclusion of several shots from the point of view of the Turkish gunners as they look down on the allied troops emerging from the troopships and attempting to move onto the beaches. Although 'documentary reconstruction' is the appropriate term for this section, there is some reliance on the cross-cutting of classical fiction cinema to achieve the effectiveness noted by Rotha. Also, the section contains some dramatised material with a discussion between officers about the viability of the mission. Lines of dialogue such as 'I don't think there is going to be very much question of getting ashore' and 'I shouldn't think there'll be very much trouble' are intercut ironically with images of the Turkish gunners lying in wait followed by several shots of men being mown down by machine-gun fire. The final shot of the section is of a soldier lying half in the sea, his head moved back and forth by the wash of the tide. It is a striking shot compositionally very similar to the shot in Eisenstein's *October* towards the end of the 'July Days' sequence when the flagbearer lies dead on the river bank. It is a powerful if downbeat ending to the sequence and a fade to black returns the film to the fictional narrative, to Edgar and Rupert who are just about to learn of their posting to Gallipoli.

The second half of the film is concerned entirely with the fictional story and though it does begin with the two friends greeting with some enthusiasm the news of their posting, the dark tone established towards the end of the first section, and reinforced in the documentary reconstruction section, is soon resumed. Edgar says goodbye to his mother (Fay Compton) who is naturally apprehensive though he reassures her that he is coming back. After he is gone, his mother is visited by a friend who discusses some minor social matter. The sequence is organised to represent the mother's anguish following Edgar's departure, achieved partly through the orchestration of the camera which moves towards the mother at key points, partly through the manipulation of the soundtrack in a sequence which, at times, obscures the neighbour's speech by reducing its volume and by overlaying it with military music and communal singing to depict the mother's anguished distraction. There are echoes of the expressionist distortions of sound that Hitchcock experimented with in *Blackmail*'s celebrated 'knife' sequence a year or so earlier and, also, an anticipation of David Lean's use of the device in *Brief Encounter* (1945), some fifteen years later. The mother faints at the end of the sequence and this is again handled in an expressionist manner through camera positioning and cutting and through the careful choice of accompanying music. With reference to this sequence, Asquith himself wrote that:

> It has been intensely interesting in this experimental period to work out the correct sounds to express certain emotions. For instance, for a woman fainting, I used a 'cello and a double bass, then two high notes on

a piano, followed by a single note on a piccolo, rather like the squeak of a bat. Sensitively used, music can play a very great part in films of the future.[14]

Much of the remainder of the film takes place in a trench, that very familiar icon of the First World War. Edgar and Rupert and their troop are literally pinned down in the trench which is being shelled by a Turkish trench mortar named 'Clara' by the men. The focus is now on the responses to war, to the fearful conditions of combat, and after some edgy moments of conflict between the two friends, Edgar, on the verge of breakdown, erupts in dramatic fashion. The sequence draws upon the film's title. Edgar, in close-up, says, 'I'd like to tell England' and the dialogue is followed by images of a soldier being shot down; the pattern – the same line of dialogue together with a variety of horrific battle images – is repeated in a powerful sequence which ends with Edgar slumping forward onto the table. His outburst, however, puts an end to the edgy period and is followed by a nostalgic sequence in which the two friends reminisce about their pre-war past, a sequence which incorporates flashbacks to their idyllic pre-war life – swimming, punting, and so on. In the final sequences, Edgar heroically charges on the Turkish trench position and immobilises 'Clara'; he is, however, shot in the course of this and later dies in a field hospital. The final images of the film are preceded by an intertitle – 'On January 8th 1916 the last British troops had left the peninsula.' Edgar's grave is marked with a wooden cross which bears the epitaph – 'Tell England, ye who pass this monument. We died for her, and here we rest content.' The words are a version of the epitaph of the Spartans at Thermopylae which Edgar has translated from the Greek. They can be, and indeed have been, interpreted as giving the film, if not exactly a pro-war tone, then at least a tone of justification for the human sacrifice, as in Jeffrey Richards trenchant characterisation of the film's attitude to war: 'While the Germans (*Westfront 1918*) and the Americans (*All Quiet on the Western Front*) were making eloquent denunciations of the war and the horrors of the trenches, the British were glorifying patriotic sacrifice and the public school code of the officer and gentleman in *Tell England*.'[15] On its release, in fact, the film did prompt similar criticism for its apparent glorification of war, and Asquith himself, in an interview, was provoked into defending the film against such a charge:

> This surely an extraordinarily naïve criticism. The fact that a great number of our troops behaved with amazing courage and endurance in the most appalling circumstances is certainly a glorious thing. But to show this seems to me far truer and more powerful anti-war propaganda than to show that all our soldiers are drunken bullies whose fate would

scarcely evoke sympathy. It is surely far more awful that splendid and noble qualities should be wasted in the futility and horror of war, as I have tried to show.[16]

The wasting of 'splendid and noble qualities in the futility and horror of war' was a key element of the predominant myth of the 'Great War', as defined by Samuel Hynes.[17] In Asquith's film the 'splendid and noble' aspects of the myth are embodied in the idealism and commitment displayed by Edgar and Rupert while the 'futility and horror' aspects are suggested in the disillusion felt by Edgar in his 'Tell England' outburst. Another aspect of the myth was the sense of a failure of leadership – 'lions led by donkeys' – and in Asquith's film this is hinted at in the representation of the commanding officers especially in the complacency of the officer presiding over the beach landing. It is this sense of disillusion that is embodied in the serious literary reflections by writers such as Robert Graves, Siegfried Sassoon, Edmund Blunden, Erich Maria Remarque, and R. C. Sherriff, the novels, plays, poems, and memoirs which appeared towards the end of the 1920s. However, as Michael Paris has suggested, other mythic strands, other understandings of the conflict, are also discernible. In particular, it was an account that suggested:

> that the war had been justified and which emphasised its heroic and sacrificial nature – another bloody but glorious page in the history of the British Empire. This interpretation of the War was expressed, not in the writings of an intellectual elite, but in mass culture – in war memorials, in adventure fictions, boys' stories, magazine illustrations and in popular histories.[18]

Asquith, of course, belonged to the social elite that generated the disenchanted view. Yet, working in a popular medium, and from a popular literary source, exerted its own pressures on the ideology of the film which 'struck an uneasy balance, reflecting the dominant public mood of wanting to remember the War as worthwhile and the dead as heroes, yet often tinged with the disenchantment that film-makers shared with other of their class'.[19]

Tell England departed significantly from Asquith's major silent pictures which were centred on working-class characters (*Underground, A Cottage on Dartmoor*), or on the relatively classless world of popular entertainment (*Shooting Stars*). The central characters in *Tell England* are upper-middle-class public schoolboys from a social milieu that was to figure prominently in many of Asquith's subsequent films. Also, the intense friendship between Edgar and Rupert introduces a possible homo-erotic element to set beside the overtly heterosexual preoccupations of

Asquith's previous films. Indeed, homo-eroticism is an important element in the literary reflection on the war identified and explored in some detail by Paul Fussell in his book, *The Great War and Modern Memory*.[20] Its understated presence in the film also raises issues about Asquith's own personal dispositions, evoked subsequently in his adaptations of the work of overtly homosexual artists such as Oscar Wilde and Terence Rattigan.

Moscow Nights (1935)

Between *Tell England* and *Moscow Nights* Asquith completed *Dance Pretty Lady*, which turned out to be his last feature for British Instructional; he then moved to Gaumont-British in 1932 and directed *The Lucky Number* for the Gainsborough production arm of the company. Apart from the two features his only other work was co-directing the English version of a multiple language film – *The Unfinished Symphony* (Willi Forst, 1934), second unit direction on Walter Forde's naval picture, *Forever England* (1935), and some script writing. After establishing himself as one of the most promising directors in British cinema in the late silent period, his career seemed to be dissolving despite the fact that he was working at the Gaumont-British organisation, a company with an annual production figure of around twenty films at the time.[21] However, as noted in the introduction, studio head, Michael Balcon, was unable to fit Asquith into the schedule of 'specialised comedies' and 'Anglo-American' subjects in which the studio specialised.[22] By 1934, Asquith's career was at a 'low ebb' – the term used by his illustrious contemporary, Alfred Hitchcock, with whom he had often been bracketed in the late 1920s, to describe his own meandering directorial career in the early 1930s. Hitchcock had ended his time at British International Pictures producing a quota picture though, in his case, linking up with Balcon at Gaumont-British led to the highly successful thriller sextet and films such as *The 39 Steps* (1935) and *The Lady Vanishes* (1938). Both directors, it seems, had problems during the period but whereas Hitchcock's association with Balcon turned out to be highly fruitful, Gaumont-British proved to be something of a dead end for Asquith.

Asquith left Gaumont-British and signed a contract with Alexander Korda's London Films, initially to work on a film to mark the Silver Jubilee of King George V in 1936 with a script written by Winston Churchill. In the event that project did not materialise and Asquith was assigned to *Moscow Nights*, an English remake of a French film, *Les*

Nuits de Moscou (Alexis Granowsky, 1934), one of the many foreign-language films that Korda had bought with a view to remaking them in English versions.[23] The star of *Les Nuits de Moscou* was Harry Baur, a popular French actor, and he, along with the director, Alexis Granowsky, were also signed up for the Korda production, with the latter to act as producer. The other principal actors were Laurence Olivier and Penelope Dudley Ward, both new contract players at Korda's London Films, in a romantic pairing that Asquith was to use again for *The Demi-Paradise* in 1943. Olivier had appeared in a small number of unremarkable films in Britain and Hollywood, and it was only Penelope Dudley Ward's second film, following a British and Dominions quota picture.

The film, a 'cliché-ridden melodramatic spy story' according to one writer,[24] 'one of Denham Studio's worst films' according to another,[25] did not bring Asquith the breakthrough he needed to get his career back on course. Like *Tell England*, *Moscow Nights* is set during the First World War, though in pre-Revolutionary Russia and away from the front line of battle. The film is organised in two interlocking generic strands. The first is a love triangle involving Captain Ignatoff, a young officer (Olivier) recuperating after a battle injury, Natasha, the young nurse (Dudley Ward) who looks after him while he is in hospital, and Peter Briochow (Baur), a wealthy middle-aged grain merchant and war profiteer whose marriage to Natasha has been arranged by her mother. The second strand – announced in the opening title, 'Espionage' – involves a spy ring organised by Madame Sabline (Athene Seyler), a fictional predecessor of Hitchcock's Miss Froy in *The Lady Vanishes*. Ignatoff incurs gambling debts to Briochow and Madame Sabline, exploiting his need for money, tries to draw him into her spy network. He is tried for high treason but found innocent after Briochow's testimony. The film concludes with Ignatoff returning to the front, being waved off by Natasha, a typical though somewhat restrained Hollywood-style ending.

There are a handful of directorial touches in the film worth singling out in relation to the stage it occupies in Asquith's career. The advent of the sound picture had diminished the use of the contrastive and associative montage techniques developed, in particular, by the Soviet film-makers of the 1920s. *Moscow Nights*, however, contains a few examples of such techniques. When Captain Ignatoff arrives at the hospital he is in a degree of shock and close shots of his being settled in the hospital bed are followed by a sequence of war images drawn from documentary footage – guns firing, bombs, explosions, tanks, cavalry, aeroplanes – conveying his fragile mental state. Later in the film, after an edgy scene in the hospital with Natasha and Briochow, Ignatoff sweeps a tray of cups off a table in anger and there is an abrupt cut to further war images – explosions, aeroplanes, bombs, and so forth – a symbolic montage embodying his rage. It is a format that is also employed subsequently when Briochow overturns a table in anger, but one which prompted Graham Greene's acerbic comment in his *Spectator* review that the 'direction is puerile, no one can drop a tray or a glass without Mr Asquith cutting to a shell-burst'.[26] Whether 'puerile' is quite the right word, the technique is at least oddly archaic in a mid-1930s film, redolent of the Soviet montage cinema of the 1920s. However, Asquith was not alone in the use of such stylistic throwbacks to the silent period; Fritz Lang in *Fury* (1936), his American debut film, followed a shot of gossiping women with a shot of clucking chickens in a similar vein. A more imaginative example of constructive montage is to be found in the film's finale, in the trial sequence when Briochow is giving his testimony, crucial evidence which will either condemn or clear Ignatoff. After the key question is put to him there is a close shot of Briochow pondering his answer followed by a shot of Ignatoff. The two shots are repeated with the camera moving slowly towards Ignatoff as the shot dissolves into one of his being blindfolded followed by shots of the firing squad and his execution. There is a shot of a cross which dissolves into the image of Briochow in the witness box just before he delivers his answer – 'No' – to the court. The anticipation of Ignatoff's fate – summarised in the montage complete with its flashforward to an imaginary event – clearly has stirred Briochow's conscience and his reply to the court exonerates him from the accusation of espionage.

The film has a number of striking location sequences representing the Russian countryside though it is not clear whether these were taken from the French original or newly shot for the remake. Part of Korda's thinking in acquiring the foreign titles for remaking was that the 'English film-maker could both use the original as a model and, if need be, keep large portions of the original footage (e.g. location and background footage, crowd and large-scale action scenes) in the adapted version'.[27] The film was not without its defenders: indeed one critic singled out Asquith's direction for specific comment: 'The situations in the story are not original, but the treatment throughout is excellent, and Mr Asquith must be complimented on almost every ground. The technical merits, the cumulative dramatic effect, the mastery of detail in this picture denotes a master director of films.'[28]

The film has been seen as an important milestone in Laurence Olivier's career, an early indication, perhaps, of the strength of Asquith's skills as a director of actors. Jeffrey Richards suggests that 'the film is illuminated and transformed by Olivier, who shows himself in complete rapport with the camera, which not only captures his dynamic good looks but shows him playing with all the understatement demanded by the film medium'.[29]

By Korda's standards it was a relatively inexpensive film, its budget of almost £60,000 dwarfed by those of his more prestigious productions such as *Things to Come* (William Cameron Menzies, 1936) and *Knight Without Armour* (Jacques Feyder, 1937).[30] Despite the positive comments on director and star, London Films sold the picture to General Film Distributors and 'it was released with no reference to Korda in the credits'.[31] The blend of romance and espionage which had worked so well for Hitchcock failed to bring similar results for Asquith. Ironically, just prior to beginning work on the film, he had written to Balcon and had congratulated him on the success of *The 39 Steps*.[32]

Pygmalion (1938)

After *Moscow Nights* Asquith left Korda and entered another period of inactivity. In 1936 he signed a contract with Max Schach, a Hungarian producer, who had been involved with *Moscow Nights* through one of his many companies, Capitol Films. Asquith's intention was to work as an independent producer in conjunction with Schach, though nothing seems to have materialised from this arrangement.[33] In fact, by 1936, Schach's production activities were beginning to run into trouble. He had only been working in Britain since 1934 but was part of a grouping which became centrally implicated in the financial crisis which hit the British film industry in the late 1930s and his career effectively ended in 1938.[34] *Pygmalion* had been gestating since late 1935 when Pascal had obtained Shaw's agreement on the project and Asquith, according to Peter Noble, became involved some time in 1937.[35] It has been seen as the film which resurrected his career and pulled him out of the trough in which he found himself during the mid-1930s. Rachael Low, for example, has suggested:

> *Pygmalion* also marked a turning point in the hitherto halting career of Anthony Asquith, who after a brilliant start in silent films had been assigned to one unsatisfactory project after another. A shy, self-effacing and cultivated man, he seems to have had no strong sense of direction in the early thirties and neither Balcon, Korda nor Schach, to all of whom he had been under contract, had realised his potential, perhaps misled by his upper-class manner.[36]

Given the nature of the enterprise and the power of the personalities involved, *Pygmalion* was, in many ways, an unpromising context for

Asquith's attempt to re-establish himself as a significant film director. The foremost personality in the process was the author of *Pygmalion*, the play on which the film was to be based, George Bernard Shaw. By the 1930s Shaw was a distinguished and venerable playwright and had been writing for the stage since the 1890s. He had a set of clear views on the relationship between cinema and theatre, and, in addition, had a highly protective attitude towards the film adaptation of his plays. The cinema, as he wrote in 1914, was 'a much more momentous invention than printing';[37] with the advent of the soundtrack it provided both the means of transcribing a play for the screen while preserving its core verbal element, and an opportunity to bring drama of the highest order with the greatest actors to a much wider audience than that for live theatre. Shaw regarded film as an extension of the theatre, as a new step in the development of dramatic art, and thought that the primacy of the verbal in dramatic art should be reflected in the process of film adaptation. As he put it in an article written in 1931:

> My plays do not consist of occasional remarks to illustrate pictures, but of verbal fencing matches between protagonists and antagonists, whose thrusts and ripostes, parries and passados, follow one another much more closely than thunder follows lightning. The first rule of their producers is that there must never be a moment of silence from the rise of the curtain to the fall.[38]

In many ways his views were at odds with the orthodox position that had been developed in the era of silent cinema that the film was a visual medium and that pictorial communication was superior to the spoken word in the context of cinema.

The other formidable individual with whom Asquith had to contend was Gabriel Pascal, the entrepreneurial brain behind the film, and yet another Hungarian working in the British cinema, 'a figure almost as colorful as Shaw himself'.[39] Pascal had persuaded Shaw that his plays should, indeed could, be filmed in compliance with the playwright's wishes to produce significant films despite the unpromising experiences of the handful of previous Shaw adaptations. In terms of the publicity for the film, it belonged to Shaw and Pascal and, indeed, in a biography of Pascal written by his wife, Asquith's name is not even mentioned in the chapter devoted to *Pygmalion*.[40] A further factor was Leslie Howard, the prominent Hollywood star selected for the role of Professor Higgins. According to Kevin Brownlow, 'Pascal chose him not only as leading actor but initially as director. Howard asked for someone to help him and Pascal hired Anthony Asquith who had been going through a bad patch.'[41] Once again, as on *Shooting Stars* and *Tell*

England, Asquith shared the direction credit, though Wendy Hiller was later to remark that 'as one who was in practically every day's shooting, I can say with confidence that I wouldn't have known Leslie was co-directing until we were shooting the tea-party scene'.[42] Also, David Lean, who worked on the film as editor, 'gave Asquith entire credit for directing the film'.[43] Yet, the creative mix on the film is further complicated by Lean's presence.

Vera Campbell, Lean's assistant cutter, quoted by Brownlow, claims that Lean should have had a co-director credit alongside Asquith and Howard:

> 'Puffin and David directed that film,' she said. 'Puffin was such a dear, and quite firm. He would never have any unpleasantness and he got on well with David. But David gradually pushed and pushed until Puffin was doing comparatively little and David was taking control as the cutter on the floor.'[44]

The accomplished montage sequences undoubtedly reflect Lean's developing skills in the cutting room though Asquith himself had displayed montage skills in his previous films. In a sense, the empirical details of creative responsibility (undoubtedly complex especially in this particular film) are secondary to the way in which responsibility was allocated in the public discussion of the film and the foregrounding of Asquith's role as director among the array of creative personalities. Basil Wright, in a review of the film in *The Spectator*, comments:

> The most important thing about *Pygmalion* is that it represents a triumph for Anthony Asquith, whose sincere cinematic sensitivity has been all too neglected by producers in recent years. The work of transferring a work so essentially uncinematic as Shaw's *Pygmalion* to the fluid terms of the screen is something from which a less assured spirit might well shrink.[45]

And, Michael Holroyd, in his biography of Shaw, suggests:

> It was Anthony Asquith who made *Pygmalion* a success. Pascal as producer was a whirlwind, stimulating, disruptive, unpredictable. There was a 'terrible row and throughout the whole shooting of the picture we were never on speaking terms', remembered Wendy Hiller. 'But as the direction was in the expert hands of Anthony Asquith we managed remarkably well.'[46]

Low's notion of the film as a 'turning point' in Asquith's career was not simply a reference to its commercial and critical success; it was also a turning point in terms of his source material. It was the first time that Asquith had been involved in the adaptation of a work written for the stage, a practice that was to play an increasingly important role in his career from *Pygmalion* onwards. Asquith's reputation had been made in the silent era as a director sensitive to cinematic values, attuned to the visual presentation of drama through *mise-en-scène*, through montage, through the resources of cinema. The confrontation with the theatre and with Shaw might have constituted something of an artistic challenge to the carefully thought through aesthetic principles which governed his silent films in particular. In fact, Shaw was persuaded to incorporate a number of additions to the filmed version amounting, on Donald Costello's calculations, to '37 per cent of the film's entire playing time' and comprising some fifteen additional sequences.[47] Some of them, including the Embassy Ball sequence, Shaw himself wrote, and some are transitional scenes with little or no dialogue. The key point is that all of them, in a range of ways, bring cinematic values to the dramatic material turning, in Basil Wright's words, 'what might so easily have been a photographed stage play into something essentially filmic'.[48]

The opening is a good example of Wright's point. The film begins in the Covent Garden market and opens on a close shot of a flower basket; the camera moves to frame Eliza (Wendy Hiller) who walks away and though the camera follows her she moves quickly out of view and, in a brief series of shots the camera begins to follow a man walking through the market ending with a long shot of the front of St Paul's Church bustling with activity. There is a dissolve to the same scene at night, now almost deserted and the man in the previous shots comes into view, walks into the foreground, and is eventually identifiable as Professor Higgins (Leslie Howard). There are some scraps of dialogue – from Eliza at the beginning, from two night watchmen at the end, but the sequence is largely a matter of sound effects, music, elaborate camera movements, and the bustle of human movement on the screen. At its very end, following the medium close shot of Higgins, there is a cut as he walks away and the camera moves towards two women near the church's portico with one saying to the other, 'What can Freddy be doing all this time?' In fact, this the first scene of the play itself and the question, a slightly truncated version of the play's opening lines.

The film also contains other sequences – some brief, some more sustained – which assert its credentials as a film rather than as a simple transcription of a play. Early in the film Eliza returns to her home and there is a short single-shot sequence which simply observes her lighting a gas lamp, playing with her caged bird, and pulling faces at herself in a mirror. The camera sustains a medium close-up image for most of the shot but moves to frame and reframe Eliza as she goes from the gas lamp to the birdcage and then to the dressing table. Though a lengthy (forty-five seconds) shot in the context of the film norms of the day – the shot is too short an element to envisage in theatrical terms and would have meant little on stage; yet on the screen it is an intimate and endearing insight into Eliza's character. In contrast to this single-shot scene, there are a number of lengthier sequences constructed on montage principles which again reflect the capacities of the medium in contrast to those of the stage. Eliza's transformation from the cockney flower seller to the sophisticated and articulate young woman is dealt with briefly in the play with Shaw providing a 'conventional stage conversation scene' based upon a short pronunciation lesson.[49] The film has two montage sequences covering Eliza's education. The first, lasting about two-and-a-half minutes precedes her first 'test' – the tea party at Mrs Higgins' house. Eliza fails this due to her stiff deportment and somewhat mechanical parroting of standard elocution exercises such as 'The rain in Spain', and so forth. The second is after the tea party and begins with Higgins resolving to complete his transformation of Eliza in time for a reception at the Transylvanian embassy; it is longer than the first with over three-and-a-half minutes of screen time. The first sequence assembles miscellaneous brief images and sounds of the processes of instruction, of Higgins taking her through the elocution exercises interspersed with images of Eliza sleeping fitfully; the second is similar but includes deportment, dancing and etiquette lessons as well, and is interspersed with images of Freddy (David Tree), an admirer whom she had met at the tea party. Both sequences utilise the traditional techniques of montage – briefly-held shots, canted framings, the use of music rather than dialogue – summarising the narrative events they depict, rendering events which occur off-stage in theatrical productions, exploiting effectively the ways in which the screen differs from the stage.

Perhaps the interaction between screen and stage is better understood by examining one of the more conventional theatrical sequences, i.e., a sequence which follows the traditional unities of time and space and represents the cut and thrust of argument and dialogue in which the political and social force of Shaw's drama resides. One of the key moments in *Pygmalion* occurs after the Embassy Ball where Eliza has been mistaken for a princess thus fulfilling the aims of Higgins' project. He has successfully transformed her from a 'flower girl' to a 'duchess' but the aftermath leaves her in a somewhat distraught state uncertain about her future and feeling used and then discarded by Higgins. The scene builds from an initial discussion between Higgins and Pickering overheard by Eliza in which Higgins expresses his relief that the enterprise is finished. It progresses into a lengthy discussion between Eliza and Higgins about the consequences of the experiment for her and touches on their feelings about and for each other. In one sense, what is important is contained in the dialogue for, as Asquith himself noted, the 'heart of a Shaw scene is nearly always a verbal one. The dialogue is closly (sic) knit, but elaborate.'[50] The film director's task, also in Asquith's own words, is 'to provide a visual accompaniment to the dialogue which would give it its fullest effect.'[51] In fact, what is striking about the sequence is the varied way in which the verbal exchanges are presented using a range of cinematic techniques. There is some brisk intercutting of shots lasting a few seconds each; there are shots several seconds long combined with camera movements in which major sections of dialogue are delivered uninterrupted by cutting; and there is a classic shot/reverse shot dialogue section towards the end of the sequence with a dozen or so shots of roughly the same length as they argue about who owns the clothes provided for Eliza's transformation. There are also examples of framing and camera movement used to counterpoint dialogue. At the beginning of the sequence, Eliza appears at the door of Higgins' drawing-room; she moves across to switch the lights on and Higgins and Pickering come into the room talking somewhat boisterously; they move out of frame still talking and the camera moves towards Eliza, eventually framing her in medium close shot as Higgins utters the line, 'What silly tomfoolery. Thank God it's all over.'

There is one further way in which the conventions of popular cinema asserted themselves over the play. In the stage version *Pygmalion*, in many respects a typical Shavian play of ideas, had ended with Eliza marrying Freddy rather than Professor Higgins, for reasons outlined in the final confrontation scene between herself and the professor. Eliza leaves after an argument with Higgins who delivers the play's final lines – 'she's going to marry Freddy' – then roars with laughter as the play ends. In the film, Eliza drives off with Freddie after the argument with Higgins – a truncated version of the argument in the play. This is followed by a montage sequence of Higgins walking around London. He returns home and accidentally switches on his phonograph which plays a recording of Eliza's untutored voice. He switches the machine off, his head drops in a disconsolate gesture; then same words – 'I washed my face and hands before I came' – are heard on the soundtrack, this time delivered in perfect received pronunciation by Eliza who has returned. The film ends with Higgins asking her – 'Where the devil are my slippers, Eliza?' – which one can interpret as a somewhat oblique version of the conventional happy ending of the popular film, maybe even a nod towards the screwball comedy. According to Bernard Dukore, Asquith shot three endings for the film, choosing 'a romantic one rather than that of Shaw, who makes it clear that Eliza will marry Freddy and that Higgins cheerfully accepts her decision'.[52] Shaw, despite the change, 'endorsed the film as being true to *Pygmalion*'.[53]

Shaw's satisfaction with a film which ostensibly departed from his insistence on the cinema as a kind of handmaiden to his dramas might be looked upon as judicious in the light of the favourable reception of the film. Indeed, in the revised version of his celebrated essay on film aesthetics, the distinguished art historian Erwin Panofsky praised the changes from the play involved in the transposition of *Pygmalion* to the screen:

> In Shaw's *Pygmalion*, for instance, the actual process of Eliza's phonetic education and, still more important, her final triumph at the grand party, are wisely omitted; we see – or rather, hear – some samples of her gradual linguistic improvement and finally encounter her, upon her return from the reception, victorious and splendidly arrayed but deeply hurt for want of recognition and sympathy. In the film adaptation, precisely these two scenes are not only supplied but strongly emphasized; we witness the fascinating activities in the laboratory with its array of spinning disks and mirrors, organ pipes and dancing flames, and we participate in the ambassadorial party, with many moments of impending catastrophe and a little counterintrigue thrown in for suspense. Unquestionably these two scenes, entirely absent from the play, and indeed unachievable on stage, were the highlights of the film; whereas the Shavian dialogue, however severely cut, turned out a little flat in certain moments.[54]

French Without Tears (1939)

French Without Tears, Asquith's next film, was his first collaboration with the two individuals – playwright Terence Rattigan and producer/ writer Anatole de Grunwald – who were to figure prominently in his subsequent career. The play on which it was based had enjoyed a long run in the West End, indeed it was 'London's biggest theatrical hit of the 1930s'.[55] Rattigan had completed the play (then titled *Gone Away*) in 1935 and, when he joined Warner Bros. as a screenwriter in 1936, he offered them the film rights to the play.[56] The studio declined but by 1938 the film rights had been acquired by Paramount and it was to be made in Britain as a quota picture, though one made in the context of the 1938 Quota Act, which encouraged American companies to make more expensive films in Britain; indeed it was subsequently described in the trade press as a 'Paramount super-film'.[57] It was made by the recently-formed Two Cities company in conjunction with the Hollywood major at Shepperton Studios. The film credits simply acknowledge Rattigan's authorship of the original play. He joined the project somewhat late in the day after a screenplay had been prepared but, according to many sources and in his own words, 'rewrote the script entirely' after working on it with de Grunwald and Asquith.[58] The principal actors were Ray Milland and Ellen Drew, drawn from Paramount's American acting roster, with one eye on the American distribution of the picture. They were supplemented by a British cast including Guy Middleton and Roland Culver who had appeared in the original London stage performance of Rattigan's play. The cast also included two French actors, Jim Gérald and Janine Darcey, with Darcey billed on the credits just below Milland and Drew but ahead of the rest of the cast. Milland, in fact, was British, born in Wales, but had been working in Hollywood as well as in Britain through the 1930s and was being groomed for stardom by the studio.

One of the primary reasons for the critical scepticism about 1930s British cinema lay in its alleged escapism, its failure to reflect the breadth of social realities, its preoccupation with the lives of the rich and the idle, its evasion of the dramatic social and political convulsions of the decade. In Michael Balcon's frequently quoted reflection on the period – 'Hardly a single film of the period reflects the agony of the times.'[59] *French Without Tears* fits perfectly into this escapist image of 1930s British cinema and, indeed, its template – Rattigan's play – was described by one theatre critic as 'a masterpiece of frivolity'.[60] *Pygmalion* investigated key ideas of class, breeding, education, language as a social instrument, and so forth, albeit with a comic orientation and, in the film version, a romantic 'battle of the sexes' dimension. *French Without Tears*, by contrast, is a comedy of manners and mores rather than ideas, a light-hearted farce set in a 'language crammer' revolving around a somewhat less than deadly femme fatale, the teasing and flirtatious Diana (Ellen Drew), and her impact on the young men in the language school and, in particular, Alan Howard (Ray Milland).

Pygmalion followed the sequence of Shaw's play adding or 'opening out' material such as Eliza's language education and the Embassy Ball sequence which occur off-stage in the play, together with some short bridging material. The play-text of *French Without Tears* underwent a more radical reconstruction for its screen realisation with the addition of several extra scenes though these were supervised, as has been noted, by the dramatist himself. The action of the play is confined to the living room of a language school but the film has additional scenes in a variety of locations, including the local railway station, a dance hall, the beach, and a number of other rooms in the school – bedrooms, hallways, the dining room, and the garden terrace. The play is opened out significantly to incorporate an impressive and lengthy countryside sequence and there is also a studio reconstruction of the town square, the venue for the carnival party and costume ball – an event which plays an off-stage role in the play. The 'reconstruction' of the play into a screenplay involved a number of changes though often this meant simply relocating the dialogue. For example, the picnic sequence contains most though not quite all of the dialogue from Act Two, Scene One of the play – Alan's discussion with Chris Neilan (David Tree) about Diana's relationship with the Commander (Roland Culver), his account of his novel, and his fight with the Commander, and an intimate discussion between Diana and the Commander.[61] Some of the dialogue from the play is repeated verbatim, some is changed slightly, and some omits elements of the original. There is also some repositioning of the dialogue elements. For example, a discussion between Alan and Chris is intercut with Diana's conversation with the Commander; what is a continuous 'scene' in the play is cut into two for the screen.

A few aspects of the film are worth singling out for attention, aspects which exploit the specific qualities of cinema while retaining the sense of the play. The film opens with a directorial touch which defines the preoccupations of the film. The opening shot of the postman cycling across a bridge is followed first by a sign for Professor Maingot's School then another which bears the inscription 'French in all its aspects.' The camera pans in a swift movement from that phrase to the postman patting the behind of a middle-aged woman – 'French' in one of its most familiar though stereotypical aspects it might be said. A film about the romantic lives of a few English 'bright young things' begins with a mild sexual exchange between two middle-aged French people.

Diana, the 'femme fatale' whose arrival precipitates the sexual jealousies and anxieties that beset the men, is introduced a little way into the film in a teasing fashion. Her brother Kenneth (Kenneth Morgan) is one of the students at the school and Professor Maingot (Jim Gérald) accompanies him to the station to meet her. The teasing (of the audience) occurs when the professor mistakes a pig-tailed schoolgirl for Diana. The camera then follows him as he walks alongside the train but it halts in front of a carriage door as the strikingly beautiful Diana – a fully-fledged woman – descends onto the platform to a fanfare of the film's signature tune on the sound track. Close-ups of Chris and Brian (Guy Middleton), their faces marked by eager approval, confirm the central role that she will now occupy in the narrative as the object of male desires. In *Pygmalion*, the 'remodelled' Eliza is also given a striking introduction at the beginning of the Embassy sequence. Higgins and Pickering are in the foreground when Eliza moves into view from the background; for a brief moment she is a hazy presence but a sharp change in focus captures her as she stands – regal, elegant, transformed – framed within the frame by the portico-style doorway. Hollywood film-makers often paid great attention to the way in which the stars made their first appearance in a film signalling their importance through *mise-en-scène* and cinematography, through image design, through spectacle. These examples show that a British film-maker such as Asquith was equally adept at star presentation.

The most obvious way in which the film has opened out the play is in the *plein-air* sequence featuring a bicycle ride and the subsequent picnicking party by the river. The bicycle ride, which anticipates Truffaut and the celebrated sequence in *Jules et Jim* (1962), is a series of relatively lengthy travelling shots presenting various characters in conversation. It includes a Renoiresque moment in one shot of Alan and Brian face on to the camera moving before them; Kenneth Lake framed between them in the background is trying to ride his bicycle with no hands, vying for attention with the foregrounded conversation. Though the deep space qualities of the *plein-air* shooting are not exploited as fully as in the work of the great French director, the sequence does evoke something of the Renoir of *Partie de campagne* (1936). In fact the sequence is used as a new location for some of the crucial dialogue in the play including Alan's account of his novel. Its subject is men fighting over a woman and, as he outlines it to the Commander, its relevance to the Diana situation becomes obvious and a fight breaks out between them.

The film passed the severest of contemporary critical tests – Graham Greene's judgement – and his comment that the film was 'a triumph for Mr. Anthony Asquith' was, in part, based on admiration for the additional material in the film, the process of 'opening out' the play and incorporating the range of locales. Indeed, he suggested that 'unlike most adaptations from stage plays it is the padding that is memorable'.[62] In both *Pygmalion* and *French Without Tears* much had been added to the plays through their transposition to the screen and although, in one sense, their success and prestige may be attributed to their illustrious sources, it is clear that Asquith's contribution as director played its role as well.

The director ended the 1930s in rather better shape than his meanderings through Gaumont-British and Korda's London Films would have suggested. *Pygmalion*, in addition to its critical and commercial success, was nominated for Academy Awards in the Best Film, Best Actor, and Best Actress categories, and won Oscars for both the adaptation and the screenplay – the latter going to Shaw himself. *French Without Tears* was 'one of the most successful British films of the thirties'.[63] However, it was drastically cut for its American release by leaving out the final sequences in which Alan tries to protect himself against Diana's wiles.

'The result', as Geoffrey Wansell has written, 'was to make the film pointless, as the *New Yorker* noted on its release in late April 1940.'[64] Nevertheless, Asquith had been launched on a trajectory – the skilled adapter – that he was to continue on, especially in the post-war period.

Notes

1 See statistics in E. Dyja (ed.), *BFI Film and Television Handbook 2000* (London: British Film Institute, 1999), p. 26.
2 S. Shafer, *British Popular Films 1929–1939. The Cinema of Reassurance* (London: Routledge, 1997), p. 3.
3 T. Dickinson, *A Discovery of Cinema* (Oxford: Oxford University Press, 1971), p. 66.
4 S. Hynes, *A War Imagined. The First World War and English Culture* (London: Pimlico, 1990), pp. 333–4.
5 *Kine Weekly* (22.9.27), pp. 16–17.
6 *Kine Weekly* (6.10.27), p. 50.
7 *Kine Weekly* (21.11.29), p. 48.
8 *Kine Weekly* (5.1.28), p. 83.
9 P. Rotha, *The Film Till Now* (London: Spring Books, 1967), p. 320.
10 P. Rotha, *Celluloid, The Film Today* (London: Longman's Green, 1931), p. 175.
11 In F. Hardy (ed.), *Grierson on Documentary* (London: Faber and Faber Ltd, 1966), p. 77.
12 'Anthony Asquith's Defence!', *The Film Weekly* (7.11.31), p. 9.
13 Rotha, quoted in Noble, *Anthony Asquith* (London: British Film Institute, 1951), p. 16.
14 *Observer* (11.2.31), quoted in Noble, *Anthony Asquith*, p. 17.
15 J. Richards, *Visions of Yesterday* (London: Routledge & Kegan Paul, 1973), p. 153.
16 'Anthony Asquith's Defence!', *The Film Weekly* (7.11.31), p. 9.
17 Hynes, *A War Imagined*, p. x.
18 M. Paris, 'Enduring Heroes' in Paris (ed.), *The First World War and Popular Cinema. 1914 to the Present* (New Brunswick, New Jersey: Rutgers University Press, 2000), p. 53.
19 *Ibid.*
20 P. Fussell, *The Great War and Modern Memory* (Oxford: Oxford University Press, 1977), Ch. VIII.
21 M. Balcon, *A Lifetime in Films* (London: Hutchinson, 1969), p. 61.
22 Balcon letter, quoted in Noble, *Anthony Asquith*, p. 21.
23 K. Kulik, *Alexander Korda. The Man Who Could Work Miracles* (London: Virgin Books, 1990), p. 125.
24 *Ibid.*, p. 145.
25 R. Armes, *A Critical History of British Cinema* (London: Secker & Warburg, 1978), p. 102.
26 G. Greene, *The Pleasure Dome* (London: Secker & Warburg, 1972), p. 36.
27 Kulik, *Alexander Korda*, p. 125.
28 *The Sunday Times* (10.11.35) – BFI cuttings collection: *Moscow Nights*.
29 J. Richards, *The Age of the Dream Palace. Cinema and Society in Britain 1930–1939* (London: Routledge & Kegan Paul, 1984), p. 165.
30 Budget details in J. Sedgwick, *Popular Filmgoing in 1930s Britain. A Choice of Pleasures* (Exeter: University of Exeter Press, 2000), p. 234. *Ibid.*, p. 166.
31 Richards, *The Age of the Dream Palace*, p. 166.

32 Letter from Asquith to Balcon dated 10.6.35. BFI Special Collection Balcon Collection, C79.

33 Letter from Asquith to Balcon dated 25.2.36 mentions his commitment to Schach. Balcon Collection, C79.

34 See R. Low, *Film-making in 1930s Britain* (London: George Allen & Unwin, 1985), pp. 198–208.

35 Noble, *Anthony Asquith*, p. 23.

36 Low, *Film-making in 1930s Britain*, p. 215.

37 'The Cinema as a Moral Leveller', *New Statesman* (27.6.14), reprinted in B. F. Dukore, *Bernard Shaw on Cinema* (Carbondale and Edwardsville: Southern Illinois University Press, 1997), p. 9.

38 G. B. Shaw, 'My First Talkie', *Malvern Festival Book*, August (1931), reprinted in Dukore, *Bernard Shaw on Cinema*, pp. 76–7.

39 D. P. Costello, *The Serpent's Eye. Shaw and the Cinema* (Notre Dame and London: University of Notre Dame Press, 1965), p. 43.

40 V. Pascal, *The Disciple and His Devil* (London: Michael Joseph, 1970), Ch. 5.

41 K. Brownlow, *David Lean* (London: Faber and Faber, 1996), p. 121.

42 B. McFarlane, *An Autobiography of British Cinema* (London: Methuen, 1997), p. 295.

43 *Ibid.*, pp. 124.

44 *Ibid.*, p. 123.

45 B. Wright, *The Spectator* (14.10.38), quoted in Noble, *Anthony Asquith*, p. 24.

46 M. Holroyd, *Bernard Shaw. Vol. III 1918–1950. The Lure of Fantasy* (London: Chatto and Windus, 1991), p. 391.

47 Costello, *The Serpent's Eye*, p. 68. In fact, there are sixteen additional scenes using Costello's method of analysis. He omits to mention that Eliza's education is represented in two montage sequences, one before the tea party at Mrs Higgins' house as well as the one after it which he does discuss.

48 B. Wright, *The Spectator* (14.10.38), quoted in Noble, *Anthony Asquith*, pp. 24–5.

49 Costello, *The Serpent's Eye*, p. 59.

50 A. Asquith, 'The Play's the Thing', *Films and Filming*, February (1959), p. 13.

51 A. Asquith , 'Shakespeare, Shaw and the screen', in G. Elvin, *Anthony Asquith. A Tribute* (London: British Film Institute, 1968), n. p.

52 Dukore, *Bernard Shaw on Cinema*, p. 135.

53 Costello, *The Serpent's Eye*, p. 79.

54 E. Panofsky, 'Style and Medium in the Motion Pictures', in D. Talbot (ed.), *Film: An Anthology* (Berkeley and Los Angeles: University of California Press, 1967), pp. 21-2. The essay originally appeared in 1934 but was published in a revised version in the 1940s.

55 D. Rebellato, 'French Without Tears', introduction to T. Rattigan, *French Without Tears* (London: Nick Hern Books, 1995), p. xxvi.

56 M. Darlow and G. Hodson, *Terence Rattigan. The Man and His Work* (London: Quartet Books, 1979), p. 75.

57 *Kine Weekly* (19.10.39), p. 19.

58 Quoted in Noble, *Anthony Asquith*, p. 26.

59 M. Balcon, *A Lifetime in Films* (London: Hutchinson, 1969), p. 99.

60 The London *Evening Standard*'s critic quoted in G. Wansell, *Terence Rattigan. A Biography* (London: Fourth Estate, 1996), p. 83.

61 The character is called 'Kit Neilan' in the play.

62 Greene, *The Pleasure Dome*, p. 248.

63 Low, *Film-making in 1930s Britain*, p. 263.

64 Wansell, *Terence Rattigan*, p. 109.

Wartime British cinema   **4**

Asquith, with a now established reputation as one of Britain's leading film-makers, was ideally placed to play a key role in the specific demands placed upon the British cinema in the wartime period. Yet, neither *Pygmalion* nor *French Without Tears*, the films which had helped to consolidate his standing, prefigured the active engagement with wartime subject matter which Asquith was to demonstrate during the period of conflict. Indeed, most of his wartime films – six out of the eight features – have wartime subject matter and can be seen in the context of the industry's contribution to the war effort. All are particularly far removed from the lightness and frivolity of *French Without Tears*.

Film production during the war period was subject to many constraints with the well-documented shortages of studio space, labour, materials, and so forth. exacerbating the problems for British film-makers working in an industry subject to cyclical bouts of instability. Despite this, for many critics and historians, it was a period in which British cinema flourished. As Charles Barr has argued:

> By the end of the war, a positive reading of 'mainstream' British cinema for the first time became convincingly available, both in Britain and abroad. It was a cinema unproblematically British in personnel (after a decade of foreign infiltration that was resented by many), it dealt with current realities of British life, it was on the whole intelligently supported by the state, was popular with British audiences, and earned respect abroad.[1]

Barr is correct to note that the 'foreign infiltration' of the British film industry in the 1930s had been controversial, with critics lamenting 'the preponderance of aliens in key positions in the industry'.[2] Yet it is worth noting, in the context of Asquith, that 'aliens', such as the Hungarian Gabriel Pascal and the Russian-born Anatole de Grunwald, had played a significant role in his career before the war, and that Italians Filippo Del Giudice and Mario Zampi, as well as de Grunwald, were to play key roles in his wartime career.

The war itself, of course, was a highly dramatic subject touching all sections of society in personal ways, and its representation whether in fiction or documentary fed a keen public interest. But it was not simply a matter of the intrinsic interest of the subject matter; in particular critics noted the ways in which documentary techniques – location shooting, the use of non-professionals in acting roles – moved into what Barr calls 'a productive coalition'[3] with fictional film-making to produce a new 'realist' cinema. Some documentary film-makers of the 1930s, the most notable being Alberto Cavalcanti, Pat Jackson, and Harry Watt, changed career direction somewhat surprisingly given the sceptical position taken previously on mainstream commercial cinema in the public pronouncements of the documentarists. Many fiction film-makers incorporated documentary-style sequences in their dramatic films to strengthen their authenticity and to reinforce their realism. To take a well-known example, Noël Coward's celebrated naval picture, *In Which We Serve* (1942), opens with a brief documentary sequence shot by Anthony Havelock-Allan and Ronald Neame in a Newcastle ship-yard, depicting the building of the HMS *Torrin*, the destroyer which featured in the film.[4] The sequence sets the scene effectively for the dramatic episodes which follow, providing what many critics took to be a guarantor of authenticity for the fictionalised events of the film. In a reciprocal gesture, key films from the documentary sector combined fictional and dramatic elements with their documentary subjects. Harry Watt's *Target for Tonight* (1941), Humphrey Jennings' *Fires Were Started* (1943), Pat Jackson's *Western Approaches* (1944), and John Boulting's *Journey Together* (1945) are a formidable quartet of exemplars blending the hitherto separate cinematic modes of fact and fiction, and indicating that the 'productive coalition' worked in both directions.

Many commentators have suggested that the 'positive reading of "mainstream" British cinema for the first time' (to quote Barr) was due to the emergence of a number of gifted film-makers who had worked in the film industry through the troublesome 1930s and who began to realise their talents in a series of exceptional pictures. Michael Powell (as part of a team with Emeric Pressburger), Carol Reed, David Lean (co-director with Coward of *In Which We Serve* and Asquith's erstwhile editor), Frank Launder and Sidney Gilliat, and Ronald Neame were among the film-makers who established significant reputations during this period after lengthy apprenticeships as 'quota quickie' directors, screenwriters, cinematographers and editors in the 1930s. Their maturing as directors can be attributed to the period of apprenticeship in the 1930s and the stimulus of the wartime subject matter. Asquith's career stage, however, was a little different; although only slightly older than most of these, he had already established a certain reputation with his earliest films – *Underground* and *A Cottage on Dartmoor* – and the war period for him was less the emergence of a new significant film director than a revival of his early promise shown in the late silent period, a renewal in a period of film-making possibly more congenial to his qualities as a film-maker.

Wartime film – the contexts

There were important changes in British cinema during the early war years affecting both the commercial structure of the industry and, in the context of the war effort, its relationship with the state. The former has mainly to do with the emergence of the powerful Rank group, the latter with the central role played by the Ministry of Information which had responsibility for wartime propaganda and information across the media. The Rank group, by 1941, had absorbed the Gaumont-British and Gainsborough companies, the Odeon cinema chain, and even Alexander Korda's Denham Studio complex following the difficulties that London Films had run into in the late 1930s. The group had developed a substantial power-base in the industry through the previous decade, building the large modern Pinewood studio, and establishing a powerful distribution arm with General Film Distributors; unusually for a British concern, it also became part-owner of an American company, Universal. Though a minor firm, lacking the resources of an MGM or a Paramount, Universal did produce a number of film cycles which were popular and successful both in the USA and in Britain, including those featuring the young singing star, Deanna Durbin, and the comedy duo Abbott and Costello. The Rank group benefited greatly from this link as distributor of Universal's films in Britain and, as Geoffrey Macnab has suggested, a 'steady stream of top-notch material, starting with *Showboat* and the first of the Deana Durbin vehicles in 1936, helped establish GFD as Britain's prime distribution company'.[5] What the group lacked at the start of the war was a consistent indigenous production supply and steps were taken to remedy this through the setting up of the Independent Producers group in 1942. This was a loose amalgamation of film-makers backed by Rank which at various times included Powell and Pressburger, Leslie Howard, Launder and Gilliat, Ronald Neame, Anthony Havelock-Allan and David Lean. Rank also established a working relationship with Filippo Del Giudice's Two Cities company. Such arrangements provided Rank with a steady flow of 'prestige' material made by some of the leading film-makers of the day and its acquisition of the Gainsborough studio with its strong generic traditions provided a stream of popular material to complement the 'quality' films from the affiliated companies. Rank was dominant though there were other companies which contributed key films to the wartime British cinema. Ealing was especially important though it eventually fell within the Rank sphere of influence through a distribution deal with the company, and other significant firms were the Associated British Picture Corporation, British National, and the American-backed quota firms. In terms of numbers and prestige, however, many of the most significant wartime titles from the mainstream cinema came from Rank or one of its associates. The list of Rank titles includes *Millions Like Us* (Frank Launder and Sidney Gilliat, 1943), *The Life and Death of Colonel Blimp* (Michael Powell and Emeric Pressburger, 1943), *The Gentle Sex* (Leslie Howard, 1943), *The Way Ahead* (Carol Reed, 1944), *A Canterbury Tale* (Powell and Pressburger, 1944), *This Happy Breed* (David Lean, 1944), *Henry V* (Laurence Olivier, 1945), and Asquith's *We Dive at Dawn* (1943) and *The Way to the Stars* (1945).

Wartime British cinema, however, also includes the substantial contribution from the documentary sector not only the notable documentary-drama films already mentioned, but also the newsreels, and the 1,400 short films sponsored by the Ministry of Information.[6] To an extent the growth in the documentary sector was a development from the 1930s. Grierson's film group (the GPO film unit) was taken over by the Ministry of Information and renamed the Crown Film Unit, but key films of the period also came from independent documentary groups such as Paul Rotha's Strand Films, and from the film units set up by the Army, Navy, and the RAF. Many discussions of the wartime cinema stress the contribution made by figures from the documentary sector who made their mark in the mainstream film industry but it is important to note the many mainstream film-makers who commuted between the sectors making commercial features one year and documentary shorts and features the next. For example, David MacDonald, Brian Desmond Hurst, John and Roy Boulting, and Carol Reed made features with war and non-war subjects, short drama documentaries, informational films, and longer service documentaries. Indeed, Ian Dalrymple, who headed the Crown Film Unit, had spent most of his pre-war career as an editor and screenwriter with the Gaumont-British/Gainsborough combine and had contributed to the Oscar-winning *Pygmalion* screenplay. While Harry Watt and Pat Jackson represented the documentarists moving towards the dramatic feature film, there were plenty of fictional film-makers whose work in documentary contributed to the status acquired by British films during the period. Although many of the documentaries came from the MOI and Services Film Units, commercial companies also contributed to actuality film-making in the period, and some of them such as Gaumont-British had their own newsreel sections.

Asquith was to contribute to both the fictional and documentary cinema, directing six features with wartime subject matter, and four documentary-style films with some fictional elements, for the Ministry of Information. In addition, Asquith directed two non-war subjects, the romantic comedy, *Quiet Wedding*, and the costume melodrama, *Fanny by Gaslight*. The war pictures ranged from films about the European resistance to Nazi tyranny both in Germany itself (*Freedom Radio*) and in occupied Belgium (*Uncensored*), to combat action at sea (*We Dive at Dawn*). In terms of tone and mood, they ranged from the light atmosphere of the comedy-thriller *Cottage to Let*, with its generic echoes of Hitchcock and Carol Reed's *Night Train to Munich* (1940), to the more sober studies of the English character in films ostensibly focused upon wartime relationships between Britain and the Soviet Union (*The Demi-Paradise*), and between Britain and America (*The Way to the Stars*). The relationship between Britain and the United States was also the focal point of one of the documentary films. *A Welcome to Britain* was really a training film aimed at American soldiers posted to Britain and designed to introduce them to the social and cultural conventions of the country. *Sight and Sound* was enthusiastic, suggesting that, 'A *Welcome to Britain* has enough entertainment value to merit a general release. It would help us too to welcome and understand better the American soldiers in our midst.'[7] The article went on to compare Asquith's film to *Know Your Ally, Britain* (1943), an American film with similar aims and intentions directed by Frank Capra; it recommended that more films about Britain's allies should be made. *Channel Incident* was a short film about Dunkirk though it fell foul of the documentarists' suspicion of the fiction film nurtured in the previous decade and 'particularly outraged the purists of the documentary movement by the way it used the precious 5-minute national weekly slot (negotiated by the Ministry for government message films) for a work of fiction-type personal identi-fication'.[8] *Rush Hour* was another in the 'the five-minute series'; it was one of the many somewhat didactic shorts – produced by the Ministry of Information on practical aspects of the war effort, in this case about the necessity of shoppers to travel between the hours of 10.00 a.m. and 4 p.m. to avoid the rush hour congestion. It was among a small number of

short films selected for a Mass-Observation survey and its report published in 1942 concluded that though enjoyed by audiences, the
effectiveness of such films as propaganda was doubtful.[9] Asquith's final
wartime short – *Two Fathers* – centred on a discussion between an
Englishman and a Frenchman about the respective contributions to the
war effort by the Englishman's son, an RAF pilot, and the Frenchman's
daughter, a nurse working for the resistance. It stressed the
contribution made by both men and women to the allied cause.

Freedom Radio (1941)

Freedom Radio, though not actually released until early in 1941, was
probably in the planning stages late in 1939, soon after the release of
French Without Tears. Indeed, in January 1940 there was an advert for
the film in *Kine Weekly* though with a different production company and
director.[10] This was a period when the kind of propaganda required
from the film industry was still unclear and when the Ministry of
Information had 'no propaganda policy and no theoretical grasp of what
propaganda itself really was'.[11] It was a period of debate on this matter –
should the documentary film be the main filter for the mixture of the
provision of information and the morale-boosting required, and what
role was there for the fictional film in this process? What role, indeed,
was envisaged for cinemagoing itself? Cinemas had been closed soon
after the declaration of war along with other entertainment and sporting
venues:

> The fear of mass slaughter in crowded places and wholesale destruction
> by enemy bombers account for an Order in Council which brought about
> their forcible closure. But as the air raids failed to materialize and no
> German bombers appeared immediately on the horizon, the govern-
> ment relented in the face of commercial and public pressure, and pro-
> ceeded to give local authorities the freedom to exercise their own
> discretion in the matter.[12]

According to R. J. Minney, Asquith's lofty social and political connections played a role in the 'public pressure' process with his mother
using her influence to lobby government ministers on behalf of the
industry.[13]

By May, 1940, when *Freedom Radio* went into production at Shepperton, after 'months of intensive preparation',[14] there were some
clearer views on the role of film. Kenneth Clark had been appointed
head of the Ministry of Information's Film Division towards the end of

1939 and his paper, 'Programme for Film Propaganda', which came in early in 1940, outlined the roles which all kinds of films – entertainment features, documentaries, newsreels – could play in the propaganda process. Films with war subjects had appeared as early as November 1939, with *The Lion Has Wings*, Korda's mixture of documentary and drama, and, in a very different vein, the comic *Old Mother Riley Joins Up* (Maclean Rogers). During 1940 the war provided a setting for films in a variety of genres – comedies, thrillers, sober dramas, and combat films. *Let George Do It* (Marcel Varnel) with George Formby, *Night Train to Munich* (Carol Reed), *Pastor Hall* (Roy Boulting), and *Convoy* (Pen Tennyson) indicated the different ways in which the war could be presented in an entertainment context. *Freedom Radio* was conceived of first and foremost in entertainment terms and *Kine Weekly* commented that it was 'not being made as a propaganda film; but obviously because of its theme, it will have an indirect, yet invaluable, propaganda appeal'.[15] However, the distinction between 'propaganda' and 'entertainment' is one that was to hover over many films of the period which took on war-relevant subject matter and the delicate task of balancing such elements is effectively demonstrated in *Freedom Radio*.

The film initially establishes a light tone of satirical comedy and of romance. Hitler's physician, Dr Karl Roder (Clive Brook), attends him and diagnoses laryngitis, advising that the Führer talks too much and should rest from speech-making for a while. The following sequence with his wife Irena (Diana Wynyard) emphasises their closeness – they are recently married – but the arrival of her brother, Otto (John Penrose), introduces a somewhat darker note when he looks out of the window to the troops marching by and passes an admiring comment. The tone is further darkened in the following sequence at Karl's annual student reunion meeting when his Jewish friend, Heini (Abraham Sofaer), is summoned by the Gestapo. The next sequence takes place the following year when the waiter informs the now smaller gathering that the club has been banned by the Nazis. The film has replaced the light satirical touch of the opening with the somewhat sombre sense of foreboding in the reunion meeting. Little is spelled out but the atmosphere changes and the serious tone is consolidated shortly after with a dramatic set-piece in a church when a service is interrupted and broken up by Nazis and the priest, a friend of Karl's who is preaching against the Nazis, is attacked and killed. As a consequence, after a chance meeting with a young radio engineer, Hans (Derek Farr), Karl sets up the underground radio station – 'Freedom Radio' – and begins broadcasting anti-Nazi material with the help of some of his old comrades and Hans' technical expertise. Thereafter, the film moves into thriller format with clandestine meetings, sabotage, and a cat-and-mouse game between Karl and the high-ranking Nazis with whom he mingles socially. The film manages two important sub-plots. Hans' fiancée, Elly (Joyce Howard) is raped by a Gestapo officer then sent to a concentration camp, and Irena, Karl's wife, is appointed as Hitler's 'Director of Popular Pageantry'. Irena, 'an interesting Leni Riefenstahl/Thea von Harbou-like character',[16] as one writer has put it, quarrels with her husband, and her status as an important Nazi official causes their estrangement from each other. However, they are eventually reunited and work and eventually die together for the anti-Nazi cause, shot during a broadcast informing the people of the impending invasion of Poland. The film ends with a Nazi broadcast announcing the end of 'Freedom Radio'; it is interrupted but the final image of the film is Hans, microphone in hand, announcing its continuation.

In common with many films of the period, *Freedom Radio* deployed documentary footage though to a limited extent. The powerful impact of the marching troops on Otto is rendered partly by a brief documentary shot. Karl's growing realisation of the horror of Nazi rule is conveyed in a montage of images of marching troops, rallies, an attack on a Jewish shop, a burning building, and so forth, superimposed on a shot of Karl walking along the canalside. Documentary footage is also used somewhat cleverly in the sabotage sequence which intercuts 1930s actuality shots of Hitler addressing massive choreographed rallies with studio shots of Hans sabotaging the sound system and replacing Hitler's speech with a Freedom Radio broadcast. Hitler is then seen descending from the podium in an actuality shot, a splendid example of 'creative geography'. There was a limited amount of location shooting in the car chase sequence when Hans escapes after sabotaging the Hitler speech. However, in the main the film is marked by a degree of 'Hollywood gloss', elaborate and expertly crafted sets presented in high-key lighting as in the impressive pillared hall outside Hitler's office in the opening sequence, or in the lavish apartment which houses a decadent party. Indeed, the trade press stories about the production of the film frequently referred to the sets, often stressing the ingenuity and economy of Paul Sheriff's art direction.[17]

Freedom Radio was an early contribution to the cycle of wartime British films which focused upon resistance movements in Europe. Films such as *Pimpernel Smith* (Leslie Howard, 1941), *The Day Will Dawn* (Harold French, 1942), initially an Asquith project, *One of Our Aircraft is Missing* (Michael Powell and Emeric Pressburger, 1942), *Secret Mission* (Harold French, 1942), *The Silver Fleet* (Vernon Sewell, 1943), and Asquith's own *Uncensored*, sketched the extent of resistance to Nazi occupation mainly in a range of small European countries including Belgium, Holland, and Norway. *Freedom Radio* was somewhat different in so far as it dealt with resistance inside Germany itself, with the leading character a Viennese doctor, and the story covering a period beginning in 1938 after Austria's incorporation into Germany, and ending just before the invasion of Poland at the beginning of September 1939. It differed from many of the films in the resistance cycle including *Pimpernel Smith, One of Our Aircraft is Missing, The Day Will Dawn*, along with *The Night Invader* (Herbert Mason, 1943), and *Escape to Danger* (Lance Comfort, 1943), which anchored their propaganda securely for a domestic audience by placing British characters among the overseas resistance groups as agents of one sort or another. What the film did have, however, was a central character played by Clive Brook. Between 1920 and 1944, he had appeared in almost one hundred films in Britain and America, including well-known Hollywood titles such as *Underworld* (1927), *Shanghai Express* (1932), and *Cavalcade* (1933), and had established a clear star persona as an upper-class British gentleman. In that sense, the film identified a German, or, to be precise, an Austrian anti-Nazi hero, with qualities comprehensible to a domestic audience in familiar, if stereotypical, national terms.

The principal propaganda element, internal German resistance to the Nazis, was not a direction with which propaganda films were to persist. Indeed, Philip Taylor has suggested that such a theme reflected a somewhat backward-looking approach to propaganda in which the Ministry of Information relied upon attitudes formed during the First World War to guide their strategy. The Ministry, he argued:

> had too readily accepted that the methods employed during the final stages of the First World War, which had allegedly proven so effective in bringing the Central Powers to their knees, could equally be applied to a war against the Axis powers ... This partially explains, perhaps, why British propagandists during the initial stages of World War Two attempted to divide the German people from its leadership on lines similar to those followed by Lord Northcliffe's Department of Enemy Propaganda at Crewe House in 1918.[18]

Films which differentiated between different kinds of Germans formed a short-lived thematic strand in the resistance cycle, a product of the early stages of the war. As James Chapman has observed of *Freedom Radio*:

> Its attitude towards the enemy belonged in essence to the phoney war period, but it was released after the blitz when public attitudes were hardening, and thus its message that there were those in Germany who opposed Hitler did not strike a chord with the British people. The idea of

internal dissent – which is also alluded to in Leslie Howard's *Pimpernel Smith* – was not to feature in film propaganda after 1941.[19]

However, whatever the propaganda of the film, one of its interesting features is that it is actually about propaganda and the media with a number of sequences reflecting on the process. An elderly lady is arrested by the Gestapo for listening to foreign broadcasts even though they are simply dance-music programmes, the Nazis are shown doctoring the news about the church attack, the young radio engineer expresses his frustration about his job – 'building radios for them to shout their lies through!', as he cries, and Karl's wife Irena is a Nazi propagandist of sorts, responsible for designing and orchestrating the massive rallies addressed by the Führer.

We Dive At Dawn (1943)

We Dive at Dawn, 'the most ambitious picture ever undertaken by Gainsborough',[20] as the trade press put it, was made in 1942 though not released until early 1943. It was the third of the four films that Asquith directed for Gainsborough and it followed the two war subjects, the spy thriller *Cottage to Let*, and the resistance film, *Uncensored*, and is one of a number of naval films made in the early years of the war. The Gainsborough studio itself had made *For Freedom* (Maurice Elvey, 1940), a blend of fiction and documentary modelled on Korda's *The Lion Has Wings* (1939), and *Neutral Port* (Marcel Varnel, 1940), but the best-known naval films were *Convoy* (Pen Tennyson, 1940) and *Ships with Wings* (Sergei Nolbandov, 1941) from Ealing, and Two Cities' *In Which We Serve* (1942). Shooting for the Noël Coward/David Lean collaboration had begun at Denham in February 1942,[21] some two months before *We Dive at Dawn* went on to the studio floor at the Gaumont-British studio in Shepherd's Bush. However, the Lean/Coward film was still shooting as Asquith's film began its production and both completed their studio stints at around the same time in May of the same year.[22] *In Which We Serve* was released some six months before *We Dive at Dawn* and was an enormous success; indeed, for many, it was the best film made in Britain during the war. In some ways it set a pattern for subsequent war films with its documentary opening, its survey of the different social classes contributing to the war effort, ordinary naval ratings as well as officers, its attention to the home front, to the families of those on active service, and its restraint and realism – characteristics which came to define the new British 'quality cinema' subsequently identified by critics of the period.

Asquith's film resembled *In Which We Serve* in many respects. It is centred on a specific vessel, the *Sea Tiger*, a submarine on a mission to pursue and destroy a Nazi battleship. The Coward picture had started in documentary fashion with the shipbuilding sequence but *We Dive at Dawn* begins with a sequence set in the submarine with the men discussing their forthcoming shore leave.[23] Following this, however, the film incorporates some location shooting as the vessel returns to base. Shots of a real submarine on the Scottish location of Holy Loch intercut skilfully with studio shots of the conning tower set the tone of authenticity clearly sought for the film.[24] It also features detailed studio realism – the reconstruction of the full-size interior of the submarine, the control room, the engine room, as well as a full-scale conning tower – all designed to replicate the *Sea Tiger* with the greatest possible accuracy. Indeed, realism was sought at the expense of shooting efficiency, as *Kine Weekly* noted in one report of production progress:

> Complete realism of undersea conditions is being obtained by the persistence of Asquith in confining all camera movements to the cramped space of the submarine's hull. Naturally, obstacles to the action such as torpedoes, bulkhead doors, iron ladders, piping and engine fittings, are not removed to facilitate the camera viewpoint but remain in the picture, so that, from the kinematographer's angle, the impression of being imprisoned under the sea is exceptionally real.[25]

The set also incorporated a complicated mechanism which enabled it to move and to simulate the gentle rocking of the vessel as well as the convulsive effects of a sudden dive. As another production report put it: 'The superbly-built reconstruction of a submarine control room is pivoted on a steel base above the deep tank on Lime Grove's biggest stage. The entire setting, with artistes, is destined to be swung suddenly downwards in the simulation of a precipitous dive to escape the menace of the Germans.'[26]

In terms of subject matter, the film also mixes material from the home front with the action at sea, exploring the private and domestic lives of crew members. *In Which We Serve* presented a spectrum of characters from all classes and, though somewhat hierarchical in attitude, the film allocates considerable time to representing the ordinary crew. Asquith's film continued in this vein and, as James Chapman has observed, the 'new realism in the representation of naval officers and men evident in *In Which We Serve* was consolidated by *We Dive at Dawn*'.[27] John Mills had played a working-class naval rating in the Lean/ Coward film; for Asquith's film he played Lieutenant Taylor, senior officer on the *Sea Tiger*, but in a relatively classless fashion compared to, say, Coward's playing of Captain Kinross. As Neil Rattigan has put it, the 'class structure is as firmly in place in *We Dive at Dawn* as in *In Which We Serve*, but the film is less concerned to rub its audience's noses in it'.[28]

The Lean/Coward film has a complex narrative structure based upon flashbacks; Asquith's film has a chronological narrative divided into four distinct sections. The first is taken up with a handful of the crew and their private and domestic entanglements following their return to port: Lt Taylor is briefly sketched as a womaniser arranging a series of dates; one crew member, Corrigan (Niall MacGinnis) prepares somewhat reluctantly for his forthcoming wedding; while another, Hobson (Eric Portman) confronts his estranged wife and her domineering brother. However, all are recalled to the submarine after a few hours, leaving the various domestic problems to be resolved. The second narrative section covers the mission – the pursuit of the *Brandenburg*, a German battleship – and it closes with a few brief shots back in England picking up the domestic elements once again. The next section deals with the *Sea Tiger*'s return to base involving action, heroics, and the refuelling of the submarine under Nazi attack. The final section back at the base sees the crewmen's various domestic problems resolved and the film ends with another submarine sailing off on a mission.

The film has a surface realism deriving partly from the location shooting, partly from the meticulous studio reconstruction of the submarine interior, and partly from the attempts at social extension, the dignified treatment of the ordinary crew members. Yet it is also a gripping suspense film with the pursuit of the battleship providing a precise narrative focus for much of the film. Following the completion of the mission, however, the submarine is attacked by destroyers and escapes when the crew throw some debris overboard including the body of a dead German airman picked up earlier. Finally, the submarine makes a detour to a Danish port to refuel, the incident handled in a 'Boys Own escapade' fashion with one of the crew, Hobson (Eric Portman), bravely going ashore alone to pave the way for the 'escapade'.[29] The episode gives the film an opportunity to represent war heroics as firstly Hobson, then others of the crew, take on the Germans, and successfully capture the oil supply with the support of the islanders. Despite the sobriety of the earlier parts of the film, it culminates in melodramatic action rather than realism. Indeed, it has been suggested that, for all the film's realism, its basic premise was inaccurate. Although British submarines had some success against German ships in the Mediterranean:

it was far less true for northern waters, where no conventional British submarine had even damaged a German heavy ship since 1939. In fact, the plot of *We Dive at Dawn* was in some ways a reversal of reality: it was the German submarine fleet, in the shape of the U-47 in October, 1939, which had sunk a British battleship – the *Royal Oak* – in Scapa Flow.[30]

We Dive at Dawn certainly juggles with a number of the elements which make up wartime British cinema – documentary, varied social depiction, melodrama, combat action – producing 'an exciting fictional documentary, with authentic backgrounds and detail' and 'great propaganda and grand adventure', to quote *Kine Weekly*'s review on its release.[31] Asquith's own attitude towards the film, which he discussed in an article written for *The Cine-Technician* stresses the importance of John Mills' performance to the authenticity of the film.[32] Indeed, for Asquith it demonstrated the value of professional acting and countered the arguments of the documentarists who preferred to use non-professionals, real people, as guarantors of authenticity.

The Demi-Paradise (1943)

Cottage to Let and *We Dive at Dawn* had focused upon 'How Britain fights' (one of the Ministry of Information's central categories of propaganda),[33] while *Freedom Radio* and *Uncensored* examined how other countries, including Germany itself, put up resistance to Nazi rule. *The Demi-Paradise* addressed 'What Britain is fighting for', another of the Ministry's central propaganda categories.[34] Ostensibly the film is about Britain's relationship with the Soviet Union or as the trade press put it, 'about mutual understanding between British and Russian peoples – an understanding that can be brought about by the two peoples equally comprehending the other's way of living'.[35] However, it is first and foremost a depiction and celebration of a portfolio of British values and beliefs, the defence of which, it was assumed, constituted the reason why Britain was engaged in the almighty struggle with Nazi Germany; indeed little attention is paid to the Soviet way of life except in incidental ways. The film provided a platform for definitions of national identity, summaries of 'Britishness' or, as critics have noted, 'Englishness', often regarded as its synonym. Indeed, there is something of an irony in the opening sequence in which Ivan (Laurence Olivier), the central character of the film and the one from whose perspective the narrative ostensibly unfolds, offers his views on England and Englishness to a sailor played by John Laurie, the archetypal Scot in the British cinema of the time.

The Demi-Paradise was made for Two Cities, by this time closely associated with the Rank Group which distributed the film; it re-united Asquith with producer and screenwriter Anatole de Grunwald on whose original story the film is based. De Grunwald brought a distinctive perspective to the material as he was actually born in Russia in 1910 though he had fled from his native country during the revolution and had lived in Britain for several years and, indeed, had been educated in a conventional English fashion at Cambridge. He was both to produce the film and write the screenplay based on his story, and to an extent the film represents a partial outsider's view of the nation and its identity. Official attitudes towards the Soviet Union were complicated by the tension between the strategic requirements of support for the Russian people in the military alliance against the Germans and ideological opposition to communism. On the whole the Ministry of Information opted to promote support for Russia in as non-political a fashion as possible, maintaining a distinction between Russia as an ally and the system of government in the Soviet Union. Indeed 1943 – the year in which *The Demi-Paradise* was released – saw a great deal of pro-Russian propaganda activity of various sorts. Early in the year there was a massive assembly at London's Albert Hall celebrating the twenty-fifth anniversary of the Red Army to which Asquith's star, Laurence Olivier, had contributed. Ian McLaine, in his study of wartime propaganda, described the extent of pro-Russian activity by the Ministry of Inform-ation in the following terms:

> In the month of September 1943, for example, meetings were organised for 34 public venues, 35 factories, 100 voluntary societies, 9 schools, 28 civil defence groups and one prison. Scores of exhibitions toured the country and by the end of the following October it was expected that the film *USSR at War* would have been seen by a total factory audience of $1^1/_4$ million. During the month the BBC broadcast thirty programmes with a Russian content to home listeners.[36]

This surge of pro-Russian propaganda was not reflected to any great extent in the commercial cinema, however, and *The Demi-Paradise* remains the only British wartime feature in which Anglo–Soviet relationships play a central role though *Tawny Pipit* (Bernard Miles and Charles Saunders, 1944) has a minor sequence involving a Russian sniper being feted at a village gathering. Hollywood also provided a handful of features set in the Soviet Union including *The Boy from Stalingrad* (Sidney Salkow, 1943), MGM's *Song of Russia* (Gregory Ratoff, 1944), *Three Russian Girls* (Fedor Ozep, 1944), and *Days of Glory* (Jacques Tourneur, 1944).

The focus of *The Demi-Paradise*, though, as mentioned previously, is the nature of Britishness or Englishness, the ideological bedrock on which the nation rested. The device used to explore this was the placing of a foreign character in a British environment, facilitating a more overt meditation on national identity. This was a familiar dramatic device and had been done previously with American characters both in wartime with *A Yank in the RAF* (Henry King, 1941) and *A Yank at Eton* (Norman Taurog, 1942), as well as in the 1930s with *A Yank at Oxford* (Jack Conway, 1937). Laurence Olivier plays Ivan Kouznetsoff, a Soviet engineer in Britain to organise a shipbuilding contract utilising a proto-type propeller which he has designed himself. The shipbuilders are a family-run company and the narrative pretext – the efforts to perfect the propeller design blending Soviet and British engineering expertise, and the building of the ship – is overlaid with a series of encounters between the Soviet visitor and members of the family designed to illustrate and explain aspects of Englishness. The film is divided into two large narrative sections. The first, set just before the war, outlines Ivan's perceptions of the British as 'humourless, arrogant, narrow-minded, hypocritical, war-like, the embodiment of capitalist and imperialist tyranny', and he 'finds the country complacent, easy-going and old-fashioned'.[37] The catalogue of vices is contested by various family members and, for example, there is a resolute defence of imperialism in terms of romantic adventurism, by Ann (Penelope Dudley Ward), a spirited young woman with whom Ivan has a romance. Yet the first section of the film ends on a somewhat muted note with Ivan's scepticism about the English erupting in a fight between him and one of the locals during the annual village pageant. The second section begins a year later after war has broken out when Ivan returns to supervise the final stages of the boat-building and to solve the problems with the propeller. Various events from the earlier part of the film are reprised, including the pageant, but this time in the context of a more sympathetic understanding of the English way of life. As Jeffrey Richards notes, his conversion is summarised in his final speech:

> Ivan's final speech brings together the ideas that have run through the film defining the national identity: a sense of duty, a sense of tradition, a sense of tolerance, a sense of humour, a sense of service, a sense of community, but also a heroic individuality which at its most potent can invent, explore and conquer and at its most pronounced can blossom as a benign and lovable eccentricity.[38]

Yet it is a specific form of national definition incorporating a conservative, pastoral, vision of England, and focused on the upper middle classes, 'a notion of Britishness derived dominantly from its ruling elite', as one writer has put it.[39] Ann herself is something of a socialite, a character comparable to Jennifer (Anne Crawford) in *Millions Like Us* (1943) though, as with the character in the Launder and Gilliat film, ultimately shown as a willing contributor to the war effort when she joins the WRNS. The rest of the family are represented as endearing mild-mannered eccentrics, especially her grandfather – Mr Runalow (Felix Aylmer) – head of the shipbuilding firm and an expert on railway timetables. The cast even includes the doyenne of English eccentrics, Margaret Rutherford, as the village historian and organiser of the annual pageant which celebrates British history and tradition. Working-class characters play a peripheral role though Tom (Jack Watling) – a pro-Soviet worker – does take the lead in urging his fellow workers on when the boat's completion is in jeopardy in a display of seamless unity with his employers. The film's somewhat idealised and narrow version of the nation's character and its lack of realism was pinpointed by C. A. Lejeune in terms reminiscent of the familiar critique of the class-bound nature of 1930s British cinema: 'I have little doubt that the British characters – the business men, the shipbuilders family, the pavement gossips, the dock-workers – would be more quickly recognised in Shaftesbury Avenue than in Portsmouth, Clydeside, or Hull.'[40]

The film is usually regarded as a fairly conservative rendition of national identity comparable to *In Which We Serve* in its benign depiction of the upper classes. Yet, it is not without its contradictions. David Lusted has suggested that the film's treatment of the romance between Ann and Ivan is not brought to the usual conclusion expected in a conventional fictional narrative. Towards the end of the film, Ann declares her love for Ivan during their second visit to the nightclub. Although they kiss both in the club and in the taxi on the way home, his response is coloured by his sense of failure. The propeller design has proved unsuccessful and he is planning to return to the Soviet Union. The romance at this point is left in the air. He solves the problem with the propeller and their last scene together is at the ship's launch. Ann, caught in an intimate two-shot with Ivan, launches the ship with a bottle of champagne in the traditional manner dedicating it to Anglo-Soviet friendship, in a prelude, one might think, to a final kiss. However, the following shots reinsert the couple into the crowd and the film then moves into the final framing sequence, picking up the action from the opening sequence. The film concludes with the romance unresolved. As Lusted suggests, 'however much the film declares itself for alliance between nations, it cannot bring itself to countenance sexual union – especially with its leading daughter'.[41] For this reason and despite the fact that the film is unequivocal in its endorsement of a set of national values and the importance of the alliance with the Soviet Union, the failure to deal with the romantic theme constitutes 'an unsettling negation of its particular *rhetoric* of nation'.[42] The film fits into Asquith's own rhetoric of nation, his own commentary on Englishness in films such as *Tell England, French Without Tears*, and *Quiet Wedding*, with a sense of the satirical and a hint of contradiction.

Fanny by Gaslight (1944)

With *Quiet Wedding*, a romantic comedy based on a successful stage play, Asquith had taken one step away from the urgencies of war, returning to the 'light comedy and affectionate satire'[43] of *French Without Tears*. Another de Grunwald/Rattigan/Asquith collaboration, it enjoyed comparable success as the film did very well both in Britain and in America. As *Kine Weekly* suggested, 'the film succeeds in its aim of providing light-hearted laughable entertainment which will take the war-strained audiences right out of themselves and provide an exhilarating hour of respite from the present-day perplexities'.[44] Although it was made during the autumn of 1940 and in the midst of the contemporary perplexities of the blitz, the film turns its back on the grim realities of war in favour of diversion and escapism. It was a notion of cinema that some in the industry espoused and it embodied the judgement that what cinema audiences wanted during the period of conflict was just as likely to be films which enhanced their feelings of well-being as those which instructed them on the rigours of war that they were experiencing in their everyday lives. Such thinking had become more widespread by the middle of the war and, in particular, Maurice Ostrer, head of production at Gainsborough where Asquith had a multi-picture contract, was 'no great believer in the serious, patriotic war setting, which an increasing number of the public must find "too near home" for complete enjoyment'.[45] The 'pure entertainment' path was exemplified by Gainsborough's 1943 production – *The Man in Grey* – a costume melodrama albeit with a framing sequence set in the wartime present. The film was a box-office success and it inaugurated a short cycle of melodramas some costume, some in contemporary settings, but all with similar female-orientated themes. The titles included *Madonna of the Seven Moons* (Arthur Crabtree, 1944), *Love Story* (Leslie Arliss, 1944), *The Wicked Lady* (Leslie Arliss, 1945), and *They Were Sisters* (Arthur Crabtree, 1945), and the films featured an array of new British stars including Phyllis Calvert, Margaret Lockwood, Patricia Roc, Jean Kent, James Mason, and Stewart Granger.

Asquith's *Fanny by Gaslight* was the second film in the cycle and featured Calvert, Granger, and Mason – three of the four stars from *The Man in Grey* – in a bid to replicate its success. Also, like some of the others, it was adapted from a best-selling historical novel. It was the final film of Asquith's Gainsborough contract and, in some ways, an odd choice for him. The critical rhetoric which greeted his films usually included terms such as 'wit', 'sensitivity', and 'irony', and comparisons with directors such as René Clair; the Gainsborough melodramas were part of 'a rich tradition of visceral, garish, flamboyant popular cinema',[46] a tradition which embodied a somewhat different set of aesthetic values from those established in Asquith's previous work.

As with *The Man in Grey*, which had the same scriptwriter, Doreen Montgomery, the film has at its centre a female character – Fanny (Phyllis Calvert). However, whereas Calvert in the previous film played an upper-middle-class woman who marries an aristocrat, in Asquith's film her social standing is much lower. Indeed her ostensible father, William Hopwood (John Laurie), is the manager of a dubious night club appropriately called 'The Shades'; however, it is revealed later in the film that he is not her biological father and that Fanny is illegitimate, her mother having married Hopwood after becoming pregnant by another man. *The Man in Grey* had used the strategy of pairing the central female character with a contrasting female character embodying a different set of values. Calvert's Clarissa is paired with the socially inferior Hesther (Margaret Lockwood) on a good/bad axis or, in terms of another reading, a restraint/desire axis. It is a pattern which is repeated in varying ways in *Madonna of the Seven Moons* with Calvert as a split personality, and *The Wicked Lady* with Lockwood paired with Patricia Roc. *Fanny by Gaslight* varies the strategy somewhat. In some respects Fanny embodies both the 'good' and the 'bad' within herself – the bad coming from her illegitimacy, and her family's low social status and doubtful occupation, the good from the fact that she is not really responsible for any of this. However, the film does include a range of contrasting female characters. Jean Kent, often cast in the morally inferior role in 1940s films, plays the contrasting figure of Lucy, like Hesther a childhood friend of the heroine, yet the antagonism between them is both mild and not developed to the same extent. Like Hesther she represents desire and, indeed, tries to draw Fanny into her *demi-monde* world of the chorus girl and the prostitute; unlike Hesther, however, her motives and the outcome of her actions are not destructive. Fanny discovers that her real father is Clive Seymore (Stuart Lindsell), a prominent politician, and his wife (Margaretta Scott), whose indiscretions lead to him committing suicide to avoid a scandal, is also presented as a contrast to Fanny – she is haughty, demanding, manipulative, uncaring. Yet, as with Lucy, the conflict is not really developed to any great extent. The final character providing contrast and conflict is Kate Somerford (Cathleen Nesbitt), sister to Harry Somerford, Fanny's lover. Her disapproval of their relationship on grounds of Fanny's doubtful background gives the film a class orientation which, though present in the other Gainsborough films, is more overtly so in *Fanny by Gaslight*. The film differs from others in the cycle by ending with a defiant Fanny declaring that she and Harry will be married. This is a stark contrast with the tragic conclusions to *The Man in Grey*, *Madonna of the Seven Moons* and *The Wicked Lady*, all of which end with the death of the central female characters.

Sue Harper has suggested that the power of the costume melo-dramas and their specific appeal to a female audience lay in 'the provision of a lascivious vitality with which female viewers could temp-orarily identify' and 'the attractions of stylish villainy'.[47] The characters embodying these qualities – attractive scheming women, handsome ruthless males – seem present in a somewhat truncated way in Asquith's film. Both Jean Kent as Lucy and Margaretta Scott as Alicia have some of the qualities of seductive wickedness possessed by Margaret Lockwood in *The Man in Grey* though both remain on the edges of the narrative. James Mason as Lord Manderstoke does, to an extent, repeat the 'com-bination of romantic allure and Sadean fascination',[48] which he had introduced in *The Man in Grey*, and despite having an instrumental narrative role he also remains on the periphery of the film and is finally killed in a duel with Harry Somerford. Though the film does have many of the qualities of the Gainsborough costume film it seems less full-blooded than the others, less focused on the attractions of trans-gression, more restrained, and with an unambiguously affirmative ending in which only James Mason's villainous Manderstoke has died.

The Way to the Stars (1945)

The Way to the Stars is often regarded as Asquith's best film of the war period and also one of the best of his entire career. However, in a sense it missed the war. It was released in June 1945, after the war had moved into its final stages and, indeed, after Germany had surrendered. As Jeffrey Richards has commented, *The Way to the Stars* was 'not only the last war film of the war but also the first war film of the peace and precursor of the post-war cycle of films such as *Angels One Five* and *The Dam Busters*'.[49] The film was a Two Cities production and involved

Asquith's usual collaborators – Anatole de Grunwald and Terence Rattigan. Though not released until the middle of 1945, its origins can be traced back to 1942 and to a Rattigan play – *Flare Path* – which Asquith had directed on the London stage.[50] The play, set in a hotel lounge near an RAF base, examined the anxieties of a group of wives waiting for their airmen husbands to return from a bombing mission. It was a great success and Twentieth Century-Fox acquired the film rights early in 1943. In the same year, Rattigan was seconded from the RAF and worked with an American screenwriter, Richard Sherman, on a film about Anglo–US relationships – a topic which had become relevant since the first American troops had arrived in Britain in 1942, but one which had not attracted British film-makers. Asquith himself had made films which featured various other nationalities including the Belgians (*Uncensored*) and the Russians (*The Demi-Paradise*), and other film-makers had portrayed the Danes, the Dutch, the French, and the Norwegians. Also, there had been a handful of Hollywood films in the early 1940s modelled to some extent on the 1930s MGM picture *A Yank at Oxford* in which the cultural interaction between Americans and the English was dramatised. *A Yank in the RAF* (Henry King, 1941) clearly acknowledged its similarly titled antecedent but titles such as *Foreign Correspondent* (Alfred Hitchcock, 1941), *One Night in Lisbon* (Edward H. Griffith, 1941), and *Eagle Squadron* (Arthur Lubin, 1942) also incorporated the Anglo–US relationship theme within their generic frameworks.[51] Some British films such as *Pimpernel Smith* (Leslie Howard, 1941) and *San Demetrio London* (Charles Frend, 1943) had American characters, and *Flying Fortress* (Walter Forde, 1942), though centred on a Canadian flier, was made in Britain by Warner Bros. at their British quota studio. Yet, the massive social impact of the arrival of US military personnel in Britain had yet to be broached in a significant way and the avoidance of the subject by British film-makers prompted *Kine Weekly*'s P. L. Mannock to complain in the following terms:

> Today ... the British Isles contain infinitely more citizens and citizenesses of the United States than at any previous period in history; and more than we can ever expect to see again after the war. In such circumstances, when much is being written about this astonishingly friendly invasion, it seems fair to ask the question: What is the British Film Industry doing about it? The answer is: Nothing.[52]

In fact the Rattigan/Sherman project had begun in March 1943, before Mannock's comments. However, though backed by the Ministry of Information and involving Twentieth Century-Fox and the distinguished Hollywood director, William Wyler, a film did not materialise.

Instead, the script produced by Rattigan and Sherman, was to form the basis of *The Way to the Stars* though not without further work on it throughout 1944 by both Asquith and de Grunwald as well as Rattigan himself.[53] The film, as a Two Cities production, started shooting in September 1944 under the title *Rendezvous* though a change to *The Way to the Stars* was announced in March 1945.[54]

The film was presented as 'a story based on the very topical theme of Anglo-American friendship';[55] however, the war was virtually over by its release in the middle of 1945 and the urgency of the theme considerably lessened. The film, originally designed to capture the exigencies of the middle years of the war and to reflect the Anglo–US collaboration, required something of a slight transformation to retain its relevance to an audience moving into peacetime. According to Geoffrey Wansell, 'Rattigan suggested that they should turn the whole story into a flash-back.'[56] The flashback, of course, was a narrative device quite familiar to Asquith who had used it in the late 1920s for *A Cottage on Dartmoor* and, during the war, for *The Demi-Paradise*. Also, as Neil Rattigan has pointed out, a number of wartime British films constructed their narratives on the basis of the flashback.[57] It was an effective device for *The Way to the Stars* repositioning the film's narrative as history and defining the tone of the film as 'nostalgic'.[58] Despite the conventional wisdom that war subjects had not been popular since around 1943, it was a major success with British audiences. However, its reception in America was much less successful despite it being included in the small number of top features that Rank released in the US through United Artists.[59]

The film opens with the camera moving into and through an abandoned RAF airfield, exploring the abandoned hangers, the derelict control tower, and the crew room still containing a few relics of the past. 'The whole sequence', as Jeffrey Richards put it, 'evokes the feeling of the recent past, recollected with sadness and pride.'[60] The nostalgic tone established, the narrative then shifts abruptly to the past, to 1940, to the year of the Battle of Britain with the airfield now a hive of activity, to a time before the Americans had entered the war. For the first twenty-five minutes or so the film introduces the principal British characters, Peter Penrose (John Mills) and David Archdale (Michael Redgrave), and Miss Todd or 'Toddy' (Rosamund John), who runs the Golden Lion, the village's residential hotel, and subsequently becomes David's wife. It establishes the ethos of the RAF mainly using the character of Squadron Leader Carter (Trevor Howard). Firstly, following an air raid on the base he complains about the ostentatious behaviour of the Hurricane pilots – the 'victory rolls' they perform over the airfield after they have repelled the German planes; he adds, though, an approving comment about their contribution to the war effort after spotting that one is missing, presumably shot down. Secondly, when Carter himself fails to return from a bombing mission in Germany, the focus is on the restrained response of the squadron and, in particular, Archdale's muted reaction which he displaces into a dressing-down for Penrose after his display of incompetence during his first training flight in a Blenheim. He also displaces his response later, into the reciting of one of his poems, when he tells Toddy about Carter's death. 'Missing' was one of two poems to feature in the film both written by the war poet John Pudney who had served in the RAF himself.[61] Carter's death while on a mission is the first of three such episodes in which key characters are killed on active service, three 'narrative marker-stones',[62] around which the emotional core of the film is built.

Indeed, it was the way in which *The Way to the Stars* dealt with such powerful emotional events in what is often called an 'understated' manner, that impressed the critics. As C. A. Lejeune wrote in the *Observer*, 'Mr Asquith's work is one more proof that the British film has at last attained its majority. It has one great merit, rare in Hollywood pictures these days, of emotional restraint.'[63] In a similar vein, the *Daily Sketch* comment that the film 'in all its admirable emotional restraint it is far more moving than any picture deliberately designed as a tear-jerker' sets the film's restrained presentation of feelings against the overt melodrama associated primarily, though not exclusively, with Hollywood conventions.[64] The first of the three deaths, that of Carter, whose character was barely sketched, might be seen as emblematic, establishing the stoical acceptance of danger which characterises the RAF community without involving the spectator with the character to any great extent. The death of David Archdale, by contrast, removes a key character and one whose emblematic significance as a heroic flier is accompanied by a greater degree of personalisation as husband and father. The groundwork for his death is carefully prepared through the device of a cigarette lighter which he uses as a talisman but which he mislays just prior to his final mission. There is also a haunting shot of Toddy before the wedding. She is preparing for the wedding and the camera moves towards her framing her reflection in a mirror. Her gaze initially is one of self-satisfied admiration; the noise of aircraft flying overhead interrupts her reverie and she moves into the frame as her look changes to one of sadness and, possibly, premonition. The episode follows a similar structure to the first – the death of Carter – though with a few variations. As Carter and the rest of the squadron fly off there are a number of shots of the villagers watching including one of Toddy and Mr Palmer (Stanley Holloway), one of the Golden Lion residents, then a fade to black. As Archdale flies off there is a single shot from the village with Toddy initially watching alone but joined by Iris Winterton (Renée Asherson), a young woman with whom Peter is involved, followed by a final shot of the planes then a fade to black. It is an important variation, shifting the emphasis from the general to the particular, from an array of shots to a single shot which anchors the second death to the personal in a concrete manner.

In neither case is the actual bombing mission shown; the film's centre of gravity, in Jeffrey Richards' words, is 'exploring the emotional impact of the war on the leading characters. It was thus not so much a film about the fighting of the war as of living with and through the war.'[65] In that sense the actual detail of the missions is less important than their tragic outcomes. The next sequence moves straight on to the returning aircrews. Although it begins with a shot from the airfield and a shot of Tiny Williams (Basil Radford), the station controller, in another small variation from the first episode, there are also separate shots of Toddy and Iris in the village watching the planes return. Archdale's death is condensed into a single shot in which the camera moves towards the pillar in the crew room to pick out the talismanic cigarette lighter left behind; a hand picks it up and the camera moves to frame Peter who uses it to light a cigarette. The camera remains on Peter initially in close-up then moves out as Peter walks out of frame. In the subsequent scene with Tiny, David's death is discussed but the point has been well-established through *mise-en-scène* and camera movement before that happens. There is a further structural similarity with the Carter episode when Peter goes to see Toddy with some of David's things. They include another poem of David's which Peter reads for Toddy just as David had recited 'Missing' for her in the earlier sequence. The poem – 'For Johnny' – is about the death of a flier and its author, John Pudney, wrote it while working as an Intelligence Officer in the RAF:

> It was first written on the back of an envelope in London during an air raid in 1941. I was, I imagine, on forty-eight hours leave from RAF Coastal Command Station at St Eval, Cornwall, where I was at the time an Intelligence Officer. There, and earlier on Fighter Stations during the Battle of Britain, I had come face to face with the deaths of men younger than myself – to have just turned thirty was to be a very old man among the squadrons. Some of these losses were very close.[66]

Elsewhere, Pudney refers to his own need for the 'tense compression of poetry to express something of what was happening daily at my elbow'.[67]

'Tense compression' is an apt phrase to apply to the ways in which Asquith's film handles the heightened emotional situations in the aftermath of the fliers' deaths. The third and final 'narrative marker' – the death of Johnny Hollis (Douglass Montgomery), an American flier – is handled in a more melodramatic fashion. Following a mission his plane crashes on the airfield as he tries to land it without endangering the lives of the villagers, marking him out as a self-sacrificing hero. Although there is a brief closeup of his commanding officer just after his plane explodes, the response to his death occurs in the following sequence when his fellow American flier, Joe Friselli (Bonar Colleano), takes his place at the village children's party, and apologises for his absence. Toddy talks to Friselli about Johnny and hands him a piece of paper to read later; it is, of course, the poem – 'For Johnny' – though, characteristically, the film leaves this understated at this point.

David Archdale's death occurs some thirty-five minutes into the film and it concludes what might be called the RAF section. Most of the squadron moves out of the base to be replaced by the American squadron though a few RAF personnel, including Tiny and Peter, remain. The film then begins to explore the Anglo–American relationship theme from the original Ministry of Information project to which Rattigan had been seconded in 1943. There is some attention to superficial cultural differences – baseball versus cricket, tea versus coffee, linguistic peculiarities – but the American dimension is basically presented through two characters: Johnny Hollis, the flier who eventually dies, and Joe Friselli. Johnny is a quiet and sensitive family man who forms a warm friendship with Toddy. Joe, by contrast, is brash and boastful, and impatient with the genteel habits of English life; he also becomes a romantic rival to Peter when he starts to court Iris towards the end of the film. Basically, despite Friselli's initial brashness, the delineation of the Americans is mildly satirical and it is not long before, differences elided, they are drawn into the host nation's way of life. This even extends to drinking British beer in the hotel bar with their RAF colleagues although their approach to social life is more vigorous than their British counterparts. As Jeffrey Richards has suggested they have 'a beneficial effect on the residents' lounge of the "Golden Lion", transforming its atmosphere from stuffy, repressed genteel decorum to cheerful, uninhibited exuberance'.[68] In many respects, like *The Demi-Paradise*, the film is really a study of Englishness which uses the foreigner dimension to illuminate indigenous character. As Harlan Kennedy has suggested, the film 'presents – without ever spelling out – a kind of "last stand" for British emotional closedness and self-control, with the Americans personifying the fresh west wind of candor and spontaneity'.[69] Also, like

The Demi-Paradise, the film is concerned predominantly with the upper-middle classes; working-class characters such as 'Nobby' Clarke (Bill Rowbotham/Owen) hover very much on the periphery of the narrative. The film has been interpreted as negating the more populist cross-class sentiments of wartime films such as Launder and Gilliat's *Millions Like Us* (1943) and Carol Reed's *The Way Ahead* (1944). In such films the co-operation of women and men from across the social spectrum is represented as central to the war effort; they are films in which the notion of 'the people's war' is embodied. By contrast, Asquith's film, according to Neil Rattigan, has a somewhat different class orientation:

> Overwhelmingly, *The Way to the Stars* demonstrates just how the notion of a people's war was no more than skin deep. Coming at the end of the war, when it might have been expected that the notion would have been more fully absorbed, *The Way to the Stars* represents the class structure as being firmly in place as ever.[70]

Like many British film-makers of the period – Powell and Pressburger, Lean, Reed – Asquith emerged from the war with an enhanced reputation, the promise of the silent films well on the way to fulfilment. In particular, *The Way to the Stars*, as Jeffrey Richards has suggested:

> was warmly welcomed by critics and public alike. *Daily Mail* readers voted it the best film of the war years. The critics mirrored the public mood well: their reviews right across the spectrum, from the *Observer* to the *Daily Sketch*, stressed its essential qualities: its Englishness, its realism, its emotional restraint.[71]

However, when Asquith resumed his career after the war, it was with a return to his pre-war success with an adaptation of a light comedy based on a play written by his collaborator on *The Way to the Stars* – Terence Rattigan. Characteristically, his films continued to shift abruptly from the dark to the light, from the comic to the serious, from the middlebrow to the popular. Some of his post-war films, the best-known ones, followed the theatrical adaptation route which he had embarked upon with *Pygmalion* but some were more modest and less prestigious genre pieces.

Notes

1 C. Barr (ed.), *All Our Yesterdays* (London: BFI Publishing, 1986), p. 11.
2 *World Film News* (September 1937), p. 20.
3 Barr, *All Our Yesterdays*, p. 11.
4 K. Brownlow, *David Lean* (London: Faber and Faber, 1997), p. 166.

5 G. Macnab, *J. Arthur Rank and the British Film Industry* (London: Routledge, 1993), p. 23.

6 J. Chapman, *The British at War. Cinema, State and Propaganda* (London: I. B. Tauris, 1998), p. 86.

7 W. Holmes, 'Mild or Bitter', *Sight and Sound*, 12:47 (October, 1943), p. 82.

8 C. Barr, 'War record', *Sight and Sound*, 58: 4 (1989), 263.

9 J. Richards and D. Sheridan (eds), *Mass Observation at the Movies* (London: Routledge & Kegan Paul, 1987), pp. 448–50. For more on the 'five-minute films' see Chapman, *The British at War*, pp. 93–108.

10 *Kine Weekly* (11.1.40). The two-page display advert for the film listed British National/Anglo-American as the companies involved and the director was Brian Desmond Hurst.

11 Chapman, *The British at War*, p. 43.

12 A. Aldgate and J. Richards (eds), *Britain Can Take It. The British Cinema in the Second World War*. Second Edition (Edinburgh: Edinburgh University Press, 1994), p. 1.

13 R. J. Minney, *Puffin Asquith* (London: Leslie Frewin, 1973), pp. 102–3.

14 *Kine Weekly* (16.5.40), p. 27.

15 *Kine Weekly* (9.5.40), p. 21.

16 R. Murphy, *British Cinema and the Second World War* (London: Continuum, 2000), p. 89.

17 *Kine Weekly* (20.6.40), p. 30; (27.6.40), p. 22.

18 P. M. Taylor, 'Techniques of Persuasion. Basic Ground Rules of British Propaganda during the Second World War', *Historical Journal of Film, Radio and Television*, 1:1 (1981), p. 57.

19 Chapman, *The British at War*, p. 223. In fact, Powell and Pressburger's *The Life and Death of Colonel Blimp* (1943) might be considered an exception to this.

20 *Kine Weekly* (16.4.42), p. 35.

21 Brownlow, *David Lean*, p. 160.

22 See *Kine Weekly* (16.4.42), p. 35, which carries reports of shooting progress on *In Which We Serve*, and an announcement of the start of Asquith's film at Shepherd's Bush.

23 A few 'documentary' shots of the submarine actually precede the interior sequence which effectively starts the film.

24 See S. P. MacKenzie, *British War Films 1939–1945* (London: Hambledon and London, 2001), pp. 83-4.

25 *Kine Weekly* (14.6.42), p. 50.

26 *Kine Weekly* (21.5.42), p. 38.

27 Chapman, *The British at War*, p. 187.

28 N. Rattigan, *This is England. British Film and the People's War, 1939–1945* (Madison, Teaneck: Fairleigh Dickinson University Press, 2001), p. 106.

29 MacKenzie, *British War Films 1939–1945*, p. 84.

30 *Ibid.*, p. 85.

31 *Kine Weekly* (22.4.43), p. 29.

32 A. Asquith, 'Realler than the Real Thing', *The Cine-Technician*, March–April 1945. See also, Murphy, *British Cinema and the Second World War*, pp. 139–41.

33 Ministry of Information document , 'Programme for Film Propaganda', reprinted in I. Christie (ed.), *Powell, Pressburger, and Others* (London: British Film Institute, 1978), p. 121.

34 *Ibid.*

35 *Kine Weekly* (15.10.42), p. 36.

36 I. McLaine, *Ministry of Morale. Home Front Morale and the Ministry of Information in World War II* (London: George Allen & Unwin, 1979), p. 203.

37 J. Richards, *Films and British National Identity. From Dickens to Dad's Army* (Manchester: Manchester University Press, 1997), p. 102.

38 *Ibid.*, p. 104.

39 D. Lusted, 'Builders and "The Demi-Paradise"', in G. Hurd (ed.), *National Fictions. World War Two in British Films and Television* (London: BFI Publishing, 1984), p. 28.

40 *Observer* (21.11.43). BFI cuttings collection: *The Demi-Paradise.*

41 Lusted, 'Builders and "Demi-Paradise"', p. 30.

42 *Ibid.* (emphasis in original).

43 P. Noble, *Anthony Asquith* (London: British Film Institute, 1951), p. 28.

44 *Kine Weekly* (23.1.41), p. 19.

45 *Kine Weekly* (8.1.42), p. 85. Quoted in R. Murphy, *Realism and Tinsel* (London: Routledge, 1989), p. 34.

46 Murphy, *Realism and Tinsel*, p. 56.

47 S. Harper, *Picturing the Past. The Rise and Fall of the British Costume Film* (London: BFI Publishing, 1994), p. 122.

48 P. W. Evans, 'James Mason: The Man Between', in B. Babington, *British Stars and Stardom* (Manchester: Manchester University Press, 2001), p. 108.

49 J. Richards, 'Our American Cousins. *The Way to the Stars*', in Aldgate and Richards (eds), *Britain Can Take It*, p. 282

50 *Flare Path* opened at the Apollo Theatre, London, in August 1942.

51 See H. M. Glancy, *When Hollywood Loved Britain. The Hollywood 'British' film 1939-45* (Manchester: Manchester University Press, 1999), pp. 111–28.

52 P. L. Mannock, 'Why No Anglo-US Subject?', *Kine Weekly* (22.9.43), p. 23.

53 M. Darlow and G. Hodson, *Terence Rattigan. The Man and his Work* (London: Quartet Books, 1979), pp. 120–9.

54 *Kine Weekly* (29.3.45), p. 27.

55 *Kine Weekly* (11.1.45), p. 174.

56 G. Wansell, *Terence Rattigan. A Biography* (London: Fourth Estate, 1996), p. 139. Also, Minney, *Puffin Asquith*, p. 111.

57 Rattigan, *This is England*, p. 79.

58 *Ibid.*, p. 116.

59 Macnab, *J. Arthur Rank*, pp. 163–4.

60 Richards, 'Our American Cousins. *The Way to the Stars*', p. 283.

61 J. Pudney, *Home and Away. An Autobiographical Gambit* (London: Michael Joseph, 1960), pp. 119–22.

62 H. Kennedy, 'How They Won the War', *Film Comment*, 32:5 (1996), p. 25.

63 Quoted in Richards, 'Our American Cousins', p. 278.

64 Quoted in Richards, 'Our American Cousins', p. 279.

65 *Ibid.*, p. 278.

66 J. Pudney, *Thank Goodness for Cake* (London: Michael Joseph, 1978), p. 74.

67 Pudney, *Home and Away*, p. 122.

68 Richards, 'Our American Cousins', p. 286.

69 Kennedy, 'How They Won the War', p. 31.

70 Rattigan, *This is England. British Film and the People's War*, p. 127.

71 J. Richards, 'National Identity in British Wartime Films', in P. M. Taylor (ed.), *Britain and the Cinema in the Second World War* (London: Macmillan Press, 1988), p. 59.

Post-war films 1 – genre and British cinema

5

The British cinema emerged from the war period with a high critical reputation, a degree of audience appeal, and with the Rank group well established as a large vertically integrated company ready to challenge the Hollywood majors in the international marketplace. Yet, the early post-war years saw the industry coping with a turbulent period of uncertainty dramatised by a trade war with Hollywood during which the American majors withheld their films from the British market for several months. The uncertainty, however, was also embodied in a series of official reports and discussion documents from government, political parties, and trade unions, posing questions about the alleged monopolistic structure of an industry effectively dominated by Rank, production costs, the state of British studios, distribution and exhibition, proposals to nationalise the industry, and so on.

Despite the critical optimism that greeted the realist war films, the wartime industry had operated under rather special conditions and a return to the operation of a commercial industry in conditions of peace meant also a return to the endemic problems besetting British cinema. Foremost in the deliberations of those who examined the industry was its fragile economic basis; as one government report put it, 'At no time since the substitution of sound for silent films has the British film production industry been on a satisfactory financial basis.'[1] These problems had, in a sense, been masked by the war, which saw the production industry operating on the basis of a much-reduced output, benefiting from a degree of government support via the propaganda mechanisms, and, for the integrated groups, an increase in exhibition income on the basis of cinema attendances, which rose continuously, peaking to record levels in 1946. Wartime production had been restricted to an annual output of between thirty-five and fifty films, a massive reduction on the 1930s annual figures which at times had hovered around the two hundred mark. After the war, although there was to be no return to the production levels of the 1930s, the industry did recover to an extent. In 1949 101 films were released and an annual figure of more than 100 films was sustained throughout the 1950s and into the 1960s.[2] The transition from the restricted and focused wartime production schedules to the reconstruction of a peacetime industry and the relative stability achieved by the industry in the 1950s was achieved in problematic circumstances, and, many have argued, at a price. For some, the ambition and quality of the wartime and immediate post-war British cinema eventually gave way to 'perhaps the most derided decade in British film history'.[3]

Post-war production

The Labour government introduced a series of measures to help the British film industry in the late 1940s including the provision of new financial support. Yet they also sowed the seeds for what many would see as an undermining of its national integrity creating conditions for an increasing involvement of the American industry in British film-making, and the rise of what became known as 'runaway' production. The origins of this lay in the proposed introduction of a tax on the British distribution earnings of American films in the context of a balance of payments crisis. The American majors responded with a boycott of the British market but, after much high-level political negotiation, the dispute was settled in 1948 with the Anglo-American Film Agreement. This set a ceiling on the amount of their distribution revenues the majors could take out of Britain and made some stipulations about how the 'frozen coin', as *Variety* termed it, could be used. One of the activities on which such revenues were permitted to be spent was, predictably, film production.[4] American investment in British production was not a new phenomenon, indeed, the Hollywood majors had been financing production in Britain since the 1920s; the terms of the Anglo-American Agreement, however, encouraged an increase in such activity and, as Robert Murphy has noted, by '1956 one third of the films made in Britain had some form of American involvement'.[5] Such involvement was to increase as the decade went on escalating to a point in the 1960s when almost the entire production industry was under-written by American capital.

American distribution revenues, then, were one important source of production finance but the Anglo-American dispute also prompted the government to explore other measures which might help the film industry. In addition to this, the quota legislation was due for renewal in

1948 and decisions about the nature and extent of government intervention in the industry were required for that. Two companies in
particular – Rank and Alexander Korda's British Lion – had attempted
to increase production in order to fill the gap left by the Hollywood
boycott. The return of American films following the agreement left both
companies in a precarious position, over-extended in terms of their
production investment, and unlikely to recoup money in the face of the
restored American competition. Rank, as a large vertically integrated
combine with substantial revenues from exhibition, was considered to
be capable of recovering under its own steam, but British Lion, which
Korda had acquired in 1946, was felt to be more seriously threatened.
The company was seen as something of a totem for the industry, and in
particular for the independent producer; its threatened demise was seen
by government as an extremely serious matter. It was argued that 'if
British Lion, the second largest production-distribution in the country,
were allowed to collapse, the rest of the industry might well follow suit'.[6]
Government loans were made to British Lion on an ad hoc basis in 1948
to solve its immediate problem, and the principle of providing state
finance for production was formalised soon after with the setting up of
the National Film Finance Corporation in 1949. Essentially it was a film
bank, through which government financial aid to the industry could be
channelled; it implemented an idea which could be traced back to the
1920s and which had been one of the recommendations of the Palache
Committee report on monopoly in the British film industry in 1944.[7]

The report had been prepared in the context of the rise of the Rank
group and the threat to independent production which many saw in the
growth of its power. Although conventional financial sources for production were still expected to provide the bulk of a film's budget, the
Corporation became a major source of high-risk capital providing the
risky 'end money' – the final proportion of the budget (30 per cent) to be
repaid out of the film's profits, and after the distributor had been paid.
Given the precarious nature of the production industry, the 'end money'
was difficult to arrange through orthodox financing concerns and was
frequently lost in the project. Although the impetus for the establishment of the corporation was the protection of independent production,
it did establish financing arrangements with the large companies. For
example, British Film-makers was set up by Rank in conjunction with
the National Film Finance Corporation and made fourteen films before
Rank withdrew from the arrangement in 1952.[8] Initially, the corporation was given a five-year treasury loan on which to operate on the
assumption that orthodox finance would take over its role once the production industry had been stabilised. However, it was to survive as an

essential bolster for the industry until the mid-1980s and was especially important in sustaining British Lion as an independent force in the industry.

The 1940s ended with greater government intervention than hitherto, with the establishment of the state-funding of production, the diversion of tax receipts to film-makers through the Eady Levy scheme, a system of subsidy for films which succeeded at the box office,[9] and a continuation of the quota system for exhibitors that had guaranteed screen time for indigenous films since the late 1920s. This is not surprising as the Labour government of the day was intervening in many other areas of public life, in industry and in welfare provision. Yet, intervention on behalf of the film production industry was not as radical as in other European countries, and was, to an extent, market-led. As Margaret Dickinson has noted, the forms of assistance 'rewarded whatever the market rewarded and could not encourage developments of a kind the trade was unlikely to foster'.[10] In that context, it is also unsurprising that the Conservative government which replaced Labour in 1951 left the various arrangements intact. The framework for the development of the British cinema in the 1950s was formed by an enlarged and flexible quota fixed according to indigenous production capacity, and by newly established sources of production finance and subsidy.

From the statistical point of view the measures were successful as through the 1950s the annual production figures doubled compared with the wartime years. As Robert Murphy has suggested, 'in the fifties film production enjoyed greater health and stability than might have been expected given the competition from television'.[11] British films were also popular with audiences enjoying commercial success if not always critical acclaim. Indeed, films such as *Doctor in the House* (Ralph Thomas, 1954), *The Dam Busters* (Michael Anderson, 1955), *Reach for the Sky* (Lewis Gilbert, 1956) and *Carry On Nurse* (Gerald Thomas, 1959) topped the popularity polls for their release years, proving more popular than their Hollywood counterparts.[12] However, though British films were produced in reasonable numbers and were doing well at the box-office, fewer people were going to see them. The social changes in the post-war period together with the competition from television were registering an effect on cinemagoing and the 1950s saw a continuous decline in the cinema audience. Measured in terms of annual cinema admissions, which had reached record levels during the wartime years, the audience began to decrease in the immediate post-war period following the record attendance figures for 1946; it continued its downward trajectory through the 1950s, and by 1960 the audience had declined to less than one third of the wartime figure.[13]

Asquith and post-war British cinema

Many of Asquith's post-war films were made as independent productions. He had spent some time working for major British companies, for example, Gaumont-British in the early 1930s and its associate studio Gainsborough in the early 1940s, but it was his work with independent producers such as Gabriel Pascal (*Pygmalion*), Mario Zampi (*French Without Tears*) and Anatole de Grunwald (*The Way to the Stars*) that had attracted significant critical attention and commercial success. It should be noted, however, that 'independence' in the context of the British cinema of the period needs some qualification as large companies such as Rank were often involved at some stage in the process even if the project originated outside of their direct control. *Pygmalion*, in fact, was distributed by Rank's General Film Distributors, and Two Cities was working as one of the Rank satellite companies in the 1940s when Asquith made *The Way to the Stars*. Indeed, the Rank Organisation had consolidated its leading position in the industry during the war period, though partly on the basis of working closely with independent companies such as Two Cities, The Archers (Powell and Pressburger), and Cineguild (Noël Coward, David Lean), though the relationship had become somewhat fraught and had begun to unravel in the early post-war period when the company moved to centralise its production operations. However, Rank remained pivotal to British production through the 1950s with its arrangements with the National Film Finance Corporation through the Group Film Scheme, and with other alliances with independent producers. Indeed, two of Asquith's 1950s titles – *The Importance of Being Earnest* and *The Young Lovers* – were made by the Rank/NFFC British Film-makers and Rank's own Group Film Producers respectively, while others – *The Woman in Question* and *The Browning Version* – were distributed by Rank's General Film Distributors.

The several hundred titles released during the period covered a variety of genres including contemporary dramas, adventure and costume films, science fiction and horror, as well as the numerous thrillers and crime films. However, as Harper and Porter have noted, the 'two genres which dominated the 1950s box-office were comedies and war films'.[14] Asquith's post-war genre films did include one war title – *Orders to Kill* – but the others are a generic miscellany including crime (*The Woman in Question*), Cold War science-fiction (*The Net*), romantic drama (*The Young Lovers*), and a hybrid – domestic melodrama mixed with sport (*The Final Test*).

The Woman in Question (1950)

The Woman in Question was directed by Asquith for Two Cities in association with Javelin Pictures, at Rank's Pinewood Studios. The origins of the project, however, lay in a new scheme for independent film production set up by theatrical producers Linnit and Dunfee known as the 'parcel system'. *The Woman in Question* was to be the first of a number of such projects and producer Harold Huth, in charge of the scheme, explained the scheme in *Kine Weekly* as follows: 'we gather together parcel deals with the idea of assisting in the making of first-class independent productions. We make all the preliminary arrangements and administer the picture, leaving everything else absolutely clear for the producer and director once they get on the floor.'[15]

However, as mentioned previously, the 'independence' enjoyed by independent producers was less than absolute and the distribution arrangement with the Rank group meant that Asquith had to cast Rank's own contract actors in the leading roles. In an interview many years later, Dirk Bogarde, one of the Rank artists who played a leading role in the film, commented that Asquith 'didn't want me at all in *The Woman in Question*, I think he wanted William Holden, but he was forced by Rank to use a contract artiste. I was one, and Susan Shaw and Jean Kent were also'.[16] The film was based on an original story by John Cresswell who also wrote the script.

The Woman in Question is a crime film, a contribution to one of the most prominent trends in the early post-war British cinema alongside titles such as *Noose* (Edmond T. Greville, 1948), *They Made me a Fugitive* (Alberto Cavalcanti, 1947), *Brighton Rock* (John Boulting, 1947), and *The Long Memory* (Robert Hamer, 1952). The contemporaneous Hollywood *film noir* has sometimes been invoked as a kindred filmic strand. For example, Julian Petley has described the British crime cycle as the 'fine crop of "*films noir*" ... which match many of their Hollywood counterparts in terms of formal stylisation, sheer physical brutality, urban sleaze and underlying existential pessimism'.[17] Asquith's film centres on the murder of a fairground fortune teller, Madame Astra/Mrs Houston (Jean Kent) and its investigation by the police. Its most striking feature is the flashback narrative structure which begins with the discovery of Astra's body, then proceeds to establish the identity of her murderer through a series of overlapping accounts of her life from the point of view of her friends, neighbours, relatives, and lovers. These are recounted to the investigating detectives and presented through flashbacks. With her death positioned at the beginning of the narrative, the film acquires the pessimism of the *film noir* taking on the fatalistic structure associated with the genre. Using the flashback as a crucial structuring element of narrative is associated with the 1940s cinema and, particularly with the Hollywood *film noir*. Exemplars include *Double Indemnity* (Billy Wilder, 1944), *The Killers* (Robert Siodmak, 1946), and *Out of the Past* (Jacques Tourneur, 1947), films in which a 'complex chronological order is ... used to reinforce the feelings of hopelessness and lost time'.[18] However, inscribing fatalism into a narrative through a complicated play with narrative time, though, perhaps, used more extensively in the American cinema than hitherto, was neither specifically American nor particularly new in the late 1940s. The French film *Le Jour se lève* (Marcel Carné, 1939), generally regarded as an important forerunner of the Hollywood *film noir*, opens with the central character hopelessly trapped in his apartment room and doomed to die, then proceeds through flashback to explain the ways in which such desperate circumstances have come about. Going further back in film history, Asquith's own 1929 picture – *A Cottage on Dartmoor* – is also structured around a flashback which explains the circumstances which lead to the predicament of the leading character – an escaped convict.

Like *Sunset Blvd* (Billy Wilder, 1950), *The Woman in Question* begins with the death of a central character; however, unlike the Wilder film which boldly uses the dead character to provide the voice-over for the flashback, Astra's story is pieced together from the multiple and sometimes conflicting perspectives of those who knew her. This links the film to another cinematic strand – the 'biographical flashback film'[19] – and to its most famous reference point, *Citizen Kane* (Orson Welles, 1941). Welles' film also opens with the death of the central character then proceeds to piece his life together through the reminiscences of his second wife and his closest friends. An important concern of Asquith's film is the identity of the murderer – it is partly at least a 'whodunnit?' – but an important related question is 'What kind of a person was Madame Astra?' Welles' film was structured entirely around establishing the true identity and character of Charles Foster Kane; *The Woman in Question* blends the concerns of the *policier* – the investigation of the murder – with questions of the true identity and character of Madame Astra. Both the biographical and crime investigation strands, in their concern with the recovery of past events, raise issues of point of view and narrational reliability. In the crime film such issues are normally resolved through the solution of the crime mystery while the biographical flashback film often leaves the enigma of identity hanging in the air. However, the Hollywood *film noir* characteristically employed the familiar combination of flashback and voice-over to blur the identity and nature of the central female character, as Karen Hollinger has suggested in relation to Hollywood *noirs*: 'Throughout the period of the 1940s, voice-over *noir* texts evidence such extreme tendencies to fragmentation and proliferation of point of view that any attempt to resolve their investigations of their female characters are rendered hopelessly inconclusive.'[20]

Though *The Woman in Question* ends with the identity of the murderer established, it certainly leaves the identity of Madame Astra 'hopelessly inconclusive' due to the proliferation of varying perspectives on her character and establishes a strong link between the film and the better-known Hollywood *noirs* of the period.

The narrative is organised into five substantial flashback sections – incidentally the same number as in *Citizen Kane* – and, indeed, was released in America with the title *Five Angles on Murder*. The five sections together constitute just under two-thirds of the film's running time, and there are also some minor flashback sequences. The major flashbacks provide perspectives on Madame Astra/Mrs Houston from the point of view of her neighbour, Mrs Finch (Hermione Baddeley), her sister Catherine (Susan Shaw), her lovers, Bob Baker (Dirk Bogarde) and Michael Murray (John McCallum), and another neighbour, Mr Pollard (Charles Victor), an older man who had asked her to marry him. They are roughly equal in length and are presented as responses to Superintendent Lodge (Duncan Macrea), the detective investigating the case. Each depicts Madame Astra in different ways: as a posh neighbour, a drunken slut, a seductress, an idealised woman, and an earthy lover. Each contains material specific to their narrators; both Baker and Murray tell of their first meeting with Madame Astra at the fairground, Pollard tells of his proposal to her, and Catherine tells of her meetings with Baker. But there are also crucial events which overlap the different sections. Indeed, the dramatic rationale for the use of flashbacks lies in the variable versions of events which are presented as common experiences across two or three of the flashback sections. For example, in the first flashback section – Mrs Finch's account – Astra's sister, Catherine, visits her when Mrs Finch is also present and is presented as a rather aggressive and argumentative young woman in contrast to Astra who appears as a calm and composed woman. The same event is then included in Catherine's account where she presents herself as a quiet, sensitive young woman concerned about her sister whereas Astra is presented as a boorish slattern and a morning drinker to boot. The discrepancies reflect the perceptions and biases of the character whose point of view governs the sequence. In another overlapping event, Baker visits Astra, makes a pass at her, and is rebuffed according to Mrs Finch's version; in Baker's version it is Astra who attempts the seduction and Baker who does the rebuffing. The episode ends with a tea tray being upset. In Mrs Finch's version, she is on the stairs and hears the crash; Astra appears and says that Mr Baker has upset the tea tray. In Baker's version the event is shown and Astra, angry at Baker's rebuff, kicks over a table. Baker then informs Mrs Finch that he accidentally upset the tea tray. Whereas the variant details in the former example can be explained in terms of point of view, the discrepancies in the latter are differences of fact so one version is 'inaccurate' within the terms of the fiction and the reliability of the various different narrative voices called into question. Though Astra is the centre of the film, all of the leading characters are presented somewhat ambiguously across the range of flashbacks.

Astra, though, is singled out towards the end of the film in a some-what schematic scene in which Superintendent Lodge reflects on the different versions of her character comprising a sequence of five images of her which reprise moments – similar images, lines of dialogue – from each of the main flashback sections. However, it is the final sequence in which the identity of the murderer is revealed that is the boldest variant on the flashback form in the film. Lodge and his partner return to speak to Mr Pollard and Lodge recounts what he thinks happened to Astra. He talks about Michael Murray and his row with her, and the flashback begins with Murray entering her house and making his way up the stairs. Lodge's voice-over continues as Michael goes into Astra's bedroom and is framed menacingly in the doorway. The shot that follows returns to Lodge and Pollard who says 'Yes, that's what happened.' The next shot returns to the flashback and to Astra sitting at her dressing table, turning to look towards the door. Lodge's voice-over says, 'She turned and saw ...' and there is a cut to Pollard standing in the doorway, not to Murray as might have been expected, a twist which reveals the identity of the murderer. It is an interesting variant on the flashback form which starts misleadingly with an event that never happened then transforms itself into the 'truth'; it mixes a 'false' flashback in the manner of Hitchcock's famous example in *Stage Fright* (1950) with a 'true' flashback which establishes what actually happened to Madame Astra.

The film remains a provocative essay in narrative structure utilising flashbacks in a bold manner. Indeed, Maureen Turim, in her study of the flashback, compares Asquith's film to Kurosawa's *Rashomon*:

> There is a British film directed by Anthony Asquith, *The Woman in Question* (1950), which uses five flashbacks to give five different per-spectives on a murder. It is a film whose dark and dry sense of humor carries a Hitchcockian tradition to an extreme where the tongue-in-

cheek suspense thriller almost defies such a categorization. It can be seen as comparable to *Rashomon* in structure, and though its tone does not insist on the same philosophical analysis, there is no reason not to analyze the play of voice in this film just as seriously.[21]

The film has many generic affinities with the British crime film – the seediness, the figure of the spiv (Dirk Bogarde), Jean Kent as femme fatale – yet its complex and innovative narrative form links it also to directions in the Hollywood crime film of the time, as well as anticipating Kurosawa's internationally acclaimed *Rashomon*. Though the basic idea for the structure probably may well have originated with the scriptwriter, John Cresswell, its experimental quality fits neatly into Asquith's inclination for cinematic experiment and the narrative innovation displayed some years previously with *A Cottage on Dartmoor*.

The Net (1952)

The Net was also made for Two Cities Films/Rank with Anthony Darnborough as producer. It attracted attention from the fan magazine *Picturegoer*, which ran a series of weekly articles following the course of its production.[22] However, on its release, critics were prone to compare it unfavourably with David Lean's *The Sound Barrier*, a film with similar subject matter, supersonic flight, which had been released some six months before Asquith's film. Apart from the comparable subject matter, a comparison between the two films was more or less inevitable as the screenplay for *The Sound Barrier* was written by regular Asquith collaborator Terence Rattigan. Although Asquith was desperately disappointed when direction of the film went to another of his erstwhile collaborators – David Lean – it was, in fact, a project which Lean himself had developed and taken to Alexander Korda. *The Net*, according to Minney, 'helped to get Asquith's acute disappointment over *The Sound Barrier* out of his system'.[23] Both films can be related to *Q Planes* (Tim Whelan, 1939) and *The First of the Few* (Leslie Howard, 1942), and a strand in British cinema which foregrounds 'Britain's technological mastery in the sky'.[24] There were, however, differences between them. Lean's film was about orthodox air travel and the breaking of the sound barrier in conventional jet aircraft, and was embedded in contemporary actuality with references to the *Comet*, the first passenger jet aeroplane. *The Net*, by contrast, had more of a science-fiction quality and was concerned with the development of a craft – a mixture of aeroplane and space ship – with a mission to fly to the edge of space. C. A. Lejeune, writing in the *Observer*, suggested that the comparison was limited arguing that 'their purpose and style are quite different. Mr Lean's film was an inquiry into the constructional and operational problems of the pioneers of the jet plane. Mr Asquith's ... is roaring melodrama.'[25]

The Net was adapted from a novel of the same name written by John Pudney, the poet and novelist whose poems had played an important part in *The Way to the Stars*. The narrative centres on a cosmopolitan group of experimental scientists – English, Scottish, Irish, German, French, and a Canadian security officer – working within the closed parameters of a government research station. Like *The Sound Barrier* much of the film is concerned with the experimental development of the craft, M7, its testing by pilots in flight conditions, its problems and failures. The film also delves into the personal lives of the group: the troubled marriage of the principal character, Heathley (James Donald) and his wife Lydia (Phyllis Calvert), Lydia's attraction to one of the other scientists, Alex Leon (Herbert Lom), and the romance between two of the junior staff, Brian Jackson (Patric Doonan) and Caroline Cartier (Muriel Pavlow). The film also has an espionage dimension, it is a Cold War film reflecting the paranoia of the 1950s, with a spy, Dennis Bord (Noel Willman), who in addition to passing on scientific secrets, attempts to hijack the M7 craft along with Heathley and to fly to his unspecified paymaster's country. In fact, the early 1950s was a period of high-profile civil service defections and shortly before *The Net* was released, John Pudney recounted an interesting anecdote in relation to his novel on which the film was based to *Daily Mirror* journalist Reg Whiteley:

> John Pudney, who wrote the original story of the new British film 'The Net' tells me that he met Donald Maclean, the missing diplomat, while finishing the book.
>
> 'Maclean was brought over to a meal by a mutual friend,' Pudney said. 'He asked me what I was writing. I told him it was a novel in which a man loses his loyalty and goes to another country.
>
> 'Maclean showed absolutely no reaction, but within ten days he had disappeared.'[26]

In addition to that uncanny brush with reality, the film mixes together a number of generic strands including science fiction, Cold War espionage, domestic melodrama, and romance. Indeed, *Kine Weekly* referred to the film as an 'espionage melodrama, domestic drama, "sound barrier" thriller, "Who-dunnit," adventure drama and semi-documentary in one'.[27] Charles Barr has added a further perspective linking the film with another title made a few years earlier – *White Corridors* (Pat Jackson, 1951). Though the primary reason for the comparison is a study of actor James Donald, who plays the leading roles in both films, Barr suggests that the films are to be admired for 'the vivid way they express particular kinds of early 1950s idealism', and *The Net* specifically expresses 'a pursuit of new technology and new frontiers, in the spirit of the 1951 Festival of Britain and the New Elizabethan Age'.[28] Both films, he suggests, 'are deceptively artful narrative structures in the "classical" tradition. They tell a public story (hospital, aircraft unit) and a personal story which are interconnected, and which move, in comparable fashion, to a joint resolution.'[29]

The film's opening sequences establish the dichotomy identified by Barr. As the credits are displayed, the films opens with a panning shot of the research station at twilight, taking in the moored M7 aircraft and ending on the station's perimeter fence where two security guards are talking. After a brief cutaway shot to the M7, Heathley and Carrington (Maurice Denham), the station's Director, arrive having a heated argument about the test plans for the craft. This is the 'public story', the tussle between scientist and bureaucrat, the scientist wanting to push the pace by having a piloted test flight, the civil servant cautious and mindful of the risks involved, insisting on a test controlled from the ground. The image itself is striking: the two are framed behind the grill of the fence, 'the net' of the film's title in which both are enveloped. The next sequence takes place at Heathley's home – a party for his colleagues – and though partly it works to introduce, somewhat schematically, the principal players in the narrative, it also establishes the private dimensions of the film, Heathley's marital problems, the romance between Brian and Caroline, and Alex Leon's interest in Lydia. Heathley arrives late and the first images are of him looking in on the gathering framed through the grill pattern of the window. Heathley joins the gathering though not before a brief conversation with his wife. She says he looks worried and he replies that it's something to do with work. 'Oh. I see' she responds. It is a brief, somewhat understated scene but it sets the tone of tension in their relationship which the film will juxtapose with the public tensions generated by Heathley's determination to fly M7 despite the opposition of the Director and a number of his colleagues including the one closest to him, Brian Jackson.

The sequence also establishes Bord, the station doctor, as a sinister character. Though he is first seen leading the party group in a song session, later in the sequence the image of bonhomie is undercut when the Director tells him that Heathley will not be allowed to conduct the piloted test while he is in charge. The scene opens with a wide shot of the two characters standing either side of a large globe. The camera moves closer as they talk about Heathley but when the Director says, 'He's not going to take her up' there is a sharp cut to a somewhat surprised-looking Bord and the scene moves into a shot/reverse shot pattern. Finally, the Director leaves and the camera returns to Bord moving to frame him from a low angle while he spins the globe accompanied by appropriately 'sinister' music on the soundtrack together with a reprise on the sound track, of the Director's comment, 'He's not going to take her up. Not while I'm in charge.'

The two sequences, the opening ten minutes of the film, establish the dramatic directions of *The Net*, 'skilfully cashing in on two worlds, that of the modern marital problem narrative and, secondly, the vogue for pseudo-scientific thrillers', as one trade paper put it.[30] Its effectiveness is not simply a matter of the skilful interweaving of narrative information, character identification, plot direction and so on; it is also a matter of the mood and tone established through *mise-en-scène*, through the music, and the creation of a tense, disquieting, sinister, tightly enclosed world in which the narrative will be played out.

Asquith's skill as a *metteur-en-scène* is exemplified in a number of ways. Shortly after the Director's death, Heathley and Bord are talking about the Director and his refusal to sanction the piloted test. The scene begins with a medium two-shot; Heathley has a model vintage aeroplane in his hand and he says, 'But he represented everything I've always been fighting against.' He goes to his desk and puts the model down and, as the camera reframes him, a large model of the M7 looms into view dominating the screen, blocking him off completely for a brief second or two. The interplay of objects – the vintage, the futuristic – is eloquent and forms a vivid commentary on the 'new technology, new frontiers' theme of the film. The sequences dealing with the relationship between Heathley's wife, Lydia, and Alex Lyon, are also of interest in terms of style and presentation. Alex and Lydia have lunch together, then he takes her to a fairground and they end up in the peepshow booth. They look at a 'What the Butler Saw' film, framed at one point ostensibly from within the peepshow machine itself, and afterwards they kiss. The setting – the fairground, frequently associated in the cinema with nightmare, fantasy, transgression, and the mildly risqué peepshow film – creates an atmosphere of mild danger, or at least a momentary ripple of disturbance in the emotional economy of the film.

In a subsequent sequence, the momentum generated by the incident is cleverly used to orchestrate a discussion between Alex and Heathley, ostensibly about the planned piloted test due the following day. It begins with a long shot of Alex sitting immobile in a chair while Heathley paces around – moving in and out of frame – talking about the flight. The camera begins to move slowly towards Alex, eventually framing him in a medium shot – the movement effectively distracting attention from the content of Heathley's monologue, and inserting instead a tense undercurrent based upon Alex's pursuit of Lydia. Alex asks Heathley about the reason for their meeting, anticipating a confrontation about Lydia; however, Heathley's real reason for the meeting is to talk about Brian's failure to support him on the question of the manned flight. Charles Barr has suggested that British films often play with the contrast between overt and underlying meaning:

> Often there is an eloquent and poignant disjunction between surface drama, as observed in talk and action, and interior drama, which may be conveyed through the eyes and/or through expressive gaps in the film's narrative structure, creating a strong sense of something *other* that is being repressed or sought in vain.[31]

The covert meanings – Alex and Lydia's meeting, the implications of their kiss – almost come to the surface at various points; Alex seems on the brink of telling Heathley about himself and Lydia but decides against it and their discussion is brought to a close when Lydia arrives. The sequence is an expert, though unremarkable, example of the way in which dialogue, camera placement and movement, and acting performance, can counterpoint each other as they develop different dimensions of the narrative exploiting the tensions between the 'surface' and the 'interior drama'.

The Net, as a genre piece, also contains two conventional action sequences of the M7 aircraft on its test flights. The sequences use process shots with a model aircraft, and a studio-constructed cockpit hydraulically operated to simulate movement in flight.[32] The final sequence, in particular, intercuts scenes of Heathley and Bord, the traitor, in the aircraft, with scenes from the base control-room, to great effect. Bord has ordered Heathley at gunpoint to fly the aircraft to another destination – by implication an unnamed communist state. Heathley disarms him by putting the aircraft into a dive and Bord accidentally severs the oxygen supply to his helmet in his attempts to regain the gun. Though he loses control of the aircraft for a brief time, Heathley manages to recover and to set the correct course for home. The final images of the film – close shots of Heathley in the aircraft; Lydia, Alex, Brian, and Caroline in the control room – reintroduce the personal emotional elements of the film after the suspense and excitements of the aerial struggle, reintegrating the public and the personal stories 'which move ... to a joint resolution'.[33]

The Young Lovers (1954)

The Young Lovers was the first of two feature films that Asquith was to direct for Anthony Havelock-Allan, a highly experienced producer, founder of the Cineguild company, and collaborator with Noël Coward and David Lean on a number of important British films during the 1940s including *In Which We Serve*, *Brief Encounter* and *Great Expectations*. The film was made for Group Film Producers, 'Rank's principal production organization',[34] in the tightly controlled circumstances of Britain's most powerful film group. Indeed, as Havelock-Allan was to reveal in an interview some years later, working for Rank had a profound effect on the course of production and, in particular, on the choice of director and stars: 'For *The Young Lovers* I had wanted Mark Robson to direct, Jimmy Stewart to star, and some very good European actress I intended to find. The Rank Organisation said they didn't have the money for an American star and wanted me to use the young American, David Knight.'[35] In 1954 James Stewart was forty-six years of age, some twenty years older than David Knight, and his casting in the lead role may well have required a revision of the film's title, even allowing for Hollywood cinema's somewhat cavalier attitude to age and leading men. It was Knight's first screen appearance and he was paired with a young French actress, Odile Versois. Perhaps more crucially, Havelock-Allan had envisaged a different style of direction for the film and, indeed, a different director:

> Puffin was the wrong director for it; it should have been made in that stark, realistic style the Americans were so good at, but Rank wanted to use Puffin. I hadn't made a film for some time and was getting lazy, so I agreed to do it as Rank wanted. It was a perfectly good film but it lacked guts; it didn't have that hard edge to it which it needed. It was intended as a blast against McCarthyism, and was written by a noted anti-Fascist, George Tabori.[36]

The Young Lovers is a 'romantic melodrama'[37] to use *Kine Weekly*'s description, though its setting against a background of the East/West conflict and the world of London's foreign embassies during the Cold War gives it something of an affinity with *The Net*. Indeed, Marcia Landy, in her comprehensive study of British film genres, locates the film in an early 1950s grouping of films which 'acknowledges international tensions and situates personal malaise within that context'.[38] Along with titles such as *The Third Man* (Carol Reed, 1949), *High Treason* (Roy Boulting, 1951), and *The Man Between* (Reed, 1953), *The Young Lovers* is embedded in the world of surveillance, of paranoia and mistrust generated by the post-war international division of the world. The film is set in London with the hero Ted Hutchens (David Knight) working as a code-breaker in the US Embassy while the heroine Anna Sobek (Odile Versois) works in a Communist trade legation office where her father is the Minister. Their chance meeting at a ballet performance leads to a romance opposed by both sides of the political division, to her pregnancy, and to her being returned to her own country in order to forestall the relationship. During her return, however, she escapes with Ted and they go on the run, pursued by both the Americans, together with British security officials, and the Communists.

The film opens with a pattern of alternating images of Ted and Anna walking separately through the London streets at night before their chance encounter at the Royal Opera House where they happen to be seated together for a ballet performance. The pattern of alternating images is repeated a number of times in the early part of the film and it both emphasises their separateness – they inhabit different and opposed worlds – and the growing intensity of their feelings for each other. Anna is taking dictation from her father but the camera slowly moves closer to her with a far-away look in her eyes; there is a dissolve to Ted and his American colleagues in a meeting with a British intelligence liaison officer, Moffatt (Joseph Tomelty) and then a similar shot of Ted with the camera moving towards him catching his far away look. A subsequent close-up of Ted dissolves into one of Anna; both are lost in romantic reverie. Ironically, Moffatt is addressing the American agents about the potential problems of chance encounters with strangers. Later, after Anna has promised her father not to see Ted again, the pattern is repeated with alternating shots of them in their offices, and in their beds, intensifying both their closeness and their separation. The images are accompanied by music from Tchaikovsky's *Swan Lake*, the well-known theme from Act II of the ballet, which is used as a *leitmotif* throughout the film. It is first heard during the opening sequences when they meet at the ballet and it prompts Anna to rush from the auditorium in tears. In the later sequence, after the alternating images, as the music reaches a crescendo, Ted and Anna meet by chance while waiting for an underground train. The *leitmotif* is also used in the film's finale over the two last images of the film – the couple on the boat and the sea now tranquil after a storm. Asquith was extremely attentive to the role of music in cinema and, for one sequence, staged the action in relation to pre-recorded music, a strategy used by Michael Powell for *Black Narcissus* (1947) some years earlier. In Asquith's own words:

> I prerecorded a piece of music in order to get a certain rhythm in the film. This was for the very opening of the picture. The scene for which it was required was shot silent. I wanted the eyes of the boy and girl to meet

for the first time at the *pas de deux* of the second Act of *Swan Lake*. To achieve this I had the music played back to make sound and vision coincide. It worked perfectly.[39]

The 'action', however, was minimal, a turn of the head, a simple glance, a brief meeting of eyes, underscored by the plaintive musical theme played on the cello. In fact, there is no dialogue during the opening six minutes or so of the film, only music and some ambient sound effects. The music governs the introduction to the narrative and presents, in lyrical fashion, the beginnings of the romance.

The lyrical dimension, the use of powerfully emotional images, continues through the first part of the film, deepening the intensity of the relationship. Towards the end of their first meeting, the couple are sitting in a restaurant and the accompanying music is coming from an accordion player. The camera moves closer to the couple, framed in a two-shot, and the music changes abruptly from the jaunty accordion music to the Tchaikovsky cello theme; the image dissolves to a shot of the river, the camera panning across to a bridge where the couple are eventually framed in a romantic shot complete with shimmering river surface and a festoon of lights. It is an appropriate setting for their first kiss and it establishes a lyricism in the presentation of their relationship which is gradually undercut by the apparently insurmountable problems that confront them across the political divide. Their first night together is a matter of low-key lighting and Tchaikovsky, together with an oddly archaic montage sequence of waves crashing against the shore following their initial passionate embrace. This is the Asquith that Graham Greene had complained about in his comments on *Moscow Nights* when he objected to the frequent use of montage sequences to underline dramatic moments in the film. The couple are subsequently shown following their love-making, sitting on the bed, discussing their future with a degree of optimism despite their different backgrounds. Sandwiched in between the two lyrical sequences, however, is an ominous scene in which Joseph (Theodore Bikel), the Legation security chief, informs Anna's father (David Kossoff) about her romance with an American. In that sense the film explicitly constructs a formidable impasse to the relationship at the same time as engaging the audience with the couple.

The narrative solution to the couple's obstacles lies in a kind of generic shift to the thriller and, specifically, the couple on the run format. It was a solution not applauded by every critic and, for example, Penelope Houston writing in *Sight and Sound* suggested it represented 'the lack of a final imaginative commitment' on Asquith's part: 'Anthony Asquith's *The Young Lovers* sympathetically establishes the relationship of the American hero and the Iron Curtain heroine, trapped between opposing ideologies; then, as though unwilling to look directly at the issues raised, it sidesteps into the less controversial and less urgent territory of the thriller.'[40] Yet the thriller sequences are expertly handled, the sequences on board the train taking Anna back to her home, the suspense skilfully engendered with the police arriving just after Ted has picked up some money from the Brighton branch of Thomas Cook, reminiscent of Hitchcock. There is even a sympathetic landlady along the lines of the innkeeper's wife in *The 39 Steps* (Hitchcock, 1935). With her help the couple evade their pursuers and, in the final images of the film, are seen sailing off in a small boat in the middle of the ocean.[41] In the context of the politics of the time, the film's theme is liberal, and critical of both sides. As Raymond Durgnat has suggested:

> [T]he sharpest repudiation of the Dulles image of the Cold War is Anthony Asquith's *The Young Lovers* (1954). The son of the American ambassador in London (David Knight) and the daughter of an East European diplomat (Odile Versois) are the Romeo and Juliet who cry 'A plague on both your houses', elope, and find happiness in flight – or death?[42]

The ambiguity of the ending, which leaves the young lovers adrift on the ocean after they have survived a mighty storm, intensifies the romantic dimensions of a film which, whatever affinities it might have with the Cold War espionage sub-genre, is centrally a romantic film in which the young lovers pursue their feelings for each other come what may. It might be seen as a restrained British variant on the theme of *amour fou* more usually associated with the Hollywood *film noir* and titles such as *Gun Crazy* (Joseph H. Lewis, 1947) and *They Live by Night* (Nicholas Ray, 1947), films which blend the intensity of romantic love with the drama of the couple on the run, the narrative pattern followed by *The Young Lovers*. It might also be linked to other romantic films of the period, as Peter Cowie has suggested: '[T]his is the type of film that one would expect from David Lean. It has the intimate love scenes, the rather drab English background, and the fear of separation from each other in the lovers that one associates with *Brief Encounter and The Passionate Friends.*'[43]

Raymond Durgnat, though appreciative of the film's liberal Cold War politics, was also impressed with Asquith's imaginative and lyrical rendition of Ted and Anna's romance. He had compared him to Max Ophuls, the great romantic director, on the basis of Asquith's 'Edwardian lyricism' evident in some of his earlier films; though he saw Asquith's career in the 1950s as something of a decline, he did concede that 'the old lyricism trickles forth one last time, after years, in *The Young Lovers* (1954)'.[44]

Orders to Kill (1958)

Orders to Kill was the second film which Asquith directed for Anthony Havelock-Allan but this time it was under the auspices of British Lion, the major refuge from the powerful combines for independent producers. As a war film it was a contribution to one of the key genres of the period and, in dealing with a resistance theme, it revisits the territory of *Freedom Radio* and *Uncensored*, films that Asquith had made during the wartime period itself. The script, an adaptation of a David Downes novel, was written by Paul Dehn who had previously worked with Asquith on a short film about the Glyndebourne opera – *On Such a Night* (1955). The film was a low-key affair with no major stars. The leading role was played by Canadian actor Paul Massie in his first significant film role, and there were strong supporting performances from the American actor Eddie Albert and from the British actor James Robertson Justice. The cast also included the legendary star of the silent screen Lillian Gish and the American-born actress Irene Worth, who had worked in the British theatre since the 1940s. Later Asquith was to comment that 'one of the very best performances I have had in my life came from Irene Worth, who'd hardly done a film before'.[45]

Asquith's film focuses upon an individual assassination mission towards the end of the war. Gene Summers (Paul Massie), a young American flier grounded following an extended tour of duty, is selected for a mission to kill a suspected double agent operating in the Parisian resistance movement as a liaison operator for a group of allied agents. The narrative follows the familiar generic pattern established by films such as Teddy Baird's *Now It Can Be Told* (1946), a dramatised documentary about the Special Operations Executive, the government agency which organised subversive activities during the war. *Orders to Kill* is divided into three narrative blocks. The first shows Summers undergoing his training and his departure for France, the middle part of the film deals with his work in France and the execution of the suspect. These sections are about equal in length, and the final part – the aftermath which deals with the impact of the experience on Summers himself – is about half the length of the other two.

The opening section follows the conventions of the genre closely outlining the various different training phases for the undercover mission – unarmed and armed combat training, interrogation methods, the learning of a new false identity, the detail of the mission, espionage techniques in general. The opening narrative block is relatively upbeat though the opening shot of the film – a close-up of a bloodied hand – warns of the dark trajectory that the narrative will take. Indeed, a close shot of Summers holding up his bloodied hand was used in the advertising of the film.[46] Summers himself displays a rather naïve approach to the mission, revelling in the 'boy's own' aspects of the training – the combat and assassination techniques, the shooting range – and even singing his instructions to the tune of an old nursery song as an *aide-mémoire*. As the *Variety* review put it, he 'approaches the job with tremendous enthusiasm as he trains for this legalized murder'.[47] This mood is sustained by the Commander (James Robertson Justice) during Gene's instructions in methods of killing – strangulation, stunning, stabbing – which occurs towards the end of his training. However, the sequence ends with Mac (Eddie Albert) speaking alone to the Commander and confiding his fears about Gene's attitude, saying, 'You know, except for one moment in his first interrogation, I don't believe he's ever stopped to think what it's really going to be like over there. He's play-acting and he's loving it.' This sequence, carefully placed at the end of the 'training' segment, darkens the film and warns of the dangers ahead as the Commander explains to Mac the necessity for inculcating such an attitude in those embarking on assassination missions. 'I've got to stop civilised men from thinking about the reality of killing a fellow human being', he says, 'because if they thought about it they'd never do it.' Yet, in the following sequence in which Gene is being briefed just prior to flying the France, he still maintains his somewhat casual attitude towards the mission and a supreme confidence in his ability to carry it out.

The second narrative block – the execution mission – introduces the character of Léonie (Irene Worth), Gene's main resistance contact for the mission, and, of course, Marcel Lafitte (Leslie French), his assassination target. His first encounter with Lafitte is by chance in a café close by his office. Shortly after this, Gene returns to the café and Lafitte arrives and sits at an adjacent table. An element of dark humour creeps in as he suggests jokingly that Gene's meal of rabbit stew is really cat stew but then offers to pay for the meal when Gene leaves. Lafitte is presented as a 'kind, bespectacled, generous and sentimental man',[48] and the sequence ends on their handshake. The image dissolves into an image of Gene in his room standing by the window, silhouetted in the moonlight; he crosses the room and sits on the bed, the camera moves towards him framing him in a powerful image of doubt. The scene is silent apart from the sound of his footsteps, but the image turns the film from the 'boy's own' adventure to the pessimistic existential tale that it eventually becomes.

Gene confides his doubts to Léonie later in the film in a tense and powerful sequence which lasts just over ten minutes. It is dominated by

Léonie who verbally chastises Gene for his doubts, his indiscreet revelations about his background, and his suggestion that they contact London about Lafitte. In the process, however, she also confides in him about the loneliness of the job and reveals her own humanity – normally masked by a rather cold exterior. Eventually Gene's boyish enthusiasm for the task is restored, his doubts banished, and he agrees to go on with the mission.

The execution itself is carried out according to the Commander's previous instructions although the process of first stunning Lafitte then stabbing him in the heart is shown to be cumbersome and protracted. He is only partially stunned from the blow with the weapon and turns to look at Gene, saying, 'Why?' To finish the job Gene has to stifle Lafitte's cries while he is struggling to open his pen-knife; he eventually abandons it in favour of a pair of scissors on the nearby desk. The physical difficulties of the killing are emphasised in a manner which anticipates Hitchcock in *Torn Curtain* (1966), leaving Gene in a traumatised state. Although he recovers some composure, taking Lafitte's money to make it look like a robbery, and altering his appearance in line with new identity details provided by Léonie, he discovers a note telling him to contact her before doing the job. He is unable to contact her and his descent into nightmare begins. In the final sequences of the film Gene is in hospital recovering from an alcoholic breakdown and, after learning that Lafitte was in fact innocent, he returns to Paris to see Lafitte's wife and to tell her of her husband's courageous role in the resistance.

For the most part the film is shot in a straightforward functional style with few striking camera angles, lighting designs, expressionist touches, and editing schemes. In particular, the first half of the film, dealing with Gene's training, has the schematic quality of a documentary; the muted expressionist outbursts are confined to sequences such as the mock interrogation which takes place, understandably, in a darkened room, and the sequence in the firing target house in the training camp. However, there are two sequences in the second half of the film which demonstrate Asquith's varied approaches to direction, the one reliant upon the long take, the other on montage. The long take predominates in the sequence when Gene expresses his doubts about Lafitte's guilt and Léonie 'delivers a furious diatribe'.[49] The major part of Léonie's diatribe, in fact, is shot in an unbroken take lasting more than two minutes; Gene is sitting while Léonie stalks around reminding him of the realities of the dirty war in which they are engaged. Around half of the sequence is taken up by three such shots in which the dilemmas and difficulties of the job are articulated. In contrast, the sequence detailing Gene's breakdown incorporates a montage sequence culminating in a brief episode with Gene trapped in the Metro during an air raid. It begins with Gene discovering Léonie's warning note; he tries to phone her but gets the 'keep away' signal agreed earlier. The montage element then begins with a medley of brief shots including Gene, making further attempts to phone, walking through the rain-washed streets, getting drunk, interwoven with a number of flashbacks of Lafitte and Léonie, Gene's bloodied hand in close-up, the blow that felled Lafitte, and so forth. The shots dissolve into each other and, in some cases – the street shots taken with a handheld camera, the out-of-focus phone receiver shots – are designed as point of view shots. The montage series ends with Gene in a Metro station; he tries to leave but is ushered back as an air raid begins. He is framed in a close shot staring up towards the Metro exit and the screen fades to black. The next time Gene appears is in his hospital bed towards the end of the film. Later, Asquith was to explain the design of the film, the move from realism to expressionism: 'I used the realistic approach in the early parts of the film. Then, as the central character was caught up with his own thoughts and conscience, I gradually moved towards a more intimate treatment. I tried to show what he was thinking.'[50]

Orders to Kill is an important representative of the change in the genre towards the end of the decade, when 'the war film took a pessimistic turn, and dealt with failure and damage'.[51] The British Second World War film produced some of the most popular films of the decade – *The Cruel Sea* (Charles Frend, 1953), *The Dam Busters*, *Reach for the Sky* – with many titles celebrating the heroic exploits of the services and exciting audiences with the dramatic world of combat in the various theatres of war. *Orders to Kill* deals with the less public face of the conflict, 'the secret war'[52] of subversion and sabotage in German-occupied Europe. Along with *Against the Wind* (Charles Crichton, 1947), *Odette* (Herbert Wilcox, 1950), *They Who Dare* (Lewis Milestone, 1953), *The Safecracker* (Ray Milland, 1957), *Carve Her Name With Pride* (Lewis Gilbert, 1958), and *Circle of Deception* (Jack Lee, 1960), the film has been identified as contributing to an important and distinctive strand of the 1950s war picture. As Nicholas Pronay has suggested, this body of films differed from the better known titles which dealt with conventional post-war themes, and 'typically explored ethical questions about war, tackled some of the more sensitive political issues not much aired in this period officially and historically'.[53] Some of the high-profile films were not entirely unquestioning about the war: *The Dam Busters* and *The Cruel Sea*, for example, contain hints of a critique at least; however, Pronay suggests that the 'subversion and sabotage' strand pushed the questioning much further with *Orders to Kill*, in particular, raising 'some central and very uncomfortable questions about Britain's wartime concentration on Subversive Operations, and on the whole complex of ethical issues involved'.[54]

Opinions of the film, however, are mixed and producer Havelock-Allan, much in the spirit of his comments on *The Young Lovers*, thought the film fell short of its potential, as he suggested in an interview:

> The next film was a story which Puffin had found, *Orders to Kill*, which again would have been better with a harder, sharper edge to it. It needed to be conceived more harshly. Both the films I did with Puffin were well made, well crafted, but the impact was soft and did not grip a world-wide audience. *Orders to Kill* was a very good story – how hard it is to kill an enemy when you get to know him personally – but the public simply didn't go for it.[55]

Perhaps the producer thought that the ending – where Gene revisits Lafitte's home and purges his guilt by giving Madame Lafitte money and heaping praise upon her husband – softened a potentially bleak scenario. Perhaps, though, he was disappointed by its box-office performance. *Kine Weekly* noted that though the film 'got raves from the critics ... it hasn't torn up any trees. It seems that the masses either want epics or X certificate hot "uns like "The Camp on Blood Island"'.[56] Though an enormously popular genre in the 1950s, the war film began to lose its appeal towards the end of the decade and *Orders to Kill* 'came rather too late in the burgeoning war film cycle to make much impact'.[57]

Asquith's genre exercises from the early 1950s, though containing much of interest – innovatory narrative structures, imaginative *mise-en-scène*, lyricism, and poetry, the radical ideological questioning of war – remain little-known films on the periphery of the mainstream British cinema of the time, and, as far as Asquith's public image is concerned, overshadowed by the theatrical adaptations. 'Asquith in the 1950s' evokes *The Importance of Being Earnest* rather than *The Young Lovers* or *Orders to Kill*.

Notes

1 *The Gater Report*, quoted in PEP, *The British Film Industry* (London: Political and Economic Planning, 1952), p. 117.

2 Statistics drawn from the *BFI Film and Television Handbook 2000* (London: British Film Institute, 1999), p. 26.

3 I. MacKillop and N. Sinyard, *British Cinema of the 1950s. A Celebration* (Manchester: Manchester University Press, 2003), p. 2.

4 For a detailed account of the episode see I. Jarvie, *Hollywood's Overseas Campaign. The North Atlantic Movie Trade, 1920–1950* (Cambridge: Cambridge University

Press, 1992), Ch. 7.

5 R. Murphy, *The Sixties* (London: BFI Publishing, 1992), p. 257.

6 K. Kulik, *Alexander Korda. The Man who could Work Miracles* (London: Virgin Books, 1975), p. 309.

7 PEP (Political and Economic Planning), *The British Film Industry* (London: PEP, 1952), p. 105.

8 S. Harper and V. Porter, *British Cinema of the 1950s. The Decline of Deference* (Oxford: Oxford University Press, 2003), pp. 38–40.

9 *Ibid.*, pp. 127-31.

10 M. Dickinson, 'The State and the Consolidation of Monopoly', in James Curran and Vincent Porter (eds), *British Cinema History* (London: Weidenfeld and Nicolson, 1983), p. 91.

11 R. Murphy, *Realism and Tinsel. Cinema and society in Britain 1939–1949* (London: Routledge, 1989), p. 230.

12 Harper and Porter, *British Cinema of the 1950s*, p. 249.

13 *BFI Film and Television Handbook 2000*, p. 30.

14 Harper and Porter, *British Cinema of the 1950s*, p. 268.

15 *Kine Weekly* (16.3.50), p. 21.

16 B. McFarlane, *An Autobiography of British Cinema* (London: Methuen, 1997), p. 68. Bogarde, in one of his autobiographical volumes, mentions that Val Guest also wanted Holden for one of his films, made shortly after *The Woman in Question*. See D. Bogarde, *Snakes and Ladders* (London: Chatto and Windus, 1978), p. 134. The film is probably *Penny Princess*.

17 J. Petley, 'The Lost Continent', in C. Barr (ed.), *All Our Yesterdays* (London: BFI Publishing, 1986), p. 111.

18 P. Schrader, 'Notes on film noir', in A. Silver and James Ursini (eds), *Film Noir Reader* (New York: Limelight Editions, 1996), p. 58.

19 M. Turim, *Flashbacks in Film* (New York & London: Routledge, 1989), p. 118.

20 K. Hollinger, 'Film Noir, Voice-Over, and the Femme Fatale', in Silver and Ursini (eds), *Film Noir Reader*, p. 247.

21 M. Turim, *Flashbacks in Film. Memory and History* (New York and London: Routledge, 1989), p. 261, n. 9. The comment is tucked away in a tantalising footnote!

22 The first part appeared in *Picturegoer and Film Weekly* (7.6.52).

23 R. J. Minney, *Puffin Asquith* (London: Leslie Frewin, 1973), p. 153.

24 I. Q. Hunter, 'Introduction. The strange world of the British science fiction film', in Hunter (ed.), *British Science Fiction Cinema* (London: Routledge, 1999), p. 7.

25 *Observer* (1.2.53) BFI cuttings collection: *The Net*.

26 R. Whiteley, 'Fiction into Truth', *Daily Mirror* (30.1.53). BFI cuttings collection: *The Net*.

27 *Kine Weekly* (15.1.53), p. 13.

28 C. Barr, '"Madness, Madness!". The Brief Stardom of James Donald', in B. Babington (ed.), *British Stars and Stardom* (Manchester: Manchester University Press, 2001), p. 162.

29 *Ibid.*

30 *Daily Film Renter* (14.1.53). BFI cuttings collection: *The Net*.

31 C. Barr, *All Our Yesterdays* (London: British Film Institute, 1986), p. 25. Emphasis in original.

32 *Kine Weekly* (11.9.52), p. 23.

33 Barr, '"Madness, Madness"', p. 162.

34 Harper and Porter, *British Cinema of the 1950s*, p. 42.

35 McFarlane, *An Autobiography of British Cinema*, p. 293.

36 *Ibid.*

37 *Kine Weekly* (26.8.54), p. 18.

38 M. Landy, *British Genres. Cinema and Society, 1930–1960* (Princeton, New Jersey: Princeton University Press, 1991), p. 181.

39 Quoted in Minney, *Puffin Asquith*, p. 154.

40 *Sight and Sound*, 25:1 (1955), p. 13.

41 Landy suggests that the boat is demolished during a storm implying that the lovers are lost at sea but they are shown to be still alive in the film's penultimate image though adrift in the middle of the ocean.

42 R. Durgnat, *A Mirror for England. British Movies from Austerity to Affluence* (London: Faber and Faber, 1970), p. 86. Ted's father is, in fact, a 'Kansas farmer', as he himself tells Anna in the film, and not the US ambassador.

43 P. Cowie, 'This England', *Films and Filming*, October (1963), p. 16.

44 Durgnat, *A Mirror for England*, p. 191.

45 Cinema Collection (Granada TV 1964–75) 3. Asquith TV interview: TX 21.1.65, p. 12. BFI Special Collection.

46 *Kine Weekly* (13.3.58), p. 34.

47 *Variety* (2.4.58), p. 6.

48 R. Murphy, *British Cinema and the Second World War* (London: Continuum, 2000), p. 200.

49 *Ibid.*, p. 201.

50 *Kine Weekly* (5.3.59), p. 20.

51 S. Harper and V. Porter, 'Cinema audience tastes in 1950s Britain', *Journal of Popular British Cinema* 2 (1999), p. 77.

52 Murphy, *British Cinema and the Second World War*, p. 81.

53 N. Pronay, 'The British Post-bellum Cinema: a survey of the films relating to World War II made in Britain between 1945 and 1960', *Historical Journal of Film, Radio and Television*, 8:1 (1988), p. 46.

54 *Ibid.*, p. 47.

55 McFarlane, *An Autobiography of British Cinema*, p. 293.

56 *Kine Weekly* (1.5.58), p. 11.

57 Harper and Porter, *British Cinema of the 1950s*, p. 111.

Post-war films 2 – adaptation and the theatre

6

The British cinema in the post-war period was not overly dependent upon the theatre for its source material. One writer has estimated that 'of the 1,033 British films of the 1950s listed in David Quinlan's *British Sound Films*, some 152 were based on stage plays'.[1] On an annual basis the figure never fell below 10 per cent of the annual production output; in some years it reached more than 20 per cent, as in 1948 when there were nineteen stage-originated features out of seventy-four films, and in 1952 when the figure was twenty-seven out of 117 films.[2] Yet for Asquith the theatre played a major role with eight of the seventeen feature films he directed between 1947 and his final film in 1964 based on stage plays of various kinds. It was this kind of film that played a key role in his image as a director often to his detriment, as in David Thomson's previously quoted description of him as 'a dull, journeyman supervisor of the transfer to the screen of proven theatrical properties'.[3] Asquith's pre-war work, particularly the silent and early sound pictures, had established his reputation as a distinctive film-maker with an awareness of the currents in the international cinema of the time and a firm grasp of the specificities of the medium. Like Hitchcock he demonstrated the film director's 'touch' and his work was praised for its innovative and experimental approach to the art of the silent film. Indeed, as has been noted in Chapter 2, his work was in tune with the aesthetic propounded by many influential critics and writers at the close of the silent period who argued that 'film was a *unique* artform, an artistic category unto itself – film as film'.[4] Yet his directorial image, as it developed in the late 1940s and through the 1950s, was built upon 'filmed theatre', that very kind of cinema which many regarded as antithetical to the art of the film. As a skilled adapter of stage drama with a number of films based on the plays of Wilde, Shaw, and Rattigan, among others, Asquith acquired a reputation as a *metteur-en-scène* rather than an *auteur*. Susan Sontag has suggested that the 'history of cinema is often treated as the

history of its emancipation from theatrical models'.⁵ Asquith appeared
to have secured his artistic emancipation early in his career but to have
succumbed subsequently to theatrical enslavement as a translator of the
work of dramatists.

Beyond genre in the post-war British film

The previous chapter established the primary image of 1950s British
films in terms of a popular cinema of genres – comedies, war films,
adventure and romantic pictures, horror and science-fiction films – as a
context for some of Asquith's post-war films. Yet there were other
aspects of the British cinema of the period which form a more appropriate framework for considering films such as *The Browning Version*
and *The Importance of Being Earnest*. Brian McFarlane has suggested two
important strands running alongside the popular cinema of genres. The
first is 'the realist strain that first made itself felt in war-time films such
as *Millions Like Us* (1943) and *San Demetrio, London* (1943)'; the second,
a literary and theatrical strand which included adaptations of Dickens,
Olivier's Shakespeare films, and *Brighton Rock*, *The Fallen Idol*, and *The
Third Man* based on the work of Graham Greene.⁶ Asquith had contributed to the 'realist' current with *We Dive at Dawn*, for example, and
the literary and theatrical strand forms an obvious context for Asquith's
best-known post-war films. Both currents can be seen as important
constituents of 'the quality film' identified by leading critics of the
period such as Dilys Powell, Richard Winnington, and C. A. Lejeune, as
representing 'a new spirit abroad in British films from 1942'.⁷

In some respects the 'quality' film constitutes a British variant of the
'art' film, and it was these films – the realist war films, David Lean's
Brief Encounter and *Great Expectations* – that were centralised in discussion of the new authentic 'British' or 'English' cinema that emerged
in the 1940s; a cinema that, in André Bazin's terms, 'was original and
free from influences from Hollywood'.⁸ The films exhibited a range of
features including 'adult' and 'humanistic' themes, emotional restraint,
attention to naturalistic detail, stylistic and narrative coherence, and a
sense of 'realism' inherited from the wartime pictures.⁹ It was not just
their intrinsic qualities which suggested an 'art cinema', however. In
America, films such as *Henry V* and *Brief Encounter* circulated through
the fast-developing 'art cinema' circuit. Many of the quality films were
successful in the prestigious European festival context; *Brief Encounter*
won the Critics' Prize at the Cannes Film Festival in 1946, *Hamlet*
(Laurence Olivier, 1948) won the Venice Film Festival's International

Grand Prize, and *The Third Man* (1949) also won the critics' prize at Cannes.

Yet, conflating these currents of British film to 'art cinema' may be misleading. Many of the quality films came from the commercially-orientated Rank group and in Britain they were screened alongside the genre films in the organisation's Odeon and Gaumont cinema chains. In addition, the same films and film directors whose work was celebrated at the European festivals enjoyed different degrees of success at Hollywood's Academy Awards – the major index of prestige in the commercial cinema. Both David Lean (in 1946) and Carol Reed (in 1949) were nominated for Oscars in the Best Director category, and Olivier's *Hamlet* actually won the Academy Award for Best Picture in 1948. The quality film was positioned in between a European cinema, which was to develop a very strong and distinctive 'art' strand during the 1950s, and the prestige American film, which tended to win the Academy Awards. Though it had elements of both kinds of cinema, it lacked the full identity of either. As Lindsay Anderson suggested in 1948: 'British cinema seems to hover between the opposite poles of France and Hollywood. Our directors never – or rarely – have the courage to tackle in an adult manner, the completely adult subject; yet, they lack also the flair for popular showmanship that is characteristic of the American cinema.'[10]

Anderson represented a new, younger critical generation compared with Lejeune, Powell, and others, and did not share the general critical enthusiasm for the quality film. Indeed, in a characteristic diatribe, he castigated some of the key quality films, including Asquith's *The Way to the Stars*, for their 'sentimental falsification of character and atmosphere'.[11] He quoted Virginia Woolf's definition of middlebrow art, a 'mixture of geniality and sentiment stuck together with a sticky slime of calves-foot jelly', and suggested that her 'phrases describe more aptly the atmosphere of those great popular and "artistic" successes of wartime – successes like *In Which We Serve*, *The Gentle Sex* and *The Captive Heart*'.[12] Where the more senior critics perceived a new realism defining the British film, Anderson saw 'reality romanticised'[13] and a cinema which remained, in Lawrence Napper's words, 'blind to both the intellectual rigours of international art cinema and the vigorous and potent entertainment provided by Hollywood'.[14]

Theatre and film

As noted previously, the relationship between film and theatre is often discussed in polemical terms with the older, traditional art form construed as a stifling influence on the newer one. For many critics and theorists, terms such as 'theatrical' and 'stage-bound' serve to distinguish films which are unduly influenced by alien aesthetic norms from those which utilise the 'proper' techniques of film. Much of this goes back to the late 1920s, the period when dialogue introduced a destabilising element into a medium which had evolved as a visually orientated art form. In the hands of the greatest directors, such as Murnau and Eisenstein, verbal elements such as the intertitle were reduced to an occasional interruption of the visual flow, or were used dynamically, integrating graphic expression into the primarily visual character of the film. The addition of synchronised speech and sound effects endangered the visual aesthetic of the silent film and threatened to reduce the medium to simple photographic recording, to relegate cinema to the status of 'canned theatre'.[15]

The relationship between film and theatre is complex because the two forms do have a number of things in common as well as the array of significant differences usually highlighted by film critics. Both forms are engaged in fictional narration, character construction, performance, visual spectacle, and dramatic structuring.[16] The relationship between them is also built on convergent though contingent factors, such as the use of theatre venues for the physical presentation of early films, the interchange of personnel between the two art forms – writers, actors, directors, producers – as well as the stage play, both historical and contemporary, as an abundant source of material for the cinema. Film historians have seen the relationship in somewhat uneven terms with the traditional art form construed as a means of rescuing the new one from its culturally inferior origins in fairgrounds, vaudeville theatres, and music halls, and improvised screening venues, facilitating its transformation into an cultural activity comparable to the established art forms. The adaptation of prestigious dramatic and literary material has been seen as a means of raising the social profile of cinema, a way of authenticating it in orthodox cultural terms, at various points in the history of the medium.

Within a few years of its invention adaptations of fragments of Shakespearean plays joined the actuality and trick films of early cinema. This trend crystallised just before the First World War in the films of companies such as Le Film d'Art in France, Autoren Film in Germany, and Série d'Or in Italy, and it also appeared in the American cinema with the work of the Vitagraph Company.[17] There were many reasons why classic literature and drama was pressed into service during the early years of cinema but the supposed prestige conferred upon film adaptations by a respectable source is one that persisted in American cinema, for example, in the glut of adaptations of British and European classic sources in the 1930s. It is also a trend which can be discerned in recent British cinema in the form of the heritage film's extensive use of Victorian and Edwardian literature. Related to this is the very familiar accusation levelled at British cinema since the 1920s, that its ambitious films are 'theatrical' in the sense of sharing a specific class-bound ethos with the traditional art form. As Stephen Lacey has suggested, the term 'connotes a particular kind of middle-class socially restricted film, carrying the same kind of associations that "well-made play" or "West End" have in the theatre'.[18] It is also frequently claimed that British cinema has, throughout its history, been unduly dependent upon stage actors and 'a style of acting that seems scaled towards the open space of a theatre auditorium rather than the enforced intimacy of the camera.'[19] Even popular actors who became major screen stars such as John Mills, Kenneth More, and Dirk Bogarde came from the stage;[20] and, of course, there was the prestigious array of 'theatrical knights' – Olivier, Redgrave, Richardson – whose origins in the theatre perhaps weighed more heavily on their screen performances.

The term 'theatrical' also connotes a range of stylistic tendencies which suppress the 'cinematic' – static camerawork, restricted camera angles, minimal editing, the uninterrupted take, and shooting in a studio. A 'theatrical' film privileges the word above the image, instrumentalising the medium at the expense of its specific aesthetic qualities.[21] Though such stylistic features are, in one sense, simply options in the range of techniques available to the film-maker, along with their alternatives – mobile camerawork, emphatic editing, the brief shot, location shooting – there has been a tendency among film theorists to privilege the alternatives as unique to cinema. As Noël Carroll has noted:

> Whereas theater narration typically relies on words, cinematic narration, it was asserted, could and should emphasise movement, image, and action. If theater was primarily verbal, cinema, ideally, was primarily visual. Likewise cinema had resources, particularly editing, that enabled film-makers to manipulate spatial and temporal transitions with more fluidity than was customary in theater. Thus, editing, or montage, was generally celebrated as the most important, essential characteristic of cinema. On this view, film was essentially visual, its natural subject of representation was animated action, and its primary means of expression was editing or montage.[22]

Asquith's undoubted cinematic credentials forged in the silent period, exemplified in films such as *Underground* and *A Cottage in Dartmoor*, and his realist credentials, established in the wartime films, provide an interesting background against which to gauge his post-war 'theatrical adaptation' period.

The Winslow Boy (1948)

The Winslow Boy was originally conceived of by Terence Rattigan as a film based on an actual historical incident – the Archer-Shee trial – which occurred a few years before the First World War. George Archer-Shee was a naval cadet expelled from naval college in 1908 after being accused of stealing a postal order from a fellow cadet. His father, convinced of his innocence, pursued the case vigorously to the highest authority and eventually proved his son's innocence. In fact, Anatole de Grunwald had asked Rattigan to write a script about British justice for Asquith to film and though Rattigan was enthusiastic about the Archer-Shee subject matter, both de Grunwald and Asquith were sceptical. Rattigan's response was to turn it into a play which opened in London in 1946.[23] It represented something of a departure for the playwright whose theatrical persona in the mid-1940s was as a writer of light comedy, an image set firmly in place by the enormous success of *French Without Tears*. *The Winslow Boy* was an altogether more serious type of play and its success took Rattigan by surprise. As he himself commented: 'It was produced at the Lyric Theatre in 1946 and, to my surprise, provided something of a critical sensation. It was generally felt to be very strange that a notoriously insincere farceur could so readily turn his hand to matters of fairly serious theatrical moment.'[24] Subsequently the film rights were bought by Alexander Korda for his recently acquired British Lion company, and early in 1948 the film went into production without much involvement from Korda himself.[25] Despite the earlier reservations, Asquith agreed to direct with de Grunwald acting as producer. In an interview with the magazine *Films and Filming*, de Grunwald suggests that his change of heart might have been prompted by a conversation he had with Ernest Bevin, the British Foreign Secretary in the post-war Labour government, who had asked him to 'make two films: one about British justice and one about the quality of British goods'. De Grunwald reflected that, 'Within three months I was shooting *The Winslow Boy*, based entirely on the idea of making a film about justice.'[26] The cast included veteran character actors Sir Cedric Hardwicke and Marie Lohr (who had worked with Asquith previously on *Pygmalion*), Margaret Leighton, a stage actress making her screen debut, and Robert Donat, a major star from the 1930s. Despite, in some respects, playing a subordinate role, Donat was the principal selling point of the film in terms of the cast, with an above-the-title billing in the pre-release trade paper advertising of the film.[27]

Writing in *The Sunday Times*, critic Cyril Ray suggested that in adapting the play for the screen, Rattigan, de Grunwald and Asquith 'have made no attempt at "pure movie"'.[28] There was, however, a certain amount of narrative restructuring. The film opens with Arthur Winslow (Sir Cedric Hardwicke) returning from his final day as a bank employee, alighting from a train, and announcing his retirement to his fellow passengers; he returns home and the first five minutes or so of the film is taken up with introducing the major characters. Despite the play's title, the 'Winslow father' is really the central character of the drama; indeed, his son, Ronnie (Neil North) – 'the Winslow boy' – is absent for much of the film and even misses the climax of the trial, having gone to the pictures. As one critic has suggested, his 'ambivalent position within the play is captured in the title which connotes both Ronnie's centrality to the story, and his personal marginality within it'.[29] The trial of Ronnie's probity, though more than a pretext, is a device on which Rattigan was able to hang meditations on justice, on the Edwardian family, and even on women's suffrage, through Arthur Winslow in particular but also through the character of his daughter, Catherine (Margaret Leighton).

The play, in contrast to the film, does open with 'the Winslow boy', indeed the first words of the play spoken by Violet, the maid (Kathleen Harrison) are, 'Master Ronnie!' It begins *in medias res* with Ronnie arriving home unexpectedly after his expulsion from naval college – hence the maid's opening exclamation – just before the rest of the family return from church. The film spends time sketching the family, defining them in thumbnail fashion – the older son Dickie's (Jack Watling) frivolous nature as he plays his gramophone and practises 'the bunny hug', daughter Catherine's (Margaret Leighton) seriousness – 'doing her envelopes' (voluntary work for the suffragette movement); there is even a montage of Ronnie's life at Osborne, the naval college, defining him sympathetically as a very normal 'schoolboy'. It is not until about eight minutes into the film that the material from Act I of the play begins with Violet's exclamation. From that point the play is then followed closely in terms of the sequence of events though there are several minor alterations to the dialogue. In a narrative sense, the film begins by establishing the terms of normality, the Winslow family life at their comfortable suburban home, before the disruptive element – Ronnie's expulsion – precipitates the drama; the play begins with the unexpected, with the enigma of Ronnie's premature homecoming creating drama and suspense from the opening moments.

In addition to that small recasting of the narrative, the film 'opens out' the play in a number of ways. The play confined its setting to the Winslow residence, indeed to a single setting – the drawing room. The key dramatic events – the debates in the House of Commons, the eventual trial, even the dramatic climax of the favourable verdict – occur off-stage. They are brought into the play, on to the stage, through various devices including the reading aloud of lengthy extracts from newspaper accounts, and through various characters reporting key incidents. For example, in the play even the dramatic climax of the trial, the verdict, is reported to Arthur Winslow by Violet, the maid. In fact Asquith's initial reservations about the viability of the project had centred on the trial of Ronnie Winslow and the difficulties that mounting such a scene presented for the stage.[30]

The film, by contrast, incorporates location-shooting – a railway station, the exterior of the Winslow house, the church, some street scenes, a golf course, the music hall – along with the two substantial studio sets of the House of Commons and the trial court. These remove the action intermittently from the Winslow drawing room where the entirety of the play is set and, in addition, some of the Winslow house sequences take place in other parts of the home – the hall, bedrooms, the garden, and the conservatory. In a sense, such opening out is relatively inconsequential, a simple exploitation of the film's capacity to move across locations in a more fluid and flexible manner than is possible on the stage. The heart of the drama can be retained while the settings provided for the screen offer a varied visual experience. But the film opened out *The Winslow Boy* in other ways, incorporating the important settings of the House of Commons and the trial court where key moments of the drama unfold. For Lejeune, this weakened the impact of the film, traducing the central impulse of the play:

> The very huddle of the characters in a stuffy Edwardian drawing room was a deliberate part of the design; the fact that all the Winslows were more or less antimacassar-bound while, their fate was being decided by fierce legal brains in the world outside added incomparably to the sense of drama. 'The Winslow Boy', in the theatre, triumphed by embracing its limits; the same 'Winslow Boy', transferred to the cinema, loses something by flouting them. Mr. Rattigan and Anthony Asquith, the director, have deliberately chosen the theatrical rather than the documentary approach to their subject; and it is in the extra scenes, the additional material, the attempts to amplify, still in theatrical terms, what has already been completely said in the theatre, that the film principally fails.[31]

It is an interesting proposition in relation to the subject of stage to screen adaptation endorsing, as it does, the confined space of the theatrical performance as the key element which injects drama into Rattigan's play. The 'opening out' or 'the attempts to amplify', in Lejeune's terms, has changed the emphasis of the work and has diluted the drama to some extent. It challenges a basic assumption about the adaptive relationship which is that the filming should avoid the static nature of performed drama by utilising cinematic techniques and by exploiting the medium's ease of mobility.

The opening-out process, though, can have other motivations, or can offer film-makers opportunities not available in the theatrical form. One critic was impressed with the film's detailed *mise-en-scène*, which he described as 'beautifully precise as to period, class and place – the Wimbledon of bank managers and retired colonels and the House of Commons of Mr Asquith's father'.[32] Another drew attention to the:

> numberless details that help to make the complete picture: the musical comedy chorus girls, unmistakably 1912 vintage ... the right proportion of top-hats and bowlers among the city gentlemen; the home of the Winslows in Wimbledon with just enough ornament and bric-à-brac in the drawing room to suggest the Edwardian influence.[33]

Despite Lejeune's strictures, a case can be made for the film's attention to such detail which gives it, in the words of one critic, a 'genuine feeling for time and place which is as rare as it is precious'.[34] The *mise-en-scène* is more than mere theatrical backdrop; it sets the motivations of the principal characters – Arthur Winslow's dogged persistence, Morton's haughty but principled commitment to justice, Catherine's restrained suffragist ideals – in the solid context of Edwardian Britain and its beliefs and values. One of the key differences between film and theatre, indeed, is the way in which the screen embeds actors in the *mise-en-scène*, as theorist Jean Mitry suggests:

> in the cinema ... the actor, instead of moving within a space serving merely as a framework, is actually part of a space "composed" with him as one of its elements; he is included within it. The essence of the cinema, apart from the mobility of its points of view, is without a doubt contained in this intimate union between the human beings and the world they live in. all the elements contained within the field of the camera – scenery, setting, objects, characters – constitute a unity of form in which and through which they are indissolubly linked together.[35]

Transposing a play to the screen also raises issues of *découpage* – the ways in which the integral space of the scene on stage is broken into a series of individual shots then combined in the editing. It also raises questions of point of view both in terms of the characters and the more general point of view on the dramatic material inscribed in the film – the film's perspective. The dramatic high spot of the play, its *pièce de théâtre*, is the cross-examination of Ronnie by Sir Edward Morton (Robert Donat), the high-profile barrister employed to defend the case. It takes place in the Winslow home some forty-five minutes into the film. Donat was the major star of the film and delaying his entrance until almost one third of the way into the film was a bold move though one which reflects the play. The text of the play is followed almost verbatim with a few slight alterations and a few lines omitted altogether. Understandably the scene is built around a shot/reverse shot structure between Ronnie and Sir Robert although there are a few shots of Arthur as he interrupts the interrogation at a couple of points. The scene builds to a crescendo in which Sir Robert accuses Ronnie of being a liar reducing him to tears as the boy protests his innocence. The sequence runs for about seven minutes and contains around one hundred shots. Though the pattern is not exact and mechanical – there are some quite brief shots at the beginning of the sequence – the *découpage* does seek to match the dramatic rhythm by gradually reducing the shot lengths as the interrogation becomes more vigorous and accusatory, and also gradually varying the scale of the shots, presenting the final images of Sir Robert and Ronnie in close-up. The pitch of the scene reduces considerably for the *coup de théâtre* which closes the sequence with Sir Robert agreeing to take the case despite having denounced Ronnie. The apparent volte-face is presented in a couple of shots each lasting several seconds by contrast to the preceding swiftly edited passage. The entire sequence both follows the scene as written for the stage, reproducing much of the dialogue verbatim, and also exploits the ability of the film to vary the perspective on events, to quicken the pace in line with dramatic intensity, and to slow matters down as it does at the end in order to emphasise the full force of Morton's parting words, 'The boy is plainly innocent. I accept the brief. Good night.' The scene is orchestrated for the cinema through the cinematography – the variations in scale and length of shot – and through the editing.

The play's ending is altered slightly for the film but in a way which lifts out more explicitly romantic nuances which are barely there in the play. In the film Morton arrives at the Winslow home just after Arthur and Catherine have been told of the trial's result; Ronnie arrives soon after having been at the pictures. Arthur and Ronnie go off to meet the press leaving Morton and Catherine alone for the final scene. Their discussion is quite personal covering such topics as Sir Robert's restrained emotions and Catherine's 'feministic activities', and the film moves towards a somewhat muted though nevertheless tangible romantic conclusion. He questions the value of her political activities, declaring them to be a 'lost cause', but she replies, 'How little you know women, Sir Robert.' As he leaves she says that they are unlikely to meet again, but his jaunty and flirtatious reply, 'How little you know men, Miss Winslow' – a play on her own words – concludes the film on a romantic note.

The Browning Version (1951)

The Browning Version is based on a one-act play which Rattigan wrote in 1946 though it was not until 1948 that the play was performed as one part of a double bill entitled *Playbill*.[36] It was a highly successful play as C. A. Lejeune commented in her review of the film: 'The Browning Version ... has become a firm favourite with the British public. It has been done on the stage by professionals and amateurs; it has been broadcast both on sound radio and television; and everywhere it has proved itself capable of arousing in an audience a peculiar and sustained affection.'[37]

The film version was made by the Javelin/Two Cities production team (de Grunwald, Asquith) that had made *The Woman in Question* with Terence Rattigan adapting his own play for the screen. The key roles of Andrew Crocker-Harris, his wife, Millie, and her lover Frank Hunter were played by Michael Redgrave, Jean Kent, and Nigel Patrick respectively though other names were bandied around in the press prior to production. Eric Portman, who had played the Crocker-Harris role on stage, and Anthony Steel were mentioned, together with Margaret Lockwood who, according to one report, turned the part of Millie down 'because she did not think she was suited for the role of the schoolmaster's erring wife'.[38] Michael Redgrave, in fact, won the Best Actor award at the Cannes Film Festival for his performance as Crocker-Harris while Terence Rattigan won the award for the best screenplay. The film was included as one of the Best Foreign Films in the American National Board of Review awards and was given a Bronze Bear as one of the best dramatic films in the Berlin Film Festival. It played at a number of European festivals including Karlovy Vary and was described in a Czech film magazine as 'an exception to present-day British film production, which is under the influence of Hollywood'.[39] Asquith was enthusiastic about the production having read the play in manuscript. His direction, according to the critics, was 'so unobtrusive ... that we are hardly aware of his part in the collaboration until the final shot of the sunny quadrangle with speech-day groups, a couple of figures running, and some bars of Beethoven'.[40] Penelope Houston, writing in *Sight and Sound*, suggested that his 'aim as director seems to have been to obtrude his own personality as little as possible; discreet, accomplished, his handling always takes its cue from the writing'.[41]

On stage *The Browning Version*, like *The Winslow Boy*, is confined to a single drawing-room set. However, whereas the events of *The Winslow Boy* span some two years, *The Browning Version* covers a short passage of time in the early evening before dinner on the day before Crocker-

Harris is due to retire from his job as a schoolmaster due to ill-health. In the transition to the screen, though, the time has been extended somewhat, running from the morning of the day before Crocker-Harris' retirement to the day itself and the climactic farewell ceremony. The film accordingly opens the play out considerably from the single-room set to include a range of locales, other rooms in the Crocker-Harris house including the dining room, the bedroom, the garden, as well as the drawing room; also, further afield, the school grounds, the chapel, and assembly hall, classrooms, the school cricket ground, and the headmaster's house.

There is a degree of invention for the screen, additional minor elements which embed the core drama in a realist setting, a filling-in of the background to the drama along the lines of the opening of *The Winslow Boy*. Indeed, the film begins with almost twenty minutes of material not in the play, in which the life of the school is sketched through the morning prayers, a chemistry lesson, a group of pupils discussing Crocker-Harris before he arrives in the classroom, Crocker-Harris' lesson, the annual cricket match, and the prize-giving ceremony at the end of term. After the lengthy scene-setting and character intro-ductions, the material of the play and the film converge with a lengthy sequence set mainly in the Crocker-Harris drawing room. It begins where the play begins, with Taplow arriving at the Crocker-Harris house for his extra lesson and subsequently incorporates the early events of the play – Taplow's discussion with Frank Hunter, Millie's arrival and her intimate conversation with Frank, Crocker-Harris' return and the lesson with Taplow. It follows the play closely, though with minor dialogue alterations and excisions, and some of Millie and Frank's conversation takes place in the garden rather than the drawing room as in the play. The film sequence ends at the point in the play just before the headmaster arrives to inform Crocker-Harris of the governors' refusal to grant him a pension and to ask him to speak before his junior colleague at the prize-giving ceremony despite the seniority which entitles him to speak last.

The film also follows the play closely in a subsequent lengthy sequence in which Taplow gives Crocker-Harris a leaving present – the Robert Browning translation of the *Agamemnon* from which the play derives its title. The gift precipitates some heated exchanges between Millie and the men and the sequence, both on stage and in the film, contains the dramatic heart of the work. The transposition of the play to the screen has involved partly replicating the stage presentation in these two lengthy sequences though they comprise less than a third of the film's running time, and partly an opening out of the film to incorporate a variety of settings which provide the film with a degree of naturalism. However, some of the important dramatic moments in the play are skilfully redeployed among the new settings including the unfortunate news about the pension which takes place during the cricket match, Crocker-Harris' confession of failure to his successor, Gilbert, set in the classroom where his unhappy career has been conducted, and his harsh diagnosis of his marriage to Millie which he confides to Hunter when they are left alone after the dinner at the headmaster's house.

As in the case of *The Winslow Boy*, some critics considered that the film's opening out of the play was a problem. It has been suggested that 'by allowing characters to leave the play's one room, the dynamic economy of the writing was clouded';[42] yet it could be argued that the distribution of some of the crucial dramatic moments across the film does provide the depth and insight into the character of Crocker-Harris while observing the cinematic protocols which require the variations in setting as the play is transformed into a film. Indeed, it could also be argued that the scene in which Crocker-Harris learns about his nickname – 'the Himmler of the lower fifth' – and confesses his failure to Gilbert is most appropriately filmed in the empty classroom where he has spent his career.

The centrepiece of the play, the dramatic high spot, is the scene where Taplow gives Crocker-Harris the book. In one sense, the film follows the play closely for the scene, using the same dialogue with a few minor alterations. It is dominated by a lengthy shot lasting around two minutes in which Taplow presents Crocker-Harris with the book and, while the boy is out of the room, the schoolmaster breaks down in tears at the gesture. As Asquith himself was later to comment, the 'scene is played through without any change of camera angle, or cut. There is no movement. What, then, makes this into a film scene and not just a film record of the stage scene?'[43] It is not an obviously 'cinematic' sequence yet, as he suggests, the choices made in how to present the somewhat simple incident in film form, are, in themselves, transformative. The choices of camera angle and position, its proximity to the actors – it is a medium close shot framing Redgrave from the waist up – the actors' own positioning and movement inevitably transform the material into something different to the scene as it would be played on stage. Asquith answered his own question in the following terms:

What makes it a film scene is firstly, the extreme intimacy which the camera establishes between actor and audience. This enables Redgrave to express the finest shades of thought and emotion in a way that would be literally invisible on the stage. Then the camera angle enables the audience to see Redgrave's mental processes as he instinctively turns from the boy towards the camera, and at the same time, the eager response to them reflected in Brian Smith's face. Further it is not only the proximity of the actors, but the momentary exclusion of their surroundings which gives such an intensely concentrated effect.[44]

As with the interrogation scene in *The Winslow Boy* the sense of the play, the specifics of the drama as originally written, remains, but the resources and techniques of cinema have been mobilised to deliver an experience which belongs to the film.

A point on which many critics are agreed is the baneful effect of the amplified ending devised for the film. During the final moments of the play, Crocker-Harris announces to Millie that he doesn't expect her to join him in his new post, implying their imminent separation; the phone rings, it is the headmaster, and Crocker-Harris, in an uncharacteristic act of defiance, tells him that he intends to exercise his right to speak last at the prize-giving. The play concludes somewhat abruptly with his line, 'Come along my dear. We mustn't let our dinner get cold.' The film deals somewhat differently with what is no more than a page of dialogue in the play. Their discussion of separation occurs at the end of the sequence at the headmaster's house and the sequence which follows it shows Millie's departure the next morning. The film then continues with a number of sequences going beyond the ending of the play and including the prize-giving ceremony itself. In contrasting the endings of play and film Lejeune suggested that the play had 'by far the nobler and more dramatic ending'.[45] Yet, the abrupt ending, though effective on stage, would have been at odds with the popular cinema's convention of ending a narrative in a more gradual fashion.[46]

The extended ending also enabled the film to intensify the emotional void between Crocker-Harris and his wife. Apart from a brief exchange between herself and Taplow at the beginning, Millie's departure sequence has no dialogue; though she and her husband are together on the screen for some of the time, their wordless non-interaction, conveyed effectively through a mixture of camera movement and close shots, point up the drastic and irreparable state of their relationship. The film also depicts the prize-giving ceremony which is simply alluded to in the play, and includes Crocker-Harris' speech in which he deviates from his prepared notes and simply apologises for failing his pupils. Their enthusiastic response may be construed as some kind of redemption for Crocker-Harris, as may the gesture after the ceremony when he obliquely reveals to Taplow that the boy has won his promotion to the science fifth for the following year. In the sense that the play ends abruptly without the intimations of the future, without a strong sense of closure, it does present a harsher vision than the film, and one more in accord, perhaps, with the work as 'a study in heroic failure, the tragedy of a man who could not *communicate*'.[47]

According to Wansell, *The Browning Version* represented Rattigan's 'first major dramatic exploration of a theme to which he was to return persistently in the years ahead – the pain and loneliness that lie behind the restraint and reticence of English society, and especially the upper-middle classes'.[48] 'Restraint and reticence', however, can be traced back, for example, to the Asquith/Rattigan collaboration, *The Way to the Stars*, and such qualities are frequently invoked in the familiar characterisation of the British cinema as a cinema of understatement.

The Importance of Being Earnest (1952)

The Importance of Being Earnest, with its 'unchallenged canonical status ... witnessed by its probably being the most quoted play in the English language after *Hamlet*',[49] had been filmed only once – in Argentina – prior to Asquith's film, though there had been a television version for the BBC in Britain in 1938. The play, first published in 1895, was due to come out of copyright in the early fifties and there was interest from various quarters in a screen adaptation. Actor Michael Denison, impressed by seeing the famous John Gielgud/Edith Evans stage performance of the play, persuaded his studio – the Associated British Picture Corporation – to register the title for production.[50] However, the Rank Organisation eventually acquired the registration rights from them and *The Importance of Being Earnest* was made by the Javelin Films team though under the auspices of British Film-makers, a Rank/National Film Finance Corporation venture.[51] It was Asquith's first film in colour.

The project represented a departure for Asquith in so far as he was dealing with a classic play written in the 1890s by a canonical playwright long since dead. Though there are some parallels with the adaptation of *Pygmalion*, another classic work from a canonical playwright, the fact that Shaw was on hand to write the screenplay for the Asquith/Howard film is a key difference. The screenplay – largely Wilde's words with minor alterations and some excisions – was prepared by Asquith himself although he declined to take a credit for this and became embroiled in an argument with the Screenwriters Association.[52] The cast assembled for the film included prominent actors such as Michael Redgrave, Joan Greenwood, Margaret Rutherford, and a young newcomer, Dorothy Tutin. Though Gielgud had declined to be involved, Edith Evans, his co-star in the celebrated 1939 stage production, repeated her stage role as Lady Bracknell for the film; and, as a condition of Rank's acquisition of the film rights, Michael Denison was given the part of Algernon Moncrieff. The film was publicised on the basis of the all-star cast with a series of full-page adverts in *Kine Weekly* each featuring one of the stars together with one of Wilde's many celebrated epigrams from the play.[53] In many ways, the film is an interesting test case for the business of adapting stage plays for the screen. One of the most trenchant comments on the film came from Jympson Harman, the critic of London's *Evening News*:

> Anthony Asquith was trying to persuade me this week that his screen version of 'The Importance of Being Earnest' (Odeon, Leicester Square) is a film.
> I hope to see the day when Mr Asquith will retract that opinion. As one of the three best film directors in the country he should not be deceiving himself about photographed stage plays. We must look for the time when he will once more believe like any other true screen artist that the business of film technique is to tell a story pictorially.[54]

Harman's view, indeed, was that the project – the adaptation of a play by Wilde – was ill-considered because the playwright was 'one of the worst plot-makers who ever wrote a play'.[55] The orthodox opinion that the verbal emphasis of the stage was at odds with the visual emphasis of film underpinned the review with Wilde cast as an uncinematic artist who 'sacrificed everything for the brilliance of his verbal wit. He was in fact the exact opposite of a screenwriter.'[56]

As many have pointed out, Asquith opened the film with a clear acknowledgement of the theatrical origins of the work. The first images are of a well-dressed man and woman sitting down in a theatre box. The man picks up a programme and there are inserts of pages turning with the play's title and cast followed by a shot of a theatre proscenium arch. The curtain begins to rise and the woman picks up her opera glasses. The next shot – her point of view – is of Jack Worthing (Michael Redgrave) sitting in his bath while servants attend him. In many respects the opening signals theatre quite clearly – the box, the programme, the proscenium arch, the curtain rising; yet the point of view shot of Redgrave signals cinema. Indeed, the shot begins out of focus and masked, in binocular fashion, before a slight camera movement resituates the point of view and detaches it from the woman. The subsequent shot is a close-up of a tray of breakfast food followed by a mid-shot of Algernon Moncrieff (Michael Denison). Critics have made much of the theatrical preamble but have ignored the way in which the opening shots of the narrative are resolutely 'cinematic'.

Nevertheless, the tension between the theatrical origins of the film and its realisation as a film prompted many reservations. Milton Shulman commented: 'This is a comedy of manners where life takes a bad second place to wit. It is perfect stuff for the cramped and artificial limitations of the stage where the words are the thing. But is it for the cinema, with its emphasis on visual action and a semblance of reality?'[57] A 'semblance of reality' is often provided by the opening out of a play to a more varied range of locales than is possible on stage as, for example, in the inclusion of the school detail in *The Browning Version*, or the House of Commons and court sequences in *The Winslow Boy*. However, in the case of *The Importance of Being Earnest* very little was done apart from one exterior shot of Algernon's house and a couple of scenes in railway carriages. Also, in terms of the actual production, the theatrical influence made itself felt in various ways. The film, according to Dorothy Tutin, was shot in sequence;[58] also, as Michael Denison remembers, 'we filmed in quite large chunks, which was different from the normal method of filming. There are lots of quite long takes in it, not a lot of elaborate cutting.'[59] Edith Evans' performance attracted attention as a 'theatrical performance', elaborate and exaggerated, indeed one which has become emblematic for the film as a whole. In his notebooks Asquith commented that stage actors new to film often over-project, an indication of a less than sensitive awareness of the specificities of the medium. Yet he also suggests that Edith Evans' 'over-life size performance was desirable' in the context of the film, a special case perhaps, and one which preserves her theatrical approach for posterity despite its overblown exaggerated qualities.[60] Michael Redgrave's biographer, however, cites a certain discrepancy between the various approaches to acting in the film as a problem for Redgrave's performance with the Edith Evans performance no doubt foremost in his mind:

> Redgrave's attempts to present his acting within a convention of semi-naturalism would, I think, have been more generally admired if that convention had been more unanimously respected; in the context of the acting he seemed all-too-scrupulously avoiding the theatrical extravagance in which the other players indulged; and, although it was an admirable demonstration of subtle adjustments in scale, it failed in the last resort because of loyalty to a lost cause.[61]

Edith Evans' exaggerated vocal delivery was not the only instance of her unwillingness to submit to the disciplines of film acting, as one of Minney's anecdotes indicates. When it was pointed out to her that failure to hit her chalk marks on her entry to a particular scene removed her from the camera's gaze, her response was 'I always feel the camera should come to *me* instead of me go to the *camera*.'[62] Indeed, Geoff

Brown, in the course of a study of the theatre/film relationship in British cinema, saw in Evans' remark a summary of Asquith's approach to the filming of plays in general, suggesting that 'Asquith displayed a similar attitude to Rattigan, Shaw, and his other dramatic subjects: the camera always came to the play.'[63]

The Importance of Being Earnest, along with the Rattigan adaptations, and *Carrington VC*, *The Doctor's Dilemma*, and *Libel*, have built an image for Asquith as the British cinema's foremost translator of various kinds of drama – classic theatre, quality middlebrow work, popular plays – to the screen. Whatever judgement critics made at the time, or subsequently, about the appropriate methods for transposing drama, or the difficulties that the aesthetics of the theatre posed for notions of the 'cinematic', Asquith's own position was clear. As he wrote in *Films and Filming* towards the end of the decade:

> I believe that there is only one test of the validity of a work of art – does it 'come off'? And I don't think it matters a hang whether the source of a film is a play, a novel or an original story. What does matter is that the director should have truly imagined or, in the case of a play or novel, re-imagined his material in terms of his medium.[64]

Close analysis of passages from the films certainly indicates a 're-imagining' in terms of cinema however closely elements from the play – the dialogue – survive the journey to the screen.

Notes

1 S. Lacey, 'Too theatrical by half? *The Admirable Crichton* and *Look Back in Anger*', in I. MacKillop and N. Sinyard (eds), *British Cinema of the 1950s* (Manchester: Manchester University Press, 2003), p. 157.

2 Figures drawn from D. Gifford, *The British Film Catalogue 1895–1985* (Newton Abbot/London: David and Charles, 1986).

3 D. Thomson, *The New Biographical Dictionary of Film* Fourth Edition (London: Little, Brown, 2003), p. 35.

4 N. Carroll, 'Introducing Film Evaluation', in C. Gledhill and L. Williams (eds), *Reinventing Film Studies* (London: Arnold, 2000), p. 269.

5 S. Sontag, 'Theatre and Film', in *Styles of Radical Will* (New York: Delta, 1970), p. 100.

6 B. McFarlane, 'Outrage: *No Orchids for Miss Blandish*', in S. Chibnall and R, Murphy (eds), *British Crime Cinema* (London: Routledge, 1999), p. 42.

7 J. Ellis, 'The Quality Film Adventure: British Critics and the Cinema 1942–1948', in A. Higson (ed.) *Dissolving Views* (London: Cassell, 1996), p. 67.

8 A. Bazin, 'The evolution of film language', in P. Graham (ed.), *The New Wave* (London: Secker & Warburg, 1968), p. 33.

9 See Ellis, 'The Quality Film Adventure: British Critics and the Cinema 1942–1948', in Higson (ed.), *Dissolving Views*, pp. 66–93.

10 L. Anderson, 'Alfred Hitchcock', *Sequence* 9, Autumn (1949), p. 113.

11 L. Anderson, 'Angles of Approach', *Sequence* 2, Winter (1947), p. 6.

12 *Ibid.*

13 *Ibid.*

14 L. Napper, 'British Cinema and the Middlebrow', in J. Ashby and A. Higson (eds), *British Cinema, Past and Present* (London: Routledge, 2000), p. 110.

15 V. F. Perkins, *Film as Film* (London: Penguin Books, 1972), p. 16.

16 R. Armes, *Action and Image. Dramatic structure in cinema* (Manchester: Manchester University Press, 1994).

17 For Europe, see S. Neale, 'Art Cinema as Institution', *Screen* 22:1 (1981); for America, B. Uricchio and R. Pearson, *Reframing Culture. The Case of the Vitagraph Quality Film* (Princeton, New Jersey: Princeton University Press, 1993).

18 Lacey, 'Too theatrical by half?', p. 160.

19 *Ibid.*, p. 159.

20 *Ibid.*, p. 157.

21 *Ibid.*, pp. 159–60, for a detailed catalogue of the connotations of the term 'theatrical' in relation to film.

22 Carroll, 'Introducing Film Evaluation', p. 269.

23 G. Wansell, *Terence Rattigan. A Biography* (London: Fourth Estate, 1946), p. 152.

24 T. Rattigan, 'Preface', in *The Collected Plays of Terence Rattigan*. Volume One (London: Hamish Hamilton, 1953), p. xvii.

25 K. Kulik, *Alexander Korda. The Man Who Could Work Miracles* (London: Virgin Books, 1990), p. 301.

26 'The Champagne Set' – interview with de Grunwald, Films and Filming, February (1965), p. 7.

27 *Kine Weekly* (26.8.48), pp. 10–11.

28 *The Sunday Times* (26.9.48), quoted in P. Noble, *Anthony Asquith* (London: British Film Institute, 1951), p. 40.

29 D. Rebellato, 'Introduction', in T. Rattigan, *The Winslow Boy* (London: Nick Hern Books, 1999), p. xxiv.

30 Wansell, *Rattigan. A Biography*, p. 154.

31 C. A. Lejeune, 'At the Films. Stage Translations'. *Observer* (26.9.48) – BFI Cuttings Collection: The Winslow Boy.

32 C. Ray, *The Sunday Times* (26.9.48) – quoted in Noble, *Anthony Asquith*, p. 40.

33 *Ibid.*

34 *Time and Tide* (2.10.48) – BFI cuttings collection: *The Winslow Boy.*

35 J. Mitry, *The Aesthetics and Psychology of the Cinema* (London: The Athlone Press, 1998), pp. 318–19.

36 The first performance was at the Phoenix Theatre, London in September, 1948, as part of a double bill – *Playbill*. The other play was *Harlequinade*.

37 C. A. Lejeune, 'Films – "The Browning Version"', *Britain Today*, June (1951), p. 33 – BFI cuttings collection: *The Browning Version.*

38 See press material in the Anthony Asquith Collection, British Film Institute Library Special Collections, Item 28. The Lockwood story is from the *Evening News* (26.8.50).

39 *Ibid.* The Karlovy Vary story is from the *Daily Film Renter* (6.8.51).

40 William Whitebait, *New Statesman and Nation* (31.3.51), quoted in Noble, *Anthony Asquith*, p. 43.

41 P. Houston, 'Review: *The Browning Version*', *Sight and Sound* 19 (New Series): 12, April 1951, p. 475.

42 In the introduction to T. Rattigan, *The Browning Version* (London: Nick Hern Books, 1994), p. xx.

43 A. Asquith, 'The Play's the Thing', *Films and Filming*, February (1959), p. 13.

44 *Ibid.*

45 Lejeune, 'Films – "The Browning Version"', p. 35.

46 See V. F. Perkins, *Film as Film*, p. 134.

47 R. Findlater, *Michael Redgrave. Actor* (London: William Heinemann Ltd., 1956), p. 97 (emphasis in original).

48 *Ibid.*, p. 170.

49 A. Sanders, *The Short Oxford History of English Literature* (Oxford: Oxford University Press, 1994), pp. 477–8.

50 M. Denison, *Double Act* (London: Michael Joseph, 1985), p. 20.

51 S. Harper and V. Porter, *British Cinema of the 1950s. The decline of deference* (Oxford: Oxford University Press, 2003), p. 38.

52 Letters in the Teddy Baird Collection, British Film Institute Special Collections, Item 29, *The Importance of Being Earnest* File.

53 For example, see *Kine Weekly* (15.5.52), p. 2, featuring Margaret Rutherford.

54 *Evening News* (26.5.52) – BFI cuttings collection: *The Importance of Being Earnest.*

55 *Ibid.*

56 *Ibid.*

57 *Evening Standard* (26.6.52) – BFI cuttings collection: *The Importance of Being Earnest.*

58 B. McFarlane, *An Autobiography of British Cinema* (London: Methuen, 1997), p. 581.

59 *Ibid.*, p. 77.

60 Anthony Asquith Collection, British Film Institute Special Collections, Notebooks Item 2.

61 R. Findlater, *Michael Redgrave. Actor* (London: William Heinemann Ltd., 1956), p. 112.

62 R. J. Minney, *Puffin Asquith* (London: Leslie Frewin, 1973), pp. 141-2 (emphasis in original).

63 G. Brown, '"Sister of the Stage" British film and British Theatre', in C. Barr (ed.) *All Our Yesterdays. 90 Years of British Cinema* (London: BFI Publishing, 1986), p. 160.

64 A. Asquith, 'The Play's the Thing', *Films and Filming*, February (1959), p. 13.

The 'international' film

7

For many critics the films from the final phase of Asquith's career were a disappointment, especially the 'increasingly banal prestige productions like *The V.I.P.s* (1963) and *The Yellow Rolls-Royce* (1964)'.[1] Such films, financed by American money supplemented by various forms of state subsidy, filmed in a range of European locations, with all-star casts drawn from all parts of the globe, became the high-profile end of a trend in post-war European cinema. They were a reflection of changing Hollywood production practices which had an especially marked influence on the British cinema of the 1960s in particular. Terms such as 'runaway', 'international', and 'mid-Atlantic', were used to differentiate such films from orthodox indigenous productions, reflecting something of their economic sources, something of the geographical location of their physical production, and something of the cultural consequences of their American provenance. 'Mid-Atlantic', in particular, became a term of critical abuse, embodying the notion of a cinema of uncertain cultural identity, a characterisation of British cinema which had been offered in the late 1940s by Lindsay Anderson.

American production in Britain

It was noted in Chapter 5 that American investment in the British cinema, though not a new phenomenon, did increase in the post-war period. This was partly for reasons internal to the American film industry, including the reorganisation of the industry following the divorcement decrees in 1948, increasing labour costs, and the flight of creative personnel for reasons ranging from tax evasion to political disenchantment with McCarthyism. However, the increased investment also derived from the government restriction on the export of revenues earned in Britain by the American companies embodied in the

Anglo-American trade agreement of 1948. In order to utilise their frozen funds, some of the Hollywood majors shifted part of their annual production schedule from the traditional Los Angeles base to Britain financing wholly or partly their production costs, effectively controlling their production in terms of subject matter and genre, stars and directors, while at the same time utilising local physical and human resources, and providing a significant boost for the host industry possibly even coming to its rescue after the various crises of the late 1940s. As Ian Jarvie has suggested: 'By March 1948 British film production was nearly at a halt, and American production in Britain was uncertain. Once the agreement was in place, millions of pounds were retained for spending in the United Kingdom. The result was a boom in American production in Britain.'[2]

American finance began to feed into the British industry with films such as *Edward, My Son* (George Cukor, 1949) and *Conspirator* (Victor Saville, 1949) from MGM-British, and increased through the 1950s as the other major American companies followed MGM's lead. In the 1960s, however, the level of financing began to escalate dramatically, as Thomas Guback has noted:

> the proportion of American-financed pictures increased steadily from 43 per cent in 1962 to 71 per cent in 1966. Concerning the magnitude of finance, American sources provided almost 75 percent of the production money for British films in 1965 and 1966. The NFFC predicted that the 'corresponding proportions for 1967 and 1968 may exceed 90 percent'.[3]

Guback went on to suggest that by the middle of the decade the 'British production industry, if one can argue that a substantial *national* one does exist today, is little more than a branch of Hollywood, dependent upon American companies for both finance and distribution'.[4] Initially, as noted above, US production in Britain was simply a way of enabling the majors to get access to the non-remittable earnings from their British distribution receipts. Though the agreement on the treatment of earnings was effectively abandoned in 1954, labour costs still remained lower than in the United States, and, with the systems of production investment and subsidy – the National Film Finance Corporation, the British Film Production Fund – well-established by then, the American companies had an additional financial incentive to continue production in Britain. In this context, as Harper and Porter have noted, 'it would be the lower production costs and benefits from the British Film Fund that would attract American investment in British films'.[5] By 1965, it was estimated that 'American subsidiaries in Great Britain now receive as much as 80 per cent of the payments from the British Production Fund'.[6]

By the 1960s, then, the US involvement in the British cinema was considerable and the fears of cultural domination, periodically expressed by commentators and film-makers in Britain since the 1920s, surfaced once again. In the 1950s the US-financed films ran parallel to the indigenous cinema, the comedies, war pictures, crime, and social problem films from Rank, Ealing, British Lion, and other British concerns. The American 'runaways', medieval costume films such as *Ivanhoe* (1952) and *Knights of the Round Table* (1953), together with films such as *The African Queen* (1952) and *Captain Horatio Hornblower R. N.* (1952), bear the hallmarks of their Hollywood genesis in terms of grandeur, scale, and the presence of stars such as Humphrey Bogart, Katharine Hepburn, and Gregory Peck and directors such as John Huston and Raoul Walsh. Though they did have some British elements – location settings, minor parts played by British actors – they were probably perceived as Hollywood films by their British and American audiences regardless of their geographical origins. They were also treated by their US producers as an integral part of their overall studio production schedules. *Knights of the Round Table*, for example, despite being made at MGM's Borehamwood base and on location in Britain and Ireland, was the American company's first CinemaScope picture and was released in America in December 1953, hot on the heels of the early Twentieth Century-Fox CinemaScope films, and some six months before being released in Britain itself.

The 1960s presented a different situation; the increased level of financing meant that instead of a stream of Hollywood-originated and financed features paralleled by an authentically British strand of films, there was now almost an entire industry which was virtually Hollywood-financed. The cultural consequences were seen in 'international' films such as *The Guns of Navarone* (1961), *Lawrence of Arabia* (1962), and *Where Eagles Dare* (1968) with their multi-national casts and varied locations. Until the 1960s the major complaints about the American cinema focused upon the fact that most of the films screened in British cinemas came from Hollywood. National cultural integrity was threatened by the popularity of such films with the British audience but at least British films themselves constituted a small but effective antidote to this; Dean Martin and Jerry Lewis were counteracted by Norman Wisdom and Jerry Desmonde, and the occasional British film topped the Hollywood films at the box office. The increase in production financing by the majors in the 1960s and the fact that the British industry had become, according to Guback, 'little more than a branch of Hollywood',[7] now appeared to threaten the cultural integrity and identity of the British film itself. The threat was that the films made in the UK with US money would inevitably be 'American' rather than 'British', or 'international' and 'mid-Atlantic' rather than identifiable in terms of the indigenous culture.

In the 1950s and 1960s the American film industry adopted a more global approach to the business of film-making. By 1965 the logic of international production was commented upon in a *Variety* article headed 'New One World of Film':

> The changing economic pattern of Europe has already brought a revolution to film production which could well lead to the virtual disappearance of 'national' film industries. This is very definitely the era of co-production, in which partners have bridged the Atlantic and the English channel, and crossed the frontiers of the Continent.[8]

In 1965 Andrew Filson – Director of the Federation of British Film-makers – warned of the dangers in the situation, complaining that films such as *From Russia With Love* (1963), *Becket* (1963), and *A Hard Day's Night* (1964), despite their strong British credentials, were 'widely thought of as American films made in Britain with attitudes and styles not recognisably British'.[9] Filson was especially concerned about the fact that the Writers Guild of America in their annual awards for 1964 had named *Becket* as the Best Written American Drama of the Year. David Lean's *Lawrence of Arabia* (1962) was also claimed by Hollywood. In response to a *New York Times* editorial which claimed that American films were neither 'artistic or thoughtful' Ralph Hetzel, the acting head of the Motion Picture Association of America, commented:

> Every year many American films are produced that equal or surpass the best imported films by any standard not forgetting the basic quality of entertainment. Films cited as examples ... were 'To Kill a Mocking Bird', 'Hud', 'Days of Wine and Roses', 'A Child is Waiting', 'Cleopatra', 'Lawrence of Arabia'. These, he wrote, are all outstanding American films and had something to say and said it well.[10]

Lawrence of Arabia's assumed American identity was reinforced when the film was actually screened in Mexico at the Acapulco film festival in 1963 as the official American entry on the basis presumably of Columbia's financial involvement and the fact that it was produced by an American – Sam Spiegel.[11]

From the perspective of the European countries, major hosts to the new globalised studio system, films produced under such conditions may be regarded as a threat to the health and well-being of individual national cinemas. With its close and long-established links to the American film industry the British cinema proved especially susceptible to Hollywood's new production strategies and film historian

Thomas Guback echoed a familiar lament about the baneful effects of this when he wrote: 'One is forced to wonder whether the British industry has not lost something ... if it has not exchanged autonomy and the chance to manifest its own culture for the appetizing appeal of financial success with many 'mid-Atlantic' productions.'[12]

Asquith's final films were made in the context of a British cinema faced with, on the one hand, a degree of buoyancy and stability based on the increased availability of Hollywood finance; and, on the other, as a consequence, the potential threat to the national integrity of the cinema, the surrender to the cultural amorphousness of the mid-Atlantic film.

Asquith and the 'international film'

Asquith, in his capacity as a trade unionist, added his voice to the growing concerns about the rise of the 'international' film, and expressed his misgivings in his 1963 presidential address to the Association of Cine and Television Technicians at their annual conference:

> We are neither anti-American nor anti-European, but we have always contended that British films should express our own attitudes and beliefs. Mid-Atlantic or mid-Channel productions are no substitute. To take an example from another country, I offer no prize for the answer to the question, which is the better or more typical Italian film – 'Bicycle Thieves' or 'Sodom and Gomorrah'.[13]

Despite this, Asquith's own work in the 1960s has been seen as succumbing to the 'international' tendency, contributing to the cultural surrender predicted by Guback, along with other experienced and prestigious film-makers who effectively sacrificed their cultural integrity by making 'mid-Atlantic' films. In fact three of Asquith's five films from the 1960s were made with Hollywood backing through a company set up by Asquith's long-time collaborator, Anatole de Grunwald.[14] *The Millionairess* was made for Twentieth Century-Fox while *The V.I.P.s* and *The Yellow Rolls-Royce* were made for MGM-British. The films were relatively expensive and, indeed, one of the obvious features of the high-profile 'international' film is the magnitude of the budget. *Kine Weekly* referred to *The Millionairess* as 'one of the costliest of the year',[15] while the budget for *The V.I.P.s* was £1 million and, for *The Yellow Rolls-Royce*, £1.25 million.[16] Though less expensive than Hollywood-financed British pictures such as *The Guns of Navarone* (J. Lee Thompson, 1962) and *Lawrence of Arabia* they were considerably more expensive than, for example, the highly successful multiple Oscar-winning *Tom Jones* (Tony

Richardson, 1963) and the Beatles film *Help!* (Richard Lester, 1964).

However, Asquith did direct two other pictures in the 1960s, both of which had international dimensions of sorts though of a rather different kind compared to the de Grunwald films. *Guns of Darkness* was an Associated British Picture Corporation production and though based on a British source – the Francis Clifford thriller, *Act of Mercy* – it had a foreign setting, a fictional South American country, and the production involved extensive location shooting in Spain. The film also featured two Hollywood stars, David Niven and Leslie Caron, in the leading roles, playing an English couple caught up in a Cuban-like Latin American revolution. It was described by Raymond Durgnat as 'a rare example of a British film advocating the overthrow of the *status quo*'.[17] The second was *Two Living, One Dead*.

Two Living, One Dead (1961)

The other small-scale international film, *Two Living, One Dead*, is a curious piece, and was shown only on television in Britain, according to Minney.[18] The picture, described by Brian McFarlane as 'one of the most "missing" films of all time',[19] was a British Lion enterprise under the supervision of Asquith's long-time colleague, Teddy Baird, in conjunction with Lorens Marmstedt, the Swedish producer of Ingmar Bergman's early films. The cast was primarily British and included Virginia McKenna, Bill Travers, and Patrick McGoohan. McGoohan, who played the central role, was the star of the British television hit series *Danger Man* and subsequently a candidate for the role of James Bond when the Bond film cycle began in 1962. However, one Swedish actor – Alf Kjellin – had a key role as one of the robbery team. The film was based on a Norwegian novel published in the 1920s about the impact of a post-office robbery on the staff involved though for the Asquith film the setting was changed to Sweden. The novel had won a Nobel prize and had previously been filmed in Norway in 1937.[20] Though there is some location-shooting – the opening with a postman cycling through the town, some street scenes, the funeral of a postal worker shot during the robbery, the schoolyard – the bulk of the film takes place indoors, in the postal office, and in the homes of the leading characters.

The film concerns a group of postal service office workers whose lives are transformed by a robbery. While Berger (Patrick McGoohan) is checking a money delivery in an inner office, his colleagues, Anderson (Bill Travers) and Kester (Peter Vaughan), are attacked in an outer office by two robbers and Kester is shot. Berger, confronted by one of the robbers, surrenders the money without resistance. The nub of the film derives from this. Kester is taken to hospital but dies, while Anderson has sustained a head wound. Berger is unscathed but his lack of resistance contrasts with the apparent courage of his colleagues. This undermines him in various ways. His marriage suffers as his wife (Virginia McKenna) expresses her doubts about his behaviour and his young son, Rolf (John Moulder-Brown), is taunted at school about his cowardly father. After its quiet start – establishing the tranquil surroundings of the riverside town, Berger's solid family life, his friendship with Kester – the film plunges Hitchcock-style into a nightmare world of fear and doubt. The transition is striking; Berger is alone in his office counting the money while his two colleagues are in the outer office. The camera tracks towards him, a muffled sound from the outer office is followed by a gunshot, then another, as he gets up and heads for the door. There is a very brief shot of Berger as he sees Kester writhing on the floor and Anderson prostrate next to him; the camera holding his point of view moves towards Kester but one of the robbers suddenly moves into frame holding a gun which is now caught in close-up – a dramatic image of menace which is reflected in the subsequent shot of Berger backing into his office, a terrified look on his face. He then surrenders the money and the robbers make their getaway.

The traumatic impact of the robbery on Berger is effectively embodied in a later sequence in which the police investigator, Johnsson (Noel Willman), questions him about the robbery at the scene of the crime. Two directorial touches in particular stand out. Firstly, during the questioning Berger's gaze alights on the bloodstained floor where Kester was shot; Berger is transfixed and the sustained note on the soundtrack emphasises the way in which the experience is gradually being etched into his mind. The second example follows when Berger is trying to describe the sequence of events to Johnsson. In a single shot lasting almost two minutes, the central pretext and tone of the film is encapsulated in a low-angle *noirish* composition complete with dramatically cast shadows. The shot ends with Johnsson looming over Berger who is kneeling on the spot where Kester was lying. Johnsonn queries Berger's involvement in the robbery, saying, 'So you weren't really in it, were you? You were the only one who wasn't injured. The other two put up a fight.' The sequence is very much that of an accuser and an accused rather than a policeman and a witness, with Berger cast as the guilty man.

Gradually the guilt motif is intensified – Berger's boss demands an explanation as to why the men were allowed to take the money, the police suspect Berger of being an accomplice in the crime, supplying the thieves with inside information, the 'heroic' Anderson is promoted to Postmaster above him, and his wife gradually distances herself from him. Though there is a skein of support for Berger – his son, his son's teacher – his eventual route to 'redemption' occurs in a somewhat bizarre twist of events when he befriends Rogers (Alf Kjellin), a man who lives at the same lodging-house as Berger's colleague, Anderson. Rogers becomes his confidant, eventually revealing that he was the robber who threatened Berger in the office and admits that he would have shot him. Berger's final act is to repeat the robbery with himself as the robber and Anderson as the threatened employee. Anderson behaves similarly to Berger, surrenders the money readily, and Berger, now vindicated, does not go through with the robbery. The film concludes with Berger and his wife embracing in a somewhat desperate gesture, a kind of resolution though one which does not erase the complications of the narrative entirely.

The film is a curious mixture of genres merging the existential concerns of the art film and the *film noir*, the didactic moral tale and expressionist drama. It is comparable to a Hitchcock film in its plunge from the low-key normalities of family life into a nightmare world of fear and doubt. The film contrasts greatly with the high-budget star vehicles associated with Asquith in the 1960s, yet it fits in with the way in which his career often veered from one kind of film to another, from a prestigious classic adaptation to a modest genre film, and, in this period, from a gloomy, existential Nordic story, to the glossy world of the romantic melodrama.

The V.I.P.s (1963)

As has been suggested, one important connotation of the 'international' film is a large budget and, in this sense, *The V.I.P.s* is a paradigmatic example of the trend. A great deal of its £1 million cost went on the international galaxy of stars with Elizabeth Taylor's fee, in particular, constituting around a third of the film's budget.[21] The film also had Richard Burton from Britain, Orson Welles from Hollywood, Louis Jourdan from France, Elsa Martinelli from Italy, and Rod Taylor from Australia. In addition to the high-profile names, the film featured a number of British character actors including Margaret Rutherford, Maggie Smith, and Richard Wattis. In a minor national triumph Margaret Rutherford won an Oscar in the 1963 Academy ceremony as best supporting actress for her appearance in the film, the only Academy Award category in which the film was nominated. In fact the actress had rejected the part at first, only agreeing to appear in the film after Rattigan had rewritten the role building up its importance in the film.[22] The film had a lavish Hollywood-style score by Miklós Rózsa, who had composed the scores of several epic films including *Ben Hur* (William Wyler, 1959) and *El Cid* (Anthony Mann, 1961), and MGM Records also released a soundtrack album and a number of other records exploiting music from the film.[23]

The publicity for the film concentrated understandably on Richard Burton and Elizabeth Taylor, then at the height of their fame with the love affair that started while they were making *Cleopatra* (Joseph Mankiewicz, 1963). In one indication of the extent of that fame, *Kine Weekly's* front cover had a photograph of them simply accompanied by the words – 'She and He. The V.I.P.s' – their faces so well-known that their names were not required.[24] The sumptuousness of *The V.I.P.s* derived also from the detailed studio replication of the interior of London Airport – bars, the VIP lounge, the restaurant, the airport hotel. Apart from a few exterior shots, including the helicopter landing which ushers Taylor and Burton into the narrative, the film was shot entirely at MGM's Borehamwood studio with '28 lavish sets' including a replica of London Airport's No. 3 Building (185 feet long and 85 feet across), claimed to be 'the largest set to be constructed in Britain'.[25]

According to Rattigan's biographer, the idea for the film came from the playwright's experience of being delayed at London Airport because of fog, the plight of the characters in the eventual film; it also included a storyline derived from an incident when Vivien Leigh attempted to leave her husband, Laurence Olivier, for Peter Finch, and was 'trapped in the VIP lounge at a fog-bound Heathrow'.[26] De Grunwald's original discussions with Rattigan were about a remake of *Grand Hotel* (Edmund Goulding, 1932), a famous MGM hit film from the studio's 'golden age' and a portmanteau film with an array of characters and storylines. It reflected de Grunwald's impulse to concentrate on optimistic entertainment rather than the 'realist' pictures – *Saturday Night and Sunday Morning* (Karel Reisz, 1960), *A Kind of Loving* (John Schlesinger, 1962) – that had captured critical attention in the early 1960s. As he revealed in an interview:

> The change from the more realistic films I worked on in the 'forties to the 'entertainment' films today is a reflection of my own mood. I find that whereas I still have plenty to say, and one of these days will perhaps make films of the same type, I felt that the preoccupation with the diseases of today had driven people away from the cinema and I had resolved to get them back into the cinema.[27]

Though Rattigan was not interested in remaking *Grand Hotel* his script for *The V.I.P.s*, which did incorporate some incidents from the earlier film, certainly fulfilled de Grunwald's intention to provide the kind of entertainment values closely associated with the classic Hollywood period.

De Grunwald's first choice of director was the American Vincente Minnelli, one of MGM's most distinguished film-makers. Though well known as a director of musicals, he was also a specialist in edgy romantic melodramas such as *Some Came Running* (1959) and *Home from the Hill* (1960). When Minnelli withdrew, de Grunwald turned to Asquith. Although no stranger to romantic films, or to the representation of tangled human relationships, Asquith's cinema operated at a very different emotional temperature to the 'garish fifties and sixties dramas' of the Hollywood director.[28] The film attracted mixed notices from the critics but was praised in America, with *Variety* considering it 'a smooth and cunning brew with most of the ingredients demanded of popular screen entertainment',[29] and Bosley Crowther, in the *New York Times*, acknowledging its generic antecedent, calling it 'a lively, engrossing romantic film cut in the always serviceable pattern of the old multi-character *Grand Hotel*'.[30] British film critics were less responsive and, as has been noted previously, film historians such as Robert Murphy and Roy Armes, writing many years after its release, have been harsh and dismissive. The film, however, was an enormous success at the box office due undoubtedly to the presence of Taylor and Burton; it had a 'record-shattering run' at the MGM flagship cinema, the Empire Leicester Square, and became one of the highest-earning films of 1963 in the United States.[31]

The V.I.P.s weaves together a number of narratives in the common context of a transatlantic flight delayed because of fog. The main story concerns the marital problems of Paul and Frances Andros (Richard Burton, Elizabeth Taylor) and her plan leave Paul for the ageing French charmer, Marc Champselle (Louis Jourdan), the incident modelled on the Olivier/Leigh/Finch triangle. A second strand focuses on Les Mangrum (Rod Taylor), a brash young Australian businessman, en route to the United States in order to save his business from a takeover. A third has Orson Welles playing Max Buda, a temperamental film director, and his excitable and scatty Italian star actress, Gloria Gritti (Elsa Martinelli). Buda has to leave the country for tax reasons and the delay threatens a huge tax bill for him. There is a also a fourth, less important, story focused on Margaret Rutherford as the eccentric and slightly dotty Duchess of Brighton who is off to work in an American holiday resort in order to make some money for the upkeep of her ramshackle English country house.

The Andros story is the dramatic centrepiece of the film and occupies around half the screen time with the subsidiary stories organised around it. The Rutherford story is simple comic relief and her Duchess of Brighton is yet another variant on the English eccentric image closely associated with the actress which can be traced back to her Rowena Ventnor in Asquith's own *The Demi-Paradise*, among other films. Welles' film director is presented somewhat satirically and self-consciously, with the fictional director something of a caricature of a foreign film-maker (possibly Alexander Korda, according to some). The film displays a mild self-consciousness when Buda proclaims to the press that 'it is not the purpose of the modern cinema to entertain', the exact opposite of the view expressed by de Grunwald, the real-life producer, in his *Films and Filming* interview, and the view which guided the making of the film.

The narrative threads are kept separate for most of the film, though they do interact towards the end and, indeed, such interaction is a means of bringing the narrative to a close. Buda spots a poster of the Duchess' country house, decides that it is a perfect location for his next film, and his offer to rent it for the shooting saves her the bother of flying to her job in America. In keeping with the status of these stories, the tone is comic. Mangrum's financial problems are solved when his secretary (Maggie Smith) persuades Paul Andros, the hard-headed tycoon, to write a cheque covering the debts and saving his company. The final stages of the film are dominated, of course, by the Andros marriage, with Frances abandoning her plan to run off with Marc, and returning to Paul. In the final shot of the film the couple appear to be reconciled as they return home in a taxi. The film called for a degree of narrative ingenuity in handling a series of narrative lines, sustaining interest across them, and bringing them together at the end of the film.

In terms of style, the film was shot using the wide-screen Panavision format, ideal for the effective display of the elaborate and expensive sets but perhaps less suited to the intimate romantic dimensions of the film. Asquith had used CinemaScope for *The Millionairess*, but shortly before that had expressed the conventional misgivings about wide-screen formats and their impact on film style:

> All the trimmings and perfections of new sound systems and new screen ratios are purely secondary to this question of style. I have never used CinemaScope for instance.
>
> This is a purely personal preference, I believe that the number of compositions which can naturally be framed in the CinemaScope oblong are very few. More important, it diffuses the close-up. And the close-up is the greatest single factor in the cinema's wonderful relationship of story and audience.[32]

Asquith's misgivings are reflected in the film in a number of the sequences between Paul, Frances, and Marc, which are dominated by lengthy medium shots simply and functionally framed, lasting between one and two minutes. Medium close-ups are used occasionally but many of the intimate discussions are shot in a detached fashion, the camera some distance from the characters. There are some exceptions to this such as the tense confrontation in the airport restaurant, and in a melodramatic sequence between Paul and Frances in her hotel bedroom. In the former, Frances and Marc are sitting at a table framed in a medium shot. Paul arrives and sits between them; the camera moves towards them, framing him and Frances, eliminating Marc from the image. The sequence then adopts a more conventional but brief shot/ reverse shot pattern as the tension between them mounts, matching medium close-ups of Frances alone in the frame with similarly-scaled shots of Paul and Marc together. The hotel sequence is also built around a small number of lengthy takes interspersed with some tensely-cut passages and it builds to a dramatic climax when Paul accidentally pushes Frances' wrist into the mirrored door of a wardrobe. This generates two startling images: the first captures Paul's shocked face in close-up reflected in the shattered mirror alongside Frances' hand; the second, immediately following it, frames the couple, together with their reflection, in the mirror as he removes her hand from the glass. It is the film's one 'cinematic' moment, a break with the understated functional style to a brief moment of melodramatic image making. Asquith frequently incorporated mirrors into the *mise-en-scène* of his films, using them inventively to construct complex and disturbing images; indeed, he admitted having a 'weakness' for them, as he put it in a radio broadcast in 1946.[33] In *The V.I.P.s* the 'mirror' sequence is a rare display of imaginative *mise-en-scène* in a film which, on the whole, relies on a subservient camera enabling its stars to perform, or, as in the case with Elizabeth Taylor, to be on display in a variety of elegant costumes including her famous mink-lined raincoat.

The Yellow Rolls-Royce (1964)

Like *The V.I.P.s*, *The Yellow Rolls-Royce* has been traced back anecdotally to incidents in Terence Rattigan's life. One version suggests that 'the idea had come to him as he sat in his own Rolls in a London traffic jam, speculating on the looks of hatred, compounded with envy, he received from the occupants of other cars in the jam'.[34] Another refers to Rattigan and Asquith coming across General Allenby's Rolls-Royce while they were looking for locations for their Lawrence of Arabia project in the late 1950s.[35] Yet another traces its origins back to the conversation that de Grunwald had with the Labour Foreign Secretary, Ernest Bevin, which led to *The Winslow Boy*. Bevin had also mentioned a film about 'the quality of British goods' and de Grunwald later claimed, 'I never abandoned the other idea, although Bevin has since died, but it took a little longer with *The Yellow Rolls Royce*, nevertheless it is directly inspired by that.'[36]

The film was made at MGM-British's Borehamwood studio but it also, unlike its studio-bound predecessor, used extensive location shooting both in Britain and in various parts of Europe. It features a range of locations including London's Whitehall, an English country house (Cliveden's impressive façade and interiors), and the Ascot racecourse; tourist Italy – the leaning tower of Pisa, and the famous view of Florence from the Piazzale Michelangelo; and the Austrian landscape which stood in for the sequences set in Yugoslavia. There was even a brief shot of the Rolls-Royce being unloaded in America against the background of the Manhattan skyline at the very end of the film. In that sense the film falls prey to the 'travelogue' tendency noted by some as a corollary of the internationalising of the production of Hollywood films in the post-war period.

The V.I.P.s was dominated by its two high-profile stars whereas *The Yellow Roll-Royce* had a somewhat more egalitarian approach with all of its many stars playing central and important roles in their respective episodes; in that respect it is a more genuinely 'all-star' vehicle. The list of stars was impressive and included Rex Harrison from Britain, then enjoying substantial international fame from his appearances in *My Fair Lady* (1964) and *Cleopatra* (1963), George C. Scott and Shirley MacLaine from America, Jeanne Moreau and Alain Delon from France, Omar Sharif from Egypt, and the Swedish Ingrid Bergman, a major Hollywood figure albeit with the high spots of her career belonging to an earlier time. As with *The V.I.P.s* there were cameos from an array of familiar faces from the British cinema including Roland Culver, Lance Percival, Moira Lister, Michael Hordern, and Edmund Purdom. Perhaps the blight of 'internationalism' and its threat to cultural identity is neatly embodied in another well-known British face in the cast, Joyce Grenfell, playing an American from the Deep South complete with a deep Southern drawl!

Though *The Yellow Rolls-Royce* was publicised partly on the basis of the culturally resonant and very particularly English automobile which gave the film its title, the predominant stress was on the all-star cast as a whole, and, in particular, its 'international' character. 'Now shooting –

with the most exciting international cast ever assembled' proclaimed its advance publicity with the names of its seven stars dominating a two-page advert in *Variety*.[37] *Kine Weekly* ran stories referring to 'a star line-up claimed to be the biggest ever seen in a British studio',[38] and the eventual review of the film in *Variety* noted:

> With a British producer, who was born in Russia, the casting director must have felt free to experiment. Result is that Britain is represented by Harrison and the impressive Rolls-Royce and Jeanne Moreau bats for France as a British peeress. A Frenchman (Alain Delon) plays an Italian, an American (Scott) pinchhits for a man of Italian extraction, a Swede (Miss Bergman) plays a Yank and an Egyptian (Sharif) represents Yugoslav. This sounds like an international boxoffice parlay that should pay off handsomely.[39]

Most of the actors involved had already appeared in either British or American films, apart from Alain Delon, though he was well-known to art-house audiences through his work with Visconti and Antonioni. Elsa Martinelli had been in Howard Hawks' *Hatari!* (1962), Omar Sharif had shot to stardom in *Lawrence of Arabia* and Jeanne Moreau, like Delon familiar to art-house audiences, had also appeared in two British films – Joseph Losey's *Eva* (1962) and Carl Foreman's *The Victors* (1963). Ingrid Bergman, of course, was more a Hollywood star than a European actress despite her work with Rossellini. The trade press reviews were complimentary, with *Variety* calling it 'a sleek piece of entertainment' and 'a glossy package'.[40] *Kine Weekly* suggested that as 'a technical achievement the film is magnificent, its interiors lush and exteriors present natural beauty at its best. A delightful British picture.'[41] However, like *The V.I.P.s* it attracted less good notices from some of the influential newspaper critics. Rattigan had been particularly upset by the response to *The V.I.P.s* and had written a twenty-five-page letter to one of the film's most prominent critics, the London *Evening Standard*'s, Alexander Walker. The treatment of *The Yellow Rolls-Royce* was similar and Rattigan was again disappointed. This time the trigger was a caustic review of the film by Kenneth Tynan, better known as a theatre critic, and, indeed, one who had been a harsh critic of Rattigan's stage work especially in the 1950s.[42] However, despite the critical responses, de Grunwald had clearly gauged the public appetite for such glossy enter-tainment and the film matched its lavish predecessor at the box office, with record-breaking runs both in Britain and America.

The Yellow Rolls-Royce has a multi-stranded narrative structure with three separate stories presented serially, rather than interwoven and interrelated as in *The V.I.P.s*. The stories are linked only by the somewhat artificial device of the car which featured prominently in each of them. It is an example of the 'episodic or portmanteau' film, a form that 'British cinema seems particularly drawn to ... where a number of personal narratives are presented, generally with some linking thread.'[43] It belongs to a minor strand of British cinema which includes titles such as *Dead of Night* (Cavalcanti *et al.*, 1945), *Bond Street* (Gordon Parry, 1948), a film which de Grunwald and Rattigan had worked on, *Quartet* (Ralph Smart *et al.*, 1948), *Train of Events* (Basil Dearden *et al.*, 1949), *Trio* (Ken Annakin and Harold French, 1950), and *Encore* (French *et al.*, 1952).

The Yellow Rolls-Royce opens with an episode set in England, specifically London and the home counties, and dealing with love and leisure among the upper and middle-classes, familiar Asquith/Rattigan territory. The second and longest episode features a Chicago gangster and his fiancée on a touring holiday in Italy, and the third, set on the border of Italy and Yugoslavia in the early years of the Second World War, is about a middle-aged American woman who becomes entangled with a Yugoslavian resistance fighter. The stories are completely separate but linked by the very distinctive Rolls-Royce of the title – a Phantom – which one of the main characters in each story buys and uses. In the English episode the Marquess of Frinton (Rex Harrison) buys the car as a belated anniversary gift for his wife (Jeanne Moreau); however, it backfires on him when he discovers her in the back of the car with Fane (Edmund Purdom), one of his colleagues in the Foreign Office. The episode ends with him returning the car to the showroom and when asked 'Why?' by his chauffeur, he replies, 'It displeases me'. The car, a symbol of his marital problems, has to go. The lavish gloss of the film is best embodied in the stylishly organised sequence in the bedroom, with its colour scheme of lilac and blue picked out in various aspects of the *mise-en-scène* – furnishings, wall coverings, bed clothes, Jeanne Moreau's dressing gown, flowers, even a small detail such as Harrison's buttonhole. The understated tension between them is communicated through Moreau's acting and hesitant vocal delivery, and through the positioning of the camera in relation to the two actors which hints effectively at the problems to come. In many respects, the episode delivers the images – the lavish country house and its capacious interior, the Ascot racecourse, and the most English of automobiles – that constitute the 'mid-Atlantic' version of England designed to appeal to a broad international, and particularly American, audience.

The second episode, which begins some '20,023 miles later', is set in Italy. If the American audience is implicitly targeted through the 'heritage' Britain in the first episode, then the Italian episode mobilises 'travelogue Italy' – Pisa, Florence, the Mediterranean – the familiar icons of tourism. But there is also a strong American influence in its storyline of an Italian-American gangster, Paola Maltese (George C. Scott), visiting his roots, showing his cultural heritage to his less than interested fiancée, Mae (Shirley MacLaine), and taking her to 'meet his folks'. It was the generic pastiche which alienated Tynan, who wrote that this 'kind of Rattiganesque Runyonesque dialogue would shrivel the tongue of any self-respecting American actor who tried to speak it'.[44] The film takes a romantic turn when the couple encounter a charming and handsome young paparazzo, Stefano (Alain Delon), who proceeds to fall in love with the 'ignorant slob of a hat-check girl', to quote Paolo's description of Mae when she shows no interest in the architectural glories of Pisa's Duomo and Baptistery. As in the first episode, there is a love scene in the back seat of the Rolls-Royce between Mae and Stefano while Paolo is back in America tending to some 'business'. In contrast to her relationship with Paolo, and despite her initial resistance, there is a degree of warmth, even passion, in their developing relationship. Eventually, however, after Joey (Art Carney), Paolo's associate who is acting as her 'minder', points out what might be done to Stefano if she continues with the romance, she rejects him. The episode ends on a bittersweet note with an image of a doleful-looking Stefano tearing up his photograph of Mae as the yellow Rolls-Royce drives her out of his life.

The final episode begins in northern Italy, in a Trieste hotel, near the border with Yugoslavia, and is set in 1941. Gerda Millet (Ingrid Bergman), a wealthy middle-aged widow travelling to Yugoslavia to visit the royal family, buys the Roll-Royce. In fact the car plays a greater role in this episode than in the others. Mrs Millet meets Davitch (Omar Sharif), a young, exiled, revolutionary Yugoslavian attempting to get back to his country, and agrees to give him a lift across the border; the car is then used as ambulance as well after a German air raid; subsequently she drives Davitch back to his home village and the car is used by them to assemble his partisan fighting group. In addition, and as in the other episodes, the car plays host to a very brief romantic interlude between Gerda and Davitch.

The V.I.P.s and *The Yellow Rolls-Royce* seem self-consciously designed to achieve a kind of international identity and consequently an international circulation. The international appeal of both films is achieved by spreading the casting net widely and representing a variety of nationalities, by filming in different national locations providing an authenticity of locale, and by the simple expedient of romantic themes crossed, as in ordinary Hollywood films, by the drama and tension drawn from traditional genre themes. The Italian episode in *The Yellow*

Rolls-Royce perhaps pulls these attributes together most comprehensively. It uses familiar figures from the American gangster film; George C. Scott is a mixture of James Cagney and Edward G. Robinson in the classic instances of the genre while Shirley MacLaine is a latter-day Jean Harlow. The film places them on vacation in Italy which is displayed in its familiar travelogue splendour – Pisa, Florence, Rome, Naples – and the episode is bound together with a poignant love affair between a young Italian photographer and the gangster's moll.

In a sense, the attributes of such films may not be so markedly different from the general attributes of the Hollywood-produced American film and, perhaps, the most telling critique is that they often fail to blend the multi-national elements together as successfully as similar films produced within the Hollywood system itself. Guback's fears about the effects upon cultural expression of American financing are to some extent fulfilled in the Asquith films but whether the economic roots invariably determine the cultural results so clearly is open to question. Though *The V.I.P.s* and *The Yellow Rolls-Royce* have a kind of cultural diffuseness, the range of US-financed films made in Britain in the 1960s includes a number of titles out of which a creditable version of a national cinema could be constructed, a version that avoids the accusation of cultural surrender. *Sons and Lovers* (1960), *The L-Shaped Room* (1962), *Tom Jones* (1963), *Zulu* (1963), *Becket* (1963), *The Knack* (1965), *The Spy Who Came in from the Cold* (1965), *Funeral in Berlin* (1966), *A Man for All Seasons* (1966), *Alfie* (1966), *Far From the Madding Crowd* (1967), *The Charge of the Light Brigade* (1968), *If ...* (1968), *Women in Love* (1969), and *The Prime of Miss Jean Brodie* (1969): all of these titles involved American finance; most of them are plausibly 'British' in cultural terms.

Notes

1 R. Murphy, *Sixties British Cinema* (London: BFI Publishing, 1992), p. 91.
2 I. Jarvie, *Hollywood's Overseas Campaign. The North Atlantic Movie Trade 1920–1950* (Cambridge: Cambridge University Press), p. 237.
3 T. Guback, *The International Film Industry* (Indiana: Indiana University Press, 1969), p. 171.
4 *Ibid.*, p. 172 (emphasis in original).
5 S. Harper and V. Porter, *British Cinema of the 1950s. The Decline of Deference* (Oxford: Oxford University Press, 2003), p. 126.
6 Guback, 'American Interests in the British Film Industry', *Quarterly Review of Economics and Business* 7 (1967), 17.
7 Guback, *The International Film Industry*, p. 172.
8 *Variety* (12.5.65), p. 55.

9 *Ibid.*, p. 55, 74.

10 *Kine Weekly* (10.10.63), p. 8.

11 *Variety* (11.12.63), p. 4.

12 Guback, 'American Interests in the British Film Industry', 21.

13 Quoted in Guback, *The International Film Industry*, p. 178.

14 *Kine Weekly* (1.10.59), p. 21.

15 *Kine Weekly* (5.5.60), p. 16.

16 *Kine Weekly* (14.2.63), p. 31 (*The V.I.P.s*); *Variety* (12.8.64), p. 3 (*The Yellow Rolls-Royce*).

17 R. Durgnat, *A Mirror for England. British Movies from Austerity to Affluence* (London: Faber and Faber, 1970), p. 86.

18 R. J. Minney, *Puffin Asquith* (London: Leslie Frewin, 1973), p. 194. *The British Film Catalogue* (Gifford) suggests a 1971 release date, and the American Film Institute catalogue indicates a 1964 release in the United States.

19 McFarlane, *An Autobiography of British Cinema* (London: Methuen, 1997), p. 568.

20 Minney, *Puffin Asquith*, p. 193.

21 *Kine Weekly* (14.2.63), p. 31. Also see *Variety* (18.9.63), p. 19. Taylor's fee is reported as $1,000,000.

22 G. Wansell, *Terence Rattigan. A Biography* (London: Fourth Estate), p. 324.

23 *Kine Weekly* (4.7.63), p. 15.

24 *Kine Weekly* (25.4.63) cover; *Variety* (8.5.63), pp. 8–9.

25 *Kine Weekly* (28.3.63), Production Review, pp. iii–iv.

26 Wansell, *Terence Rattigan*, pp. 314–17.

27 'The Champagne Set', *Films and Filming* 11:5, February (1965), p. 7.

28 A. Sarris, *The American Cinema* (New York: E. P. Dutton, 1968), p. 100.

29 *Variety* (14.8.63), p. 6.

30 Quoted in Wansell, *Terence Rattigan*, p. 343.

31 See *Kine Weekly* (3.10.63), p. 10, and *Variety* (8.1.64), p. 37.

32 *Kine Weekly* (5.3.59), p. 20.

33 See transcript of radio broadcast, *The World and his Wife*, BBC Light Programme (broadcast 11.11.46). Teddy Baird Collection, Item 42, British Film Institute Special Collections.

34 M. Darlow and G. Hodson, *Terence Rattigan. The Man and His Work* (London: Quartet Books, 1979), p. 266.

35 Wansell, *Terence Rattigan*, p. 330.

36 *Films and Filming* 11: 5 (February 1965), p. 7.

37 *Variety* (6.5.65), pp. 18–19.

38 *Kine Weekly* (23.4.64), p. 19.

39 *Variety* (13.1.65), p. 6.

40 *Ibid.*

41 *Kine Weekly* (7.1.65), p. 7.

42 Wansell, *Terence Rattigan*, pp. 345–6.

43 B. McFarlane, *The Encyclopedia of British Film* (London: BFI/Methuen, 2003), p. 205. The entry is written by Luke McKernan.

44 Quoted in Wansell, *Terence Rattigan*, p. 346.

Asquith and the British cinema   8

In a career lasting from the 1920s to the 1960s Anthony Asquith directed thirty-five feature films: he also worked in a variety of capacities on other films; foreign-version direction, screenwriting, second unit work, and so on. He made a number of short films; some were drama-documentary films made for the Ministry of Information during the Second World War, others were made for charities such as the Guide Dogs for the Blind Association, and St Dunstan's, a centre for the blind. He also directed *Zero* (1960), an adaptation of a Samuel Beckett play, and a most improbable project for Asquith. He made two music films, *On Such a Night* (1955) and *An Evening with the Royal Ballet* (1963), co-directed with Anthony Havelock-Allan.

There were a number of projects which failed to materialise with *Lawrence of Arabia*, rejected by Rank in the late 1950s, the most notable. Others included some working-class subjects such as *The Window Cleaner*, 'a melodrama of London life',[1] and *Covent Garden*, about a porter 'who has ambitions to become an operatic and ballet star', which would have also engaged Asquith's passion for classical music. Both projects originated in the early 1930s though Asquith was still talking about making the Covent Garden film in the 1950s.[2] There was also a plan to make a film about lorry-drivers working on the Great North Road, inspired no doubt by his time in Catterick while shooting *The Way to the Stars* and his friendship with the family that owned a local transport café which he used subsequently as a refuge from the life that he led in London.[3] In addition, some historical pictures were discussed; *Beau Brummell*, based on a screenplay by de Grunwald,[4] and a film based on the life of Samuel Pepys planned with Teddy Baird.[5]

Though best known for his dramatic adaptations from classic drama – Shaw, Wilde, Rattigan – Asquith's work is extremely diverse in terms of subject matter, style, tone, and genre. It ranges from the avant-garde expressionism of his silent films to the highly conventionally and functionally directed star vehicles of his final years, from the light romantic escapades of *French Without Tears* to the moral seriousness of *Orders to Kill*, from the parochialism of *The Final Test* to the amorphous internationalism of *The Yellow Rolls-Royce*. Such diversity makes it somewhat difficult to summarise his work in the manner of a conventional director study. His films are drawn from a variety of sources: original screenplays (*Shooting Stars, We Dive at Dawn, The V.I.P.s*), popular novels (*Tell England, Fanny by Gaslight, The Net, Orders to Kill*), and popular plays (*Carrington VC, Libel*), as well as the middlebrow cultural material (Shaw, Wilde, Rattigan) on which his familiar public image is based.

There were three phases during his career when it might be argued that his work both earned a degree of critical approval and displayed the kind of consistency that might produce a clearer directorial image. The first, from his debut feature, *Shooting Stars*, to his first sound film, *Tell England*, from 1928 to 1931, established his presence in British cinema. Asquith's early films attracted much attention and a degree of critical praise though, as was the case with influential writers such as John Grierson and Paul Rotha, it was sometimes a grudging acknowledgment of his virtuosity and skill as a film-maker, at other times it was more flattering, as in comparisons with the French director René Clair. Such critics rarely moved to fully endorse the films but wrote often in terms of the promise his work showed. The second relatively consistent period is the war when titles such as *We Dive at Dawn* and *The Way to the Stars* were beneficiaries of the general critical approval for British wartime cinema. The third covers a short period from 1948 to 1952 and includes the Rattigan adaptations *The Winslow Boy* and *The Browning Version*, and culminates in *The Importance of Being Earnest*, the film for which Asquith is probably best known. Asquith, of course, had worked on play adaptations previously – *Pygmalion, French Without Tears* – but his reputation as a skilled transposer of stage plays was consolidated during this phase, producing perhaps the most familiar public image of the director.

In many respects the films that Asquith directed in the three periods interact with and reflect the film culture of their times. The first phase belongs to the period in which the British cinema was in the process of redefining itself in a popular film culture dominated by the Hollywood entertainment film with its hold on the imagination of the British audience, and in an intellectual film culture which was responding enthusiastically to the contrasting kinds of cinema coming from Germany, France, the Scandinavian countries, and the Soviet Union. Films such as *Shooting Stars* and *A Cottage on Dartmoor* reflect the self-conscious and experimental European art cinema of the time although drawing also on the vernacular of popular cinema. Many of Asquith's university-educated contemporaries coming to the cinema in the 1920s were influenced by the art cinema but gravitated towards the documentary movement rather than the mainstream popular cinema. Indeed, Alan Lovell has suggested that the documentary 'captured the interest in film as an art that was developing in Britain in the late 1920s',[6] and Asquith's background and cultural interests 'might have fitted more easily into the stereotype of the documentary filmmaker'. [7] Yet Asquith opted for a career in the popular cinema where his art-cinema interests and influences might struggle to find an outlet. He did begin in the documentary-orientated British Instructional company but at a point when they were steering a course towards the fictional film, a change of direction in which he played a central role writing and directing the company's first fictional narratives. Despite an overture from Grierson,[8] and though he did make the occasional documentary, Asquith remained a mainstream film-maker working in the popular cinema of stars and genres that constituted the subject matter of his first feature – *Shooting Stars*. Yet the influence of the art cinema of the 1920s was to surface intermittently; the German film's world of 'shadows and mirrors',[9] the subjective cinema from France, and the montage of the Soviet films were all echoed in his films from time to time.

The wartime period, as has been noted, is conventionally regarded as a highly successful era in British cinema, both a prelude to, and a springboard for, the emergence, later in the decade, of a distinctive British cinema, 'an artistically mature British cinema' as a contributor to *The Penguin Film Review* put it.[10] Unlike many of the directors who contributed to this 'renaissance' – David Lean, Carol Reed, Charles Frend, the Launder and Gilliat team – Asquith brought something of a track record to the job of wartime film-making and, indeed, the experience of directing or co-directing an actual war film – *Tell England*. One of the most admired features of the wartime film was the way in which documentary styles and techniques began to be used extensively in the fiction film. Asquith, for example, was to use actuality footage of a Hitler rally inserted for realist effect in dramatic sequences in *Freedom Radio*, and he filmed on location with actors performing in realist settings in *We Dive at Dawn*. Such strategies, though emerging from the context of wartime film-making, have their roots in Asquith's early film experience; in particular, the realism of the London location sequences in *Underground*, and in the romantic comedy, *The Runaway Princess*, indicated a facility for integrating documentary settings with drama, and *Tell England* drew together the combination of documentary, fiction and war subject matter which defined, for many, the cinematic glory of the wartime period.

The third period, from the late 1940s to the early 1950s, locates Asquith in the important literary-adaptation strand of British cinema and links him to film-makers such as Laurence Olivier and David Lean, with their adaptations of Shakespeare and Dickens, respectively. It was the period in which Asquith would acquire a strong profile as an adapter of stage plays but one in which his own artistic and cinematic credentials were placed at the service of the originating texts – the plays of Rattigan and Wilde. Yet, as Brian McFarlane has pointed out, Asquith was not alone in this, and that the strand of British literary cinema in the post-war years to which *The Winslow Boy*, *The Browning Version* and *The Importance of Being Earnest* belonged, was grounded in a logic of subordination: 'It was not just that these films were derived from writers of high cultural status; the *kind* of adaptation strategies they exhibited indicated a strong respect for the precursor text, and there was about them a degree of sophistication in the writing and filming that marked them out as fare for discriminating audiences.'[11] It was a logic which acknowledged that the prestige and status of the original texts placed conditions on their adaptation, that the audience expectations would be in part governed by audience preconceptions derived from an educated awareness of the cultural material being transposed. Popular genre cinema, partly at least, operates different conventions in which the audience expectations are more likely to be governed by previous instances of the genre rather than a literary source. For example, Asquith's *Fanny by Gaslight* would probably have been understood in the context of its predecessor costume melodrama, *The Man in Grey*, rather than its source-novel.

If the early years of his career fostered avant-garde tendencies, and the war years enabled Asquith to develop as a popular realist film-maker, the post-war period consolidated his position within the world of middlebrow culture. He directed three adaptations of Shaw plays – *Pygmalion*, *The Doctor's Dilemma*, and *The Millionairess*; four adaptations of Rattigan – *French Without Tears*, *While the Sun Shines*, *The Winslow Boy* and *The Browning Version*; and *The Importance of Being Earnest*, one of his best-known films and often considered to be among the very best of all filmed plays, was based on the Wilde classic. Though there are many differences between the three playwrights – Shaw's didacticism, Wilde's verbal wit and polish, Rattigan's agonised portraits of the middle classes – and although two of the dramatists are Irish, all are part of the very English repertory of middlebrow drama. This is not simply a matter of setting, though all eight plays do have a cultural and class homogeneity, at least on the surface. It is also a matter of the tone and temperament signalled in the term 'middlebrow', defined by one writer, in the context of cinema, in terms of its 'reliance on literary sources, its restraint, its formal conservatism, its provincialism, its concern with middle-class characters'. [12] Middlebrow art and culture sits in between the formal avant-garde and the popular, in 'its eschewal of certain formal and stylistic characteristics of the highbrow, as well as its avoidance of overtly formulaic popular techniques',[13] and it is tempting to see Asquith's work as oscillating between them, with the middlebrow eventually becoming the dominant strand in his directorial profile. Indeed, some writers have argued that the British cinema as a whole has been dominated by the presuppositions of middlebrow culture. This aspect of Asquith's career, particularly as represented by his Rattigan adaptations, suggests a middlebrow artist making safe, somewhat genteel, possibly bland, films, addressed to an audience uncomfortable with both the demands of modernism and the avant-garde and the immediate appeal of the popular cinema.

Raymond Durgnat invented the notion of the 'Rattigasquith'[14] to categorise the close working relationship that Asquith had with Rattigan, which spanned some ten films beginning in 1939 with *French Without Tears*, based on the Rattigan play, and ending in 1964 with Asquith's final film, *The Yellow Rolls-Royce*, scripted by Rattigan. Indeed, apart from their lengthy professional relationship, there are two related aspects of their respective profiles as artists that also draw them together. Firstly, both are often seen as archetypal middle-class English artists, part of middlebrow culture, their work marked by qualities such as 'restraint', 'inhibition', and 'understatement', especially in relation to the depiction of emotional life. Secondly, both have been discussed by gay critics, partly based on public biographical information, and partly on the intrinsic qualities of their work, especially those noted above which relate to emotional expression.

Both fell out of critical favour during the 1950s in the face of the apparently more radical and socially sensitive currents of drama and film which emerged in the 1950s. Lindsay Anderson had launched a general attack on British cinema in the 1950s, characterising it as 'snobbish, anti-intelligent, emotionally inhibited, wilfully blind to the conditions and problems of the present, dedicated to an out-of-date, exhausted national ideal'.[15] During the same period, somewhat similar critical comments were directed at the London stage – Rattigan's home – with Kenneth Tynan complaining that in the typical West End play 'the inhabitants belong to a social class derived from romantic novels, and partly from the playwright's vision of the leisured life he will lead after the play is a success – this being the only effort of imagination he is called upon to make'.[16] Reference to outdated national ideals, and to visions of a leisured life, though not completely accurate in respect of either artist, certainly capture aspects of the somewhat elevated social worlds that are often the focus of their plays and films and, in the context of the grittier, 'realist' plays and films which emerged in the theatre and cinema of the 1950s, the work of both artists began to look a little old-fashioned and perhaps out of touch. Rattigan's work was challenged by the plays of John Osborne and Shelagh Delaney, by *Look back in Anger* (1956) and *A Taste of Honey* (1958); indeed after attending the first night of the former, Rattigan had suggested that Osborne was effectively saying, 'Look, Ma, I'm not Terence Rattigan.'[17] In a similar vein, Asquith's glossy, international films of the 1960s, *The V.I.P.s* and *The Yellow Rolls-Royce*, looked somewhat dated in the era of the 'kitchen sink' narratives such as *Room at the Top* (Jack Clayton, 1959) and *Saturday Night and Sunday Morning* (Karel Reisz, 1960).

Neither Asquith nor Rattigan explicitly addressed homosexual issues in their work, which is understandable given the social and moral climate in which they worked and the systems of censorship which controlled their work. In fact, as Stephen Bourne has noted, 'in most of his films, Asquith seems preoccupied with the breakdown of hetero-sexual relationships'.[18] Indeed, it is a theme which can be traced back to his first film, *Shooting Stars*, and one which is also present in his final film, *The Yellow Rolls-Royce*. The case is much the same with Rattigan in a number of his best-known plays – *French Without Tears*, *The Browning Version*, *The Deep Blue Sea* – also focusing on heterosexual relation-ships. Yet their plays and films have been understood in gay terms. Partly, this is a matter of biography: Rattigan was certainly a practising homosexual though the situation is less clear with Asquith.[19] Partly, it is a matter of the textual characteristics of their work which might be read for the covert meanings which lie behind the ostensible subject matter. The paradigmatic film for this critical approach is David Lean's *Brief Encounter*, its gay credentials underwritten partly by its origins in a short play by Noël Coward, but also by the film's mixture of intensity and restraint, and its analysis of a romance doomed in a climate of social and moral disapproval. As Andy Medhurst has suggested, '*Brief Encounter* shows Noël Coward displacing his own fears, anxieties and pessimism about the possibility of a fulfilled sexual relationship within an oppress-ively homophobic culture by transposing them into a heterosexual context.'[20] Similarly, Richard Dyer has suggested that the film's 'subject matter – forbidden love in ordinary lives – makes an obvious appeal to gay readers'.[21]

Comparable claims have been made for a number of Asquith's films and it is also possible to pick one's way through Asquith's filmography highlighting potential gay elements as Stephen Bourne has done. *Tell England* depicts an intense relationship between the two public school-boy heroes as they fight in the trenches and there is a brief appearance of 'effeminate autograph hunter' in *Dance Pretty Lady*.[22] *Pygmalion* has a few stereotypical gay figures – hairdressers, a lesbian couple – together with Professor Higgins and Colonel Pickering, a 'bachelor couple'; *French Without Tears* is centred on a group of young men struggling with the wiles of a subversively heterosexual woman. Bourne has also identified homoeroticism in the war feature, *We Dive at Dawn*, the hint of a lesbian character, Harry Somerford's sister, Kate (Cathleen Nesbitt) in *Fanny by Gaslight*, and has suggested that *The Way to the Stars* is 'a fascinating study of the frailty of masculinity'.[23] Asquith's post-war work can also be drawn into the discussion with the hopelessly repressed Crocker-Harris in *The Browning Version*, Oscar Wilde and *The Importance of Being Earnest*, with its deceptions and double-life theme, and *The Young Lovers*, a film described by Bourne as 'a glorious, passionate plea for the understanding of forbidden love', and comparable to *Brief Encounter* in its susceptibility to a gay reading.[24]

Asquith's films can be understood in a variety of contexts – the avant-garde, the realist, the theatrical, middlebrow culture, the covert gay text, the mid-Atlantic film – but they have often been seen as typically British or, perhaps one should say, English. In an article written towards the end of Asquith's career, Peter Cowie suggested that the director 'is remarkable because ever since 1927 he has made films almost solely in, and about, England'.[25] Indeed, many of his films are concerned with aspects of English life, culture, mores and behaviour. *Tell England* is about young Englishmen fresh from public school, fighting in the First World War, *Pygmalion*, with its middle-class English professor of linguistics and cockney heroine, is about the specificities of the English language, and its relationship to class and culture, and *French Without Tears* is a light study of the sexuality of young Englishmen abroad. *The Way to the Stars* contrasts the middle-class RAF officers during wartime with their relatively classless American counterparts, while Victorian Britain, its morality and hypocrisy, is dissected in *Fanny by Gaslight* in a melodramatic mode. Asquith's post-war films reflect upon the Edwardian middle-class family, its morality and politics, in *The Winslow Boy*; on an English public school centred on a restrained and repressed school-master in *The Browning Version*; on the leisured life of the idle rich in *The Importance of Being Earnest*; and on the resonantly English world of cricket in *The Final Test*. Such films, when looked at as a composite, offer a series of meditations on the national character, on national identity, on the strengths as well as the foibles and eccentricities of the English character.

The concept of Englishness itself is broached quite explicitly in a number of the films Asquith made during the Second World War. *The Demi-Paradise, A Welcome to Britain*, and *The Way to the Stars* were made at a time when matters of national definition were embodied in one of the key aims of wartime propaganda – the representation of 'what we are fighting for'. Indeed, Raymond Durgnat has described *The Way to the Stars*, a film that 'British critics pretended to think was a tribute to Anglo-American unity', as, in fact, 'a placidly immodest tale about the Americans coming to admire everything traditionally English'.[26] The English world embodied in the titles cited above is, of course, a very particular one: the world of the English middle classes, often the upper-middle classes, albeit slightly punctured in *Pygmalion* by the working-class Doolittles, though both daughter and father are duly elevated up the class ladder in the course of the film. The image of Asquith as a chronicler of the 'rich and empty-headed'[27] is at least partly accurate, and is an image embodied in the titles of his final films, *The V.I.P.s* and *The Yellow Rolls-Royce*.

Yet Asquith's films do occasionally move away from the affluent, English middle-class world and stray into the 'lower depths'. *Underground* is centred on the intertwined lives and loves of a group of young working-class men and women including a shop assistant and an underground worker, two of the central characters in *A Cottage on Dartmoor* work in a hairdressing salon, *The Lucky Number* is about a professional footballer in the days when that was a working-class job, *We Dive at Dawn* has an array of characters drawn from across the class boundaries typical of a wartime film, and the central character of *The Woman in Question* is a fairground entertainer. A number of Asquith's films also move away from England and the English entirely. *Moscow Nights* is set in pre-revolutionary Russia during the First World War, *Freedom Radio*, in Nazi Germany towards the end of the 1930s, *Uncensored* is set in German-occupied Belgium, and *Two Living, One Dead*, in Sweden. *The Young Lovers* and *Orders to Kill*, although set entirely or partly in England, are centred on foreigners, with British characters playing only incidental roles.

Richard Dyer has drawn attention to 'three qualities of a certain strain of British cinema: 'theatricality, realism and the "filmic"'. Together, he suggests, they 'constitute for critical common sense both what British cinema does aspire to, and, for most, what it also should aspire to'.[28] These qualities have a marked presence in Asquith's cinema:

'theatricality' in the numerous drama adaptations from *Pygmalion* to *Libel*; 'realism' in his wartime pictures in particular but also evident an early film such as *Underground*; the 'filmic' in his varied and inventive uses of the techniques of cinema again evident from his silent pictures onwards. Yet, the characterisation of Asquith as a middlebrow, 'quality' film-maker, accurate in many respects, does need to be set alongside his achievements in what, for many, would be considered lesser films – genre pieces such as *The Lucky Number, Cottage to Let, Fanny by Gaslight, The Woman in Question, The Net*, and *The Young Lovers*. The genteel image of the director may be the one which locates his work in the respectable traditions of 'quality' British cinema, but something of the vigour of the popular also crept into his profile through the less prestigious routine assignments.

Notes

1 P. Noble, *Anthony Asquith* (London: British Film Institute, 1951), p. 7.
2 *Northern Despatch* (21.5.51) – in Asquith Special Collection, British Film Institute, Item 28, Cuttings Scrapbook for *The Browning Version*.
3 See R. J. Minney, *Puffin Asquith* (London: Leslie Frewin, 1973), pp. 118–19.
4 *What's On* (22.9.50) – in Asquith Special Collection, Item 28, Cuttings Scrapbook for *The Browning Version*.
5 *Kine Weekly* (14.5.53), p. 26.
6 A. Lovell and J. Hillier, *Studies in Documentary* (London: Secker and Warburg/ British Film Institute, 1972), p. 35.
7 N. Thomas, Asquith entry, *International Dictionary of Films and Film Makers 2*, Second Edition (London: St. James Press), p. 33.
8 *Ibid.*
9 See L. Eisner, *The Haunted Screen* (London: Secker and Warburg, 1973), Ch. 8.
10 A. L. Vargas, 'British Films and their Audience', *Penguin Film Review*, 8 (1949), p. 71.
11 B. McFarlane, 'Outrage: *No Orchids for Miss Blandish*', in S. Chibnall and R. Murphy (eds), *British Crime Cinema* (London: Routledge, 1999), pp. 41–2 (emphasis in original).
12 L. Napper, 'British Cinema and the Middlebrow', in J. Ashby and A. Higson (eds), *British Cinema, Past and Present* (London: Routledge, 2000), p. 110.
13 J. Baxendale and C. Pawling, *Narrating the Thirties. A Decade in the Making: 1930 to the Present* (London: Macmillan Press, 1996), pp. 49–50.
14 R. Durgnat, *A Mirror for England. British Movies from Austerity to Affluence* (London: Faber & Faber, 1970), p. 192.
15 L. Anderson, 'Get Out and Push', in T. Maschler (ed.), *Declaration* (Port Washington, NY and London: Kennikat Press, 1957), p. 139.
16 Quoted in D. Shellard, *British Theatre Since the War* (New Haven and London: Yale University Press, 1999), p. 35.
17 G. Wansell, *Terence Rattigan. A Biography* (London: Fourth Estate, 1995), p. 270.
18 S. Bourne, *Brief Encounters. Lesbians and Gays in British Cinema 1930–1971* (London: Cassell, 1996) p. 13.

19 See Minney, *Puffin Asquith*, Ch. 23.

20 A. Medhurst, 'That special thrill: *Brief Encounter*, homosexuality and authorship', *Screen* 32:2, Summer (1991), p. 198.

21 R. Dyer, *Brief Encounter* (London: British Film Institute, 1993), p. 11.

22 *Ibid.*, p. 9.

23 Bourne, *Brief Encounters*, p. 75.

24 *Ibid.*, p. 116.

25 P. Cowie, 'This England', *Films and Filming*, October (1963), p. 13.

26 Durgnat, *A Mirror for England*, p. 14.

27 R. Murphy, *Sixties British Cinema* (London: BFI Publishing, 1992), p. 265.

28 Dyer, *Brief Encounter*, p. 43.

Filmography

Boadicea 1926, 7,915 ft., b/w

Production company: British Instructional Films
Studio: Cricklewood Studios
Producer: H. Bruce Woolfe
Director: Sinclair Hill
Screenplay: Sinclair Hill, Anthony Asquith
Photography: Jack Parker
Art director: Walter Murton
Stunts: Anthony Asquith
Studio: Cricklewood Studios
Leading players: Ray Raymond (Burrus), Clifford Heatherley (Catus Deci-
    anus), Phyllis Neilson-Terry (Boadicea), Lilian Hall-Davis (Emmelyn),
    Clifford McLaglen (Marcus), Sybil Rhoda (Blondicca), Cyril McLaglen
    (Madoc)

Shooting Stars 1928, 7,089 ft., b/w

Directors: A.V. Bramble, Anthony Asquith
Production company: British Instructional Films
Producer: H. Bruce Woolfe
Screenplay: Anthony Asquith, John Orton, from a story by Asquith
Photography: Karl Fischer
Art director: Ian Campbell-Gray
Art director: Walter Murton
Studio: Cricklewood Studios
Leading players: Annette Benson (Mae Feather), Brian Aherne (Julian
    Gordon), Donald Calthrop (Andy Wilks), Chili Bouchier (Winnie), Wally
    Patch (Property Man), David Brooks (Turner), Ella Daincourt
    (Ashphodel Smythe), Tubby Phillips (Fatty)

Underground 1928, 7282 ft., b/w

Production company: British Instructional Films
Producer: H. Bruce Woolfe
Director: Anthony Asquith
Assistant director: Hal Martin
Screenplay: Anthony Asquith
Photography: Stanley Rodwell, Karl Fischer
Art director: Ian Campbell-Gray
Studio: Cricklewood Studios, Elstree Studios
Leading players: Elissa Landi (Nell), Brian Aherne (Bill), Norah Baring (Kate), Cyril McLaglen (Bert)

The Runaway Princess (Alternative titles: _Priscilla's fart ins glück, Princess Priscilla's Fortnight_) 1929, 7053 ft., b/w

Production company: British Instructional Films, Laenderfilm (Germany)
Producer: H. Bruce Woolfe
Director: Anthony Asquith, Fritz Wendhausen
Assistant director: Victor A. Peers
Screenplay: Anthony Asquith, from the novel _Princess Priscilla's Fortnight_ by Elizabeth Russell
Photography: G.A. Viragh, Henry Harris
Art director: Ian Campbell-Gray, Herman Warm
Studio: Laenderfilm Studios (Berlin), Welwyn Studios
Leading players: Mady Christians (Princess Priscilla), Paul Cavanagh (Prince of Savona), Fred Rains (the professor), Norah Baring (the forger), Claude H. Beerbohm (the detective)

A Cottage on Dartmoor (_Fången 53_ [Sweden], _Escaped from Dartmoor_ [USA]) 1929, 114 min., b/w

Production company: British Instructional Films
Producer: H. Bruce Woolfe
Director: Anthony Asquith
Assistant director: A. Frank Bundy
Screenplay: Anthony Asquith, from a story by Herbert Price
Photography: Stanley Rodwell, Axel Lindblom
Art director: Ian Campbell-Gray, Arthur Woods
Music/Music Conductor: William HodgsonStudio: Welwyn Studios
Leading players: Hans Adalbert von Schlettow (farmer Harry Stevens), Uno Henning (Joe Ward), Norah Baring (Sally), Judd Green (customer), Anthony Asquith (bespectacled man in cinema)

Tell England (The Battle of Gallipoli [USA]) 1931, 88 min., b/w

Production company: British Instructional Films
Producer: H. Bruce Woolfe
Director: Anthony Asquith, Geoffrey Barkas
Assistant director: Teddy Baird
Screenplay: Anthony Asquith, from the Ernest Raymond novel *Tell England*
Additional dialogue: A. P. Herbert
Photography: Jack Parker, Stanley Rodwell, James E. Rogers
Editor: Mary Field
Art director: Arthur Woods
Sound recording: A. F. Birch
Sound editor: Victor A. Peers
Studio: Welwyn Studios
Leading players: Carl Harbord (Edgar Doe), Tony Bruce (Rupert Ray), Fay
  Compton (Mrs Ray), Dennis Hoey (Padre), C.M. Hallard (Colonel),
  Frederick Lloyd (Captain Harding), Gerald Rawlinson (Lt. Doon), Lionel
  Hedges (Sims), Sam Wilkinson (Private Booth), Wally Patch (Instruction
  sergeant), Hubert Harben (Mr Ray)

Dance Pretty Lady (Alternative Title: *Carnival*) 1932, 64 min., b/w

Production company: British Instructional Films
Producer: H. Bruce Woolfe
Director: Anthony Asquith
Assistant director: Teddy Baird
Screenplay: Anthony Asquith, from the Compton Mackenzie novel *Carnival*
Additional dialogue: A. P. Herbert
Photography: Jack Parker
Art director: Ian Campbell-Gray
Music director: John Reynders
Choreographer and technical adviser on ballet sequences: Frederick Ashton
Sound recording: Victor A. Peers, A. F. Birch
Studio: Welwyn Studios
Leading players: Ann Casson (Jenny Pearl), Carl Harbord (Maurice Avery),
  Michael Hogan (Fuzz Castleton), Moore Marriott (Charles Raeburn),
  Flora Robson (Florrie Raeburn), Leonard Brett (Alf Raeburn), Norman
  Claridge (Jack Danby), Sunday Wilshin (Irene), Rene Ray (Elsie
  Crawford), Marie Rambert and the Marie Rambert Corps de Ballet

Marry Me (English-language version of *Mädchen zum Heiraten*
[Germany]) 1932, 85 min., b/w

Production company: Gainsborough PicturesProducer: Michael Balcon
Director: Wilhelm Thiele
Screenplay: Anthony Asquith, Angus MacPhail

Photography: Bernard Knowles
Studio: Gainsborough Studios
Leading players: Renate Müller (Ann Linden), Harry Green (Sigurd Bernstein), George Robey (Aloysius Novak), Ian Hunter (Robert Hart), Maurice Evans (Paul Hart), Charles Hawtrey (Billy Hart), Billy Carlyll (Meyer), Charles Carson (Korten), Viola Lyel (Frau Krause), Sunday Wilshin (Ida Brun), Roland Culver (Tailor)

Letting in the Sunshine 1933, 73 min., b/w

Production company: British International Pictures
Producer: John Maxwell
Director: Lupino Lane
Assistant director:
Editor: E. B. Jarvis
Screenplay: Frank Miller, from a story by Anthony Asquith
Photography: Jack Cox, Bryan Langley
Art director: David Rawnsley
Music: Idris Lewis
Studio: Gainsborough Studios
Leading players: Albert Burdon (Nobby Green), Molly Lamont (Lady Anne), Henry Mollinson (Duvine), Tonie Edgar-Bruce (Lady Warminster)

The Lucky Number 1933, 72 min., b/w

Production company: Gainsborough Pictures
Producer: Michael Balcon
Director: Anthony Asquith
Assistant director: Marjorie Gaffney
Screenplay: Anthony Asquith, Douglas Furber, from a story by Franz Schulz
Photography: Günther Krampf, Derick Williams
Art director: Alex Vetchinsky
Music: Mischa Spoliansky Studio: Gainsborough Studios
Leading players: Clifford Mollinson (Percy Gibbs), Gordon Harker (Bert), Joan Wyndham (Winnie), Frank Pettingell (Mr Brown), Joe Hayman (Douglas Macdonald), Hetty Hartley (Flora Macdonald) Esmé Percy (the chairman), Alfred Wellesley (the pickpocket), Hay Petrie (the photographer), Wally Patch (bookie), and members of Arsenal FC

Youth Will be Served 1933, 6 min., b/w

Production company: National Film Corporation
Director: Anthony Asquith
Photography: Derick Williams
Music: Louis Levy

Recordist: A. L. M. Douglas
Recorded at Shepherd's Bush Studios
Leading players: Gordon Harker (delivery man), Martita Hunt (school
teacher), Marjorie Hume (mother), Desmond Tester

The Unfinished Symphony 1934, 90 min., b/w

Production company: Cine-Allianz-Tonfilmproduktion, Gaumont-British
Producer: Willi Forst, Arnold Pressburger
Director (German version): Willi Forst
Director (English version): Anthony Asquith
Screenplay: Benn Levy
Photography: Franz Planer
Leading players: Marta Eggerth (Caroline Esterhazy), Hans Jaray (Franz
Schubert), Cecil Humphreys (Salieri), Helen Chandler (Emmie Passenter),
Ronald Squire (Count Esterhazy), Esmé Percy (Huettenbrenner)

Forever England 1935 (Born for Glory [USA]) 79 min., b/w

Production company: Gaumont-British
Producer: Michael Balcon
Director: Walter Forde
Second Unit director: Anthony Asquith
Assistant director: Ralph D. Hogg
Editor: Otto LudwigDesigner: Alfred Jünge
Screenplay: John Orton from the novel by C. S. Forrester
Photography: Bernard Knowles
Music director: Louis Levy
Studio: Shepherd's Bush Studios
Naval Advisor: R. W. Wilkinson
Leading players: John Mills (Albert Brown), Betty Balfour (Elisabeth Brown),
Lt. Barry MacKay (Somerville), Jimmy Hanley (Ginger)

Moscow Nights 1935 (I Stand Condemned [USA]) 74 min., b/w

Production company: London Film Productions, Capitol Film Corporation
Producer: Alexis Granowsky
Director: Anthony Asquith
Editor: William Hornbeck, Francis D. Lyon
Art director: Vincent Korda
Screenplay: Anthony Asquith, Erich Siepman, from the novel by Pierre
Benoît
Photography: Philip Tannura
Studio: Worton Hall, Denham
Leading players: Harry Baur (Peter Brioukow), Laurence Olivier (Captain

Ivan Ignatoff), Penelope Dudley Ward (Natasha), Robert Cochran (Polonsky), Morton Selten (General Kovrin), Athene Seyler (Madame Anna Sabine), Walter Hudd (doctor), Kate Cutler (Madame Kovrin), C. M. Hallard (court president), Edmund Willard (prosecutor), Charles Carson (officer of the defence), Morland Graham (Brioukow's servant), Hay Petrie (spy), Anthony Quayle (officer)

The Story of Papworth: The Village of Hope 1935, 18 min., b/w

Director: Anthony Asquith
Producer and scenario: Major Lloyd
Photography: Francis Carver
Epilogue: C. Aubrey Smith
Leading players: Madeleine Carroll (the introducer), Gordon Harker (a working man – Henry Hawkins), Mabel Constanduros (Mrs Hawkins), Nicholas Hannen (the Vicar), Owen Nares (Dr Strong, the doctor)

Lest We Forget 1937, 8 min., b/w

Production company: British Pictorial Productions
Producer: Major Lloyd
Director: Anthony Asquith
Leading players: Flora Robson (the visitor), Derrick de Marney (a clerk), Nicholas Hannen (a settler), Charles Laughton (appellant)

Pygmalion 1938, 96 min., b/w

Production company: Pascal Film Productions
Producer: Gabriel Pascal
Director: Leslie Howard, Anthony Asquith
Assistant director: Teddy Baird
Editor: David Lean
Screenplay: George Bernard Shaw, W. P. Lipscomb, Cecil Lewis, Ian Dalrymple, from the play by Shaw
Photography: Harry Stradling
Art director: Laurence Irving, John Bryan
Music: Arthur Honegger
Studio: Pinewood Studios
Leading players: Leslie Howard (Professor Henry Higgins), Wendy Hiller (Eliza Doolittle), Wilfred Lawson (Doolittle), Marie Löhr (Mrs Higgins), Scott Sunderland (Colonel Pickering), Jean Cadell (Mrs Pearce), David Tree (Freddy Hill), Everley Gregg (Mrs Eynsford Hill), Leueen MacGrath (Clara), Esmé Percy (Count Aristid Karpathy), Violet Vanbrugh (ambassadress), Iris Hoey (Ysabel, society reporter), Viola Tree (Perfide, society reporter), Irene Brown (Duchess), Kate Cutler (grand old lady)

French Without Tears 1939, 84 min., b/w

Production company: Two Cities/Paramount Pictures
Producer: Mario Zampi
Director: Anthony Asquith
Production manager: Theo Lageard
Assistant director: Teddy Baird
Supervising editor: David Lean
Screenplay: Anatole de Grunwald, Ian Dalrymple, Terence Rattigan, from
the Rattigan play
Photography: Bernard Knowles
Camera operator: Jack Hildyard
Art director: Paul Sheriff
Assistant art director: Carmen Dillon
Music: Nicholas Brodszky Studio: Pinewood Studios
Leading players: Ray Milland (Alan Howard), Ellen Drew (Diana Lake),
Janine Darcey (Jacqueline Maingot), David Tree (Chris Neilan), Roland
Culver (Commander Bill Rogers), Guy Middleton (Brian Curtis), Kenneth
Morgan (Kenneth Lake), Jim Gérald (professor Maingot), Margaret
Yarde (Marianne), Toni Gable (Chi-Chi)

Guide Dogs for the Blind 1939, b/w

Production company: Guide Dogs for the Blind Association
Director: Anthony Asquith
With Leslie Banks, Vivien Leigh, Lee Tracy

Channel Incident 1940, 5 min., b/w

Production company: Ministry of Information
Producer: Anthony Asquith
Director: Anthony Asquith
Screenplay: Dallas Bower
Director of photography: Bernard Knowles
Editor: Ralph Kemplen
Studio: D and P Studios
Players: Peggy Ashcroft (woman), Gordon Harker (Ferris), Robert Newton
(Tanner), Kenneth Griffith (Johnny)

Freedom Radio (A Voice in the Night [USA]) 1940, 90 min., b/w

Production company: Two Cities Films/Columbia Pictures
Producer: Mario Zampi
Associate producer: Theo Lageard
Production manager: John Cornfield

Director: Anthony Asquith
Assistant director: Michael Anderson, Stanley Irving
Continuity: Peggy McClafferty
Casting director: Noel Arthur
Original story: Wolfgang Wilhelm, George Campbell
Screenplay and dialogue: Jeffrey Dell, Basil Woon, Anatole de Grunwald
Scenario contributions: Roland Pertwee, Bridget Boland, Louis Golding, Gordon Wellesley
Photography: Bernard Knowles
Camera: Cyril Knowles
Editor: Reginald Beck
Art director: Paul Sheriff
Assistant art director: Carmen Dillon
Music: Nicholas Brodszky
Musical director: Muir Mathieson
Studio: Shepperton
Leading players: Clive Brook (Dr Karl Roder), Diana Wynyard (Irena Roder), Raymond Huntley (Rabenau), Derek Farr (Hans Glazer), Joyce Howard (Elly Schmidt), Howard Marion-Crawford (Kummer), John Penrose (Otto), Morland Graham (Father Landbach), Ronald Squire (Rudolf Spiedler), Reginald Beckwith (Emil Fenner), Clifford Evans (Dressler), Bernard Miles (Captain Muller), Gibb McLaughlin (Doctor Weiner), Muriel George (Hanna), Martita Hunt (Frau Lehmann), Hay Petrie (Sebastian), Manning Whiley (SS trooper), Katie Johnson (Granny Schmidt), George Hayes (policeman), Everley Gregg (Maria Tattenheim), Marie Ault (woman customer), Abraham Sofaer (Heini), Joan Hickson (Katie), Pat McGrath (Kurt), Ken Annakin (Radio announcer)

Rush Hour 1941, 6 min., b/w

Production company: Twentieth Century Productions Ltd
Producer: Edward Black
Director: Anthony Asquith
Script: Arthur Boys, Rodney Ackland
Photography: Arthur Crabtree
Editor: Alfred Roome
Leading players: Muriel George (Violet), Joan Sterndale-Bennett (Lil), Beatrice Varley (shopper), Charles Victor (inspector), Hay Petrie (conductor)

Cottage to Let (Bombsight Stolen [USA]) 1941, 90 min., b/w

Production company: Gainsborough Pictures
Producer: Edward Black
Director: Anthony Asquith

Assistant director: Michael Anderson
Screenplay: Anatole de Grunwald. John Orton, from the play by Geoffrey Kerr
Photography: Jack Cox
Editor: R. E. Dearing
Art director: Alex Vetchinsky
Musical director: Louis Levy
Studio: Shepherd's Bush Studios
Leading players: John Mills (Flight Lieutenant George Perry), Leslie Banks (John Barrington), Michael Wilding (Alan Trently), Alastair Sim (Charles Dimble), Jeanne de Casalis (Mrs Barrington), Carla Lehmann (Helen Barrington), George Cole (Ronald Mittsby)

Quiet Wedding 1941, 80 min., b/w

Production company: Conqueror Productions, Paramount British Productions
Producer: Paul Soskin
Director: Anthony Asquith
Assistant director: Michael Anderson
Screenplay: Terence Rattigan, Anatole de Grunwald, from the play by Esther McCracken
Photography: Bernard Knowles
Editor: Reginald Beck
Art director: Paul Sheriff
Assistant art director: Carmen Dillon
Music: Nicholas Brodszky
Studio: Shepherd's Bush
Leading players: Margaret Lockwood (Janet Royd), Derek Farr (Dallas Chaytor), Marjorie Fielding (Mildred Royd), A. E. Matthews (Arthur Royd), David Tomlinson (John Royd), Sydney King (Denys Royd), Margaretta Scott (Marcia Royd), Muriel Pavlow (Miranda), Athene Seyler (Aunt Mary Jarrow), Peggy Ashcroft (Flower Lisle), Roland Culver (Boofy Ponsonby)

Uncensored (Alternative title: *We Shall Rise Again*) 1942 108 min., b/w

Production company: Gainsborough Pictures
Producer: Edward Black
Director: Anthony Asquith
Screenplay: Rodney Ackland, Terence Rattigan, adaptation/story by Wolfgang Wilhelm, based on novel by Oscar Millard
Photography: Arthur Crabtree
Editor: R. E. Dearing
Art director: Alex Vetchinsky
Music director: Louis Levy
Studio: Shepherd's Bush

Leading players: Eric Portman (Delage), Phyllis Calvert (Julie Lanvin), Griffith Jones (Father de Gruyte), Peter Glenville (Charles Neele)

A Welcome to Britain 1943, 60 min., b/w

Production company: Strand Film company/Ministry of Information
Producer: Arthur Elton
Director: Anthony Asquith, Burgess Meredith
Screenplay: Burgess Meredith, Samuel Spewack
Photography: Jo Jago
Music: William Alwyn
Leading players: Burgess Meredith (himself), Felix Aylmer (the country schoolmaster), Carla Lehmann (the unknown girl), Bob Hope (himself), Beatrice Lillie, Beatrice Varley, Johnnie Schofield

We Dive at Dawn 1943, 98 min., b/w

Production company: Gainsborough Pictures
Producer: Edward Black
Director: Anthony Asquith
Story and screenplay: J. B. Williams, Val Valentine, Frank Launder
Photography: Jack Cox
Editing: R. E. Dearing
Art director: Walter Murton
Musical director: Louis Levy
Studio: Shepherd's Bush Studios
Leading players: John Mills (Lt Freddie Taylor), Eric Portman (L/Seaman Hobson), Reginald Purdell (CPO Dickie Dabbs), Niall MacGinnis (PO Mike Corrigan), Louis Bradfield (Lt Brace), Jack Watling (first officer)

The Demi-Paradise (Adventure for Two [USA]) 1943 115 min., b/w

Production company:
Producer: Anatole de Grunwald
Director: Anthony Asquith
Assistant director: George Pollock
Screenplay: Anatole de Grunwald
Photography: Bernard Knowles
Supervising editor: Jack Harris
Editor: Renee Woods
Supervising art director: Paul Sheriff
Art director: Carmen Dillon
Music: Nicholas Brodszky
Music director: Muir Mathieson
Studio: Denham Studios

Leading players: Laurence Olivier (Ivan Kouznetsoff), Penelope [Dudley] Ward (Ann Tisdall), Marjorie Fielding (Mrs Agnes Tisdall), Margaret Rutherford (Rowena Ventnor), Felix Aylmer (Mr Runalow), George Thorpe (Herbert Tisdall), Leslie Henson (himself), Guy Middleton (Richard Christie), Michael Shepley (Walford), Edie Martin (Miss Winifred Tisdall), Joyce Grenfell (Mrs Pawson) Jack Watling (Tom Sellars), John Laurie (British sailor), George Cole (Percy)

Two Fathers 1944, 13 min., b/w

Production company: Crown Film Unit
Producer: Arthur Elton
Director: Anthony Asquith
Script: Anthony Asquith, from a story by V. S. Pritchett
Photography: Jonah Jones
Editor: Terry Trench
Art director: Edward Carrick
Music: Clifton Parker
Sound recording: Ken Cameron
Studio: Crown Studios, Beaconsfield
Leading players: Bernard Miles (The Englishman), Paul Bonifas (The Frenchman

Fanny by Gaslight (Man of Evil [USA]) 1944, 108 min., b/w

Production company: Gainsborough Pictures
Producer: Edward Black
Director: Anthony Asquith
Screenplay: Doreen Montgomery, from the novel by Michael Sadlier
Additional dialogue: Aimee Stuart
Photography: Arthur Crabtree
Editing: R. E. Dearing
Art direction: John Bryan
Costumes: Elizabeth Haffenden
Music score: Cedric Mallabey
Music direction: Louis Levy
Studio: Gainsborough Studios
Leading players: Phyllis Calvert (Fanny), James Mason (Lord Manderstoke), Stewart Granger (Harry Somerford), Wilfred Lawson (Chunks), Jean Kent (Lucy Beckett), Margaretta Scott (Alicia), Ann Stephens (Fanny as a child), Gloria Sydney (Lucy as a child), Nora Swinburne (Mrs Hopwood), Cathleen Nesbitt (Kate Somerford), Helen Haye (Mrs Somerford), John Laurie (William Hopwood), Stuart Lindsell (Clive Seymore), Amy Veness (Mrs Heaviside)

The Way to the Stars (Johnny in the Clouds [USA]) 1945, 109 min., b/w

Production company: Two Cities Films
Producer: Anatole de Grunwald
Director: Anthony Asquith
Assistant director: George Pollock
Screenplay: Terence Rattigan, Anatole de Grunwald, from a scenario by
    Rattigan and Richard Sherman, poems by John Pudney
Photography: Derick Williams
Editor: Fergus McDonell
Supervising art director: Paul Sheriff
Art director: Carmen Dillon
Music: Nicholas Brodszky
Studio: Shepherd's Bush and Denham
Leading players: Michael Redgrave (David Archdale), John Mills (Peter
    Penrose), Rosamund John (Miss Todd), Douglass Montgomery (Johnny
    Hollis), Stanley Holloway (Mr Palmer), Renée Asherson (Iris Winter-
    ton), Felix Aylmer (Reverend Charles Moss), Basil Radford (Tiny Williams),
    Bonar Colleano (Joe Friselli), Trevor Howard (Squadron Leader Carter),
    Jean Simmons (a singer), Joyce Carey (Miss Winterton), Tryon Nichol
    (Colonel Rogers), Bill Rowbotham/Owen (Sergeant 'Nobby' Clarke),
    Johnnie Schofield (Jones, Penrose's batman)

While the Sun Shines 1947, 81 min., b/w

Production company: International Screenplays
Producer: Anatole de Grunwald
Associate producer: Teddy Baird
Director: Anthony Asquith
Assistant director: Jack Clayton
Screenplay: Terence Rattigan, Anatole de Grunwald, from the play by
    Rattigan
Director of photography: Jack Hildyard
Editor: Frederick Wilson
Art director: Tom Morahan
Music: Nicholas Brodszky
Leading players: Ronald Howard (the Earl of Harpenden), Barbara White
    (Lady Elizabeth Randall), Ronald Squire (the Duke of Ayr and Stirling),
    Brenda Bruce (Mabel Crum), Bonar Colleano (Joe Mulvaney), Michael
    Allan (Colbert), Miles Malleson (Horton), Margaret Rutherford (Dr
    Winifred Frye), Cyril Maude (old Admiral), Garry Marsh (Mr Jordan),
    Joyce Grenfell (Daphne),

The Winslow Boy 1948, 117 min., b/w

Production company: London Film Productions, British Lion Film Corporation
Producer: Anatole de Grunwald
Associate producer: Teddy Baird
Director: Anthony Asquith
Screenplay: Terence Rattigan, Anatole de Grunwald, from the Rattigan play
Director of photography: Freddie Young
Exterior photography: Osmond Borrodaile
Editor: Gerald Turney-Smith
Art director: Andre Andrejew
Music: William Alwyn
Leading players: Robert Donat (Sir Robert Morton), Cedric Hardwicke (Arthur
  Winslow), Neil North (Ronnie Winslow), Margaret Leighton (Catherine
  Winslow), Marie Löhr (Grace Winslow), Jack Watling (Dickie Winslow),
  Kathleen Harrison (Violet, the maid), Basil Radford (Desmond Curry),
  Francis L. Sullivan (attorney-general), Mona Washbourne (Miss Barnes)

The Woman in Question (*Five Angles on Murder* [USA]) 1950, 88 min., b/w

Production company: Javelin Films, Vic Films
Producer: Teddy Baird
Executive producer: Joseph Janni
Director: Anthony AsquithAss
Assistant director: George Pollock
Original story and screenplay: John Cresswell
Photography: Desmond Dickinson
Editor: John D. Guthridge
Art director: Carmen Dillon
Music: John Wooldridge
Studio: Pinewood Studios
Leading players: Jean Kent (Agnes 'Astra' Houston), Dirk Bogarde (Robert
  'Bob' Baker), John McCallum (Michael Murray), Susan Shaw (Catherine
  Taylor), Hermione Baddeley (Mrs. Finch), Charles Victor (Albert Pollard),
  Duncan MacRae (Superintendent Lodge), Lana Morris (Lana Clark), Joe
  Linnane (Chief Inspector Butler), Vida Hope (Shirley Jones), Duncan
  Lamont (Barney), Bobby Scroggins (Alfie Finch)

World Without Shadow 1950, b/w

Director: Anthony Asquith
Listed in the BFI's Film Index International, but no further credits or
  information available. There is also a title – *World Without Shadows* –
  listed in Gifford's *The British film catalogue. Vol. 2, Non-fiction film 1888–*

1994, produced by Rank Screen Services but with a 1960 release date. Both the BFI and Gifford mention St Dunstan's School for the Blind as the subject matter of the titles.

The Browning Version 1951, 90 min., b/w

Production company: Javelin Films
Producer: Teddy Baird
Director: Anthony Asquith
Assistant director: George Pollock
Screenplay: Terence Rattigan from his own play
Director of photography: Desmond Dickinson
Editor: John D. Guthridge
Art director: Carmen Dillon
Leading players: Michael Redgrave (Andrew Crocker-Harris), Jean Kent (Millie Crocker-Harris), Nigel Patrick (Frank Hunter), Ronald Howard (Gilbert), Brian Smith (Taplow), Wilfrid Hyde-White (Frobisher), Bill Travers (Fletcher)

The Importance of Being Earnest 1952, 92 min., col.

Production company: British Film-Makers, Javelin Films
Producer: Teddy Baird
Director: Anthony Asquith
Original play: Oscar Wilde
Director of photography: Desmond Dickinson
Technicolor colour consultant: Joan Bridge
Film editor: John D. Guthridge
Art director: Carmen Dillon
Music: Benjamin Frankel
Studio: Pinewood Studios
Leading players: Michael Redgrave (Ernest Worthing), Michael Denison (Algernon Moncrieff), Edith Evans (Lady Augusta Bracknell), Joan Greenwood (Gwendolen Fairfax), Dorothy Tutin (Cecily Cardew), Richard Wattis (Seton), Walter Hudd (Lane), Margaret Rutherford (Miss Letitia Prism), Miles Malleson (Canon Chasuble), Aubrey Mather (Merriman)

The Net (*Project M7* [USA]) 1952, 86 min., b/w

Production company: Javelin Films/Two Cities
Producer: Anthony Darnborough
Director: Anthony Asquith
Assistant director: George Pollock
Script: William Fairchild, from the novel by John Pudney
Director of Photography: Desmond Dickinson

Editor: Frederick Wilson
Art director: John Howell
Music: Benjamin Frankel
Studio: Pinewood Studios
Leading players: James Donald (Michael Heathley), Phyllis Calvert (Lydia Heathley), Herbert Lom (Alex Leon), Noel Willman (Dr Dennis Bord), Robert Beatty (Sam Seagram), Muriel Pavlow (Caroline Cartier), Walter Fitzgerald (Sir Charles Cruddock), Patric Doonan (Brian Jackson), Maurice Denham (Carrington), Marjorie Fielding (Mama), Cavan Watson (Ferguson), Herbert Lomas (George Jackson), Hartley Power (General Adams), Hal Osmond (Lawson), Hal Osmond (Fisher), Geoffrey Denton (Inspector Carter)

The Final Test 1953, 91 min., b/w

Production company: A.C.T. Films
Producer: R. J. Minney
Director: Anthony Asquith
Assistant director: Anthony Hearne
Screenplay/original TV Play: Terence Rattigan
Photography: William McLeod
Editor: Helga Cranston
Art director: R. Holmes Paul
Music/music conductor: Benjamin Frankel
Technical adviser: Alf Gover
Cricket commentary: John Arlott
Studio: Pinewood Studios
Leading players: Jack Warner (Sam Palmer), Ray Jackson (Reginald 'Reggie' Palmer), Robert Morley (Alexander Whitehead), Adrianne Allen (Aunt Ethel), Brenda Bruce (Cora), George Relph (Syd Thompson), Stanley Maxted (Senator), Joan Swinstead (Miss Fanshawe), John Glyn-Jones (Guinness drinker) and Len Hutton, Denis Compton, Alec Bedser, Godfrey Evans, Jim Laker, Cyril Washbrook (members of the England cricket team)

The Young Lovers (*Chance Meeting* [USA]) 1954, 95 min., b/w

Production company: Group Film Productions (Rank)
Producer: Anthony Havelock-Allan
Director: Anthony Asquith
Assistant director: Robert Asher
Screenplay: George Tabori, Robin Estridge
Director of photography: Jack Asher
Editor: Frederick Wilson
Art director: John Howell, John Box

Leading players: Odile Versois (Anna Szobek), David Knight (Ted Hutchens), David Kossoff (Anton Szobek), Joseph Tomelty (Moffatt), Theodore Bikel (Joseph), Paul Carpenter (Gregg Pearson), Peter Illing (Dr Weissbrod), John McLaren (Colonel Margetson), Jill Adams (Judy), Betty Marsden (Mrs Forrester)

Carrington VC (Court-Martial [USA]) 1954, 105 min., b/w

Production company: Romulus Films, Remus Films
Producer: Teddy Baird
Director: Anthony Asquith
Assistant director: Basil Keys
Screenplay: John Hunter, from the play by Dorothy and Campbell Christie
Director of photography: Desmond Dickinson
Editor: Ralph Kemplen
Art director: Wilfrid Shingleton
Studio: Shepperton Studios
Leading players: David Niven (Major 'Copper' Carrington, V.C.), Margaret Leighton (Valerie Carrington), Noëlle Middleton (Captain Alison Graham), Allan Cuthbertson (Lt.-Col. Henniker), Victor Maddern (Bombardier Owen), Raymond Francis (Major James Mitchell), Geoffrey Keen (The President, court-martial), Newton Blick (The Judge-Advocate, Mr Tester-Terry), Mark Dignam (the prosecuting officer), Robert Bishop (Captain Foljambe, Prosecutor's assistant), Maurice Denham (Lt.-Col Reeve), Laurence Naismith (Major R. E. Panton), Clive Morton (Lt.-Col T. B. Huxford), Michael Bates (Major Broke-Smith), Stuart Saunders (Sergeant Crane), John Glyn-Jones (Evans, the reporter), John Chandos (Rawlinson, the adjutant), R. S. M. Brittain (the Sergeant-Major)

On Such a Night 1955, 37 min., col.

Production company: Screen Audiences
Associate producer: Francis Edge
Production supervisor: Donald Wynne
Director: Anthony Asquith
Artistic director (Glyndebourne): Carl Ebert
Screenplay: Paul Dehn
Photography: Frank North
Editor: Anthony Harvey
Music director: Benjamin Frankel
Leading players: David Knight (David Cornell), Marie Löhr (Lady Falconbridge), Josephine Griffin (Virginia Ridley), Allan Cuthbertson, Peter Jones

Orders to Kill 1958, 111 min., b/w

Production company: Lynx Productions, British Lion Film Corporation
Producer: Anthony Havelock-Allan
Director: Anthony Asquith
Screenplay: Paul Dehn, from a story by Donald C. Downes
Adaptation: George St. George
Photography: Desmond Dickinson
Editor: Gordon Hales
Art director: John Howell
Music/Music Conductor: Benjamin Frankel
Studio: Shepperton Studios
Leading players: Paul Massie (Gene Summers), Eddie Albert (Major 'Mac' MacMahon), Lillian Gish (Mrs Summers), James Robertson Justice (Naval Commander), Leslie French (Marcel Lafitte), Irene Worth (Léonie), John Crawford (Kimball), Lionel Jeffries (Interrogator), Nicholas Phipps (lecturer lieutenant), Sandra Dorne (blonde), Jacques Brunius (Commander Morand), Robert Henderson (Colonel Snyder), Miki Iveria (Louise), Lillabea Gifford (Mauricette Lafitte), Anne Blake (Madame Lafitte)

The Doctor's Dilemma 1959, 98 min., col.

Production company: Comet Productions
Producer: Anatole de Grunwald
Associate producer: Pierre Rouve
Director: Anthony Asquith
Assistant director: Kip Gowans
Script: Anatole de Grunwald, from the play by George Bernard Shaw
Photography: Robert Krasker
Editor: Gordon HalesArt director: Paul Sheriff
Music: Joseph Kosma
Studio: MGM British Studios
Leading players: Dirk Bogarde (Louis Dubedat), Leslie Caron (Jennifer Dubedat), Alastair Sim (Cutler Walpole), Robert Morley (Sir Ralph Bloomfield Bonington), John Robinson (Sir Colenso Ridgeon), Felix Aylmer (Sir Patrick Cullen), Michael Gwynn (Dr Blenkinsop)

Libel 1959, 100 min., b/w

Production company: Comet Productions, MGM
Producer: Anatole de Grunwald
Associate producer: Pierre Rouve
Director: Anthony Asquith
Assistant director: David Middlemas

Screenplay: Anatole de Grunwald, Karl Tunberg, based on the play by Edward Wooll
Director of photography: Robert Krasker
Editor: Frank Clarke
Art director: Paul Sheriff
Music: Benjamin Frankel
Studio: MGM British Studios
Leading players: Dirk Bogarde (Sir Mark Loddon/Frank Welney/No. 15), Olivia de Havilland (Lady Margaret Loddon), Paul Massie (Jeffrey Buckenham), Robert Morley (Sir Wilfred), Wilfrid Hyde-White (Hubert Foxley), Anthony Dawson (Gerald Loddon), Richard Wattis (the judge), Richard Dimbleby (himself)

The Millionairess 1960, 90 min., col.

Production company: Twentieth Century-Fox/Anatole de Grunwald Ltd
Producers: Dimitri de Grunwald, Pierre Rouve
Director: Anthony Asquith
Assistant director: Frank Hollands
Screenplay: Wolf Mankowitz, Riccardo Aragno, from the play by George Bernard Shaw
Director of photography: Jack Hildyard
Editor: Anthony Harvey
Art director: Harry White
Music: Georges Van Parys
Studio: MGM British
Leading players: Sophia Loren (Epifania Parerga), Peter Sellers (Dr Ahmed El Kabir/Parerga), Alastair Sim (Julius Sagamore), Dennis Price (Dr Adrian Bland), Gary Raymond (Alastair), Alfie Bass (fish curer), Vittorio de Sica (Joe), Miriam Karlin (Maria, Joe's wife), Noel Purcell (professor), Virginia Vernon (Polly Smith), Basil Hoskins (first secretary), Graham Stark (butler), Diana Coupland (nurse)

Zero 1960, 12 min., b/w

Production company: Sapphire Films, American Film Theatre
Producer: Barney Rosset
Executive producer: Ely Landau
Director: Anthony Asquith
Screenplay: Samuel Beckett, based on his play *Mime Without Words*
Leading player: Zero Mostel (Zero)

Two Living, One Dead (Två Levande Och En Död [Sweden]) 1961, 92 min., b/w

Production company: Swan Productions, Wera
Producer: Teddy Baird
Associate producer: Lorens Marmstedt
Director: Anthony Asquith
Script: Anthony Asquith, Lindsay Galloway
Director of photography: Gunnar Fischer
Leading players: Virginia McKenna (Helen Berger), Patrick McGoohan (Berger), Bill Travers (Anderson), Alf Kjellin (Rogers), Peter Vaughan (Kester), Pauline Jameson (Miss Larsen), Michael Crawford (Nils), Noel Willman (Johnsson)

Guns of Darkness 1962, 102 min., b/w

Production company: Cavalcade Films, Associated British Picture Corporation, Concorde
Producer: Thomas Clyde
Executive producer: Ben Kadish
Director: Anthony Asquith
Assistant director: David Tomblin
Script: John Mortimer, from the novel by Francis Clifford
Photography: Robert Krasker
Editor: Frederick Wilson
Art director: John Howell
Music/music conductor: Benjamin Frankel
Leading players: Leslie Caron (Claire Jordan), David Niven (Tom Jordan), James Robertson Justice (Hugo Bryant), David Opatoshu (President Rivera), Eleanor Summerfield (Mrs Bastian), Ian Hunter (Dr Swann), Derek Godfrey (Hernandez), Richard Pearson (Bastian), Sandor Elès (Lt. Gomez)

The V.I.P.s 1963, 119 min., col.

Production company: Metro-Goldwyn-Mayer British Studios, Taylor Productions
Producer: Anatole de Grunwald
Production adviser: Margaret Booth
Associate producer: Roy Parkinson
Director: Anthony Asquith
Screenplay: Terence Rattigan
Director of photography: Jack Hildyard
Editor: Frank Clarke
Art director: William Kellner
Music: Miklós Rózsa

Studio: MGM British

Leading players: Elizabeth Taylor (Frances Andros), Richard Burton (Paul Andros), Louis Jourdan (Marc Champselle), Elsa Martinelli (Gloria Gritti), Margaret Rutherford (Duchess of Brighton), Maggie Smith (Miss Mead), Rod Taylor (Les Mangrum), Orson Welles (Max Buda), Linda Christian (Miriam Marshall), Dennis Price (Commander Millbank), Richard Wattis (Sanders), David Frost (reporter), Ronald Fraser (Joslin), Michael Hordern (airport director), Robert Coote (John Coburn), Martin Miller (Dr Schwutzbacher)

An Evening with the Royal Ballet 1963, 85 min., col.

Production company: B.H.E. Productions, Ltd
Producer: Anthony Havelock-Allan
Associate producer: Richard Goodwin
Directors: Anthony Havelock-Allan, Anthony Asquith
Assistant directors: René Dupont, Jack Causey, Michael Birket
Photography: Geoffrey Unsworth, Christopher Challis
Editors: Richard Marden, Jim Clark
Leading performers: Margot Fonteyn, Rudolf Nureyev

The Yellow Rolls-Royce 1964, 122 min., col.

Production company: Metro-Goldwyn-Mayer
Producer: Anatole de Grunwald
Associate producer: Roy Parkinson
Director: Anthony Asquith
Script: Terence Rattigan
Photography: Jack Hildyard
Editor: Frank Clarke
Art directors: Vincent Korda (European sequences), William Kellner (European sequences), Elliot Scott (English sequences)
Music: Riz Ortolani
Studio: MGM British
Leading players: Rex Harrison (Marquess of Frinton), Jeanne Moreau (Marchioness of Frinton), Edmund Purdom (John Fane), Moira Lister (Lady St Simeon), Roland Culver (Norwood), Michael Hordern (Harmsworth), Shirley MacLaine (Mae Jenkins), George C. Scott (Paolo Maltese), Alain Delon (Stefano), Art Carney (Joey), Ingrid Bergman (Mrs. Gerda Millett), Omar Sharif (Davich), Joyce Grenfell (Miss Hortense Astor)

Select bibliography

Aldgate, A. and Richards, J. (eds), *Britain Can Take It. The British Cinema in the Second World War*. Second Edition, Edinburgh, Edinburgh University Press, 1994.

Anderson, L., 'Angles of Approach', *Sequence* 2, Winter 1947, pp. 5–8.

Anderson, L., 'Get Out and Push', in T. Maschler (ed.), *Declaration*, Port Washington, NY and London, Kennikat Press, 1957, pp. 136–60.

Armes, R., *A Critical History of British Cinema*, London, Secker and Warburg, 1978.

Asquith, A., 'In Praise of Westerns', *The Picturegoer*, June 1928, pp. 12–13.

Asquith, A., 'Ballet and the Film', in C. Brahms (ed.), *Footnotes to the Ballet*, London, Peter Davies Ltd., 1936, pp. 231–52.

Asquith, A., 'Wanted – A Genius', *Sight and Sound*, Spring 1938, pp. 5–6.

Asquith, A., 'Realler than the Real Thing', *The Cine-Technician*, March–April 1945, pp. 26–7.

Asquith, A., 'A Style in Film Direction', *The Cine-Technician*, July–August 1951, pp. 94–5, 103.

Asquith, A., 'The Directorial Touch', *The Cine-Technician*, Sept.–Oct. 1951, pp. 126–7.

Asquith, A., 'Days with Chaplin. Hollywood Memories of the Nineteen Twenties', *The Cine-Technician*, Nov.-Dec. 1952, pp. 122–5.

Asquith, A., 'The Play's the Thing', *Films and Filming*, February 1959, p. 13.

Asquith, A., 'Shakespeare, Shaw and the screen', in G. Elvin, *Anthony Asquith. A Tribute*, London, British Film Institute, 1968.

Balcon, M., *My Life in Films*, London, Hutchinson, 1971.

Barr, C., *All Our Yesterdays*, London: BFI Publishing, 1986.

Barr, C., '"Madness, Madness!" The Brief Stardom of James Donald', in B. Babington (ed.), *British Stars and Stardom*, Manchester, Manchester University Press, 2001, pp. 155–66.

Belfrage, C., *All is Grist*, London, Parallax Press, n.d.

Bogarde, D., *Snakes and Ladders*, London, Chatto and Windus, 1978.

Brown, G., '"Sister of the Stage". British Film and British Theatre', in C. Barr (ed.), *All Our Yesterdays. 90 Years of British Cinema*, London, BFI Publishing, 1986.

Brown, G., 'A Cottage on Dartmoor', *Monthly Film Bulletin*, 47:504, January 1976, p. 14.

Brownlow, K., *David Lean*, London, Faber and Faber, 1996.

Carroll, N., 'Introducing Film Evaluation', in C. Gledhill and L. Williams (eds), *Reinventing Film Studies*, London: Arnold, 2000, pp. 265–78.

Chapman, J., *The British at War. Cinema, State and Propaganda*, London, I. B. Tauris, 1998.

Chibnall, S., 'Purgatory at the End of the Pier: Imprinting a Sense of Place through *Brighton Rock*', in A. Burton, T. O'Sullivan, and P. Wells (eds), *The Family Way. The Boulting Brothers and British Film Culture*, Trowbridge, Wiltshire, Flicks Books, 2000, pp. 134–42.

Costello, D. P., *The Serpent's Eye. Shaw and the Cinema*, Notre Dame and London, University of Notre Dame Press, 1965.

Cowie, P., 'This England', *Films and Filming*, October 1963, pp. 13–17.

Darlow, M. and Hodson, G., *Terence Rattigan. The Man and His Work*, London, Quartet Books, 1979.

de Grazia, V., 'Mass Culture and Sovereignty: The American Challenge to European Cinemas, 1920–1960', *Journal of Modern History* 6, March 1989, pp. 53–87.

Denison, M., *Double Act*, London, Michael Joseph, 1985.

Dickinson, M., 'The State and the Consolidation of Monopoly', in J. Curran and V. Porter (eds), *British Cinema History*, London, Weidenfeld and Nicolson, 1983, pp. 74–95.

Donald, J., Friedberg, A., and Marcus, L. (eds), *Close Up 1927–1933. Cinema and Modernism*, London, Cassell, 1998.

Drazin, C., *The Finest Years. British Cinema of the 1940s*, London, Andre Deutsch, 1998.

Drazin, C., *Korda. Britain's Only Movie Mogul*, London, Sidgwick and Jackson, 2002.

Dukore, B. F., *Bernard Shaw on Cinema*, Carbondale and Edwardsville, Southern Illinois University Press, 1997.

Durgnat, R., *A Mirror for England. British Movies from Austerity to Affluence*, London, Faber & Faber, 1970.

Dyer, R., *Brief Encounter*, London, British Film Institute, 1993.

Dyja, E. (ed.), *BFI Film and Television Handbook 2000*, London, British Film Institute, 1999.

Ellis, J., 'The Quality Film Adventure: British Critics and the Cinema 1942–1948', in A. Higson (ed.), *Dissolving Views*, London, Cassell, 1996, pp. 66–93.

Findlater, R., *Michael Redgrave Actor*, London, William Heinemann, Ltd., 1956.

Fussell, P., *The Great War and Modern Memory*, Oxford: Oxford University Press, 1977.

Gifford, D., *The British Film Catalogue 1895–1985*, Newton Abbot and London, David and Charles, 1986.

Gifford, D., *The British Film Catalogue. Vol. 2, Non-fiction Film 1888–1994*,

Fitzroy Dearborn, 2001.

Gledhill, C., 'Between Melodrama and Realism. Anthony Asquith's *Underground* and King Vidor's *The Crowd*', in J. Gaines (ed.), *Classical Hollywood Narrative. The Paradigm Wars*, Durham, NC, Duke University Press, 1992, pp. 129–67.

Gledhill, C., 'Taking it Forward: Theatricality and British Cinema Style in the 1920s', in L. Fitzsimmons and S. Street (eds), *Moving Performance. British Stage and Screen, 1890s–1920s*, Wiltshire, Flicks Books, 2000.

Gledhill, C., *Reframing British Cinema 1918–1928. Between Restraint and Passion*, London, BFI Publishing, 2003.

Greene, G., *The Pleasure Dome*, London, Secker and Warburg, 1972.

Guback, T., 'American Interests in the British Film Industry', *Quarterly Review of Economics and Business* 7, 1967, pp. 7–21.

Guback, T., *The International Film Industry*, Indiana, Indiana University Press, 1969.

Hardy, F. (ed.), *Grierson on Documentary*, London, Faber and Faber Ltd, 1966.

Harper, S., *Picturing the Past. The Rise and Fall of the British Costume Film*, London, BFI Publishing, 1994.

Harper, S. and Porter, V., 'Cinema audience tastes in 1950s Britain', *Journal of Popular British Cinema* 2, 1999, pp. 66–82.

Harper, S. and Porter, V., *British Cinema of the 1950s. The Decline of Deference*, Oxford, Oxford University Press, 2003.

Higson, A. (ed.), *Young and Innocent? The Cinema in Britain 1896–1930*, Exeter, University of Exeter Press, 2002.

Hollinger, K., 'Film Noir, Voice-Over, and the Femme Fatale', in A. Silver and J. Ursini (eds), *Film Noir Reader*, New York, Limelight Editions, 1996, pp. 243–58.

Holroyd, M., *Bernard Shaw. Vol. III 1898–1950. The Lure of Fantasy*, London, Chatto and Windus, 1999.

Houston, P., 'Review: *The Browning Version*', *Sight and Sound*, April 1951, p. 475.

Hunter, I. Q., 'Introduction. The Strange World of the British Science Fiction Film', in I. Q. Hunter (ed.), *British Science Fiction Cinema*, London, Routledge, 1999, pp. 1–15.

Hurd, G. (ed.), *National Fictions. World War Two in British Films and Television*, London, BFI Publishing, 1984.

Hynes, S., *A War Imagined. The First World War and English Culture*, London, Pimlico, 1990.

Jarvie, I., *Hollywood's Overseas Campaign. The North Atlantic Movie Trade, 1920–1950*, Cambridge, Cambridge University Press, 1992.

Kashner, S., 'A First-Class Affair', *Vanity Fair*, No. 515, July 2003, pp. 111–25.

Kennedy, H., 'How They Won the War', *Film Comment*, October 1996, pp. 24–34.

Kulik, K., *Alexander Korda. The Man Who Could Work Miracles*, London, Virgin Books, 1990.

Lacey, S., 'Too theatrical by half? *The Admirable Crichton* and *Look Back in Anger*', in I. MacKillop and N. Sinyard (eds), *British Cinema of the 1950s*, Manchester, Manchester University Press, 2003, pp. 157–67.

Landy, M., *British Genres. Cinema and Society, 1930–1960*, Princeton, New Jersey, Princeton University Press, 1991.

Low, R., *The History of the British Film 1928–1929*, London, George Allen & Unwin ltd., 1971.

Low, R., *Film-making in 1930s Britain*, London, George Allen & Unwin, 1985.

Mackenzie, S. P., *British War Films, 1939–1945*, London, Hambledon and London Ltd., 2001.

MacKillop, I. and Sinyard, N. (eds), *British Cinema of the 1950s*, Manchester, Manchester University Press, 2003.

McLaine, I., *Ministry of Morale. Home Front Morale and the Ministry of Information in World War II*, London, George Allen & Unwin, 1979.

Macnab, G., *J. Arthur Rank and the British Film Industry*, London, Routledge, 1993.

Manvell, R., 'Revaluations – 3. Shooting Stars, 1928', *Sight and Sound*, June 1950, pp. 172–4.

Massie, P., 'What Asquith Did For Me', *Films and Filming*, February 1958, pp. 11, 28.

McFarlane, B., 'Outrage: *No Orchids for Miss Blandish*', in S. Chibnall and R. Murphy (eds), *British Crime Cinema*, London, Routledge, 1999, pp. 37–50.

McFarlane, B., *An Autobiography of British Cinema*, London, Methuen, 1997.

McFarlane, B., *The Encyclopedia of British Film*, London, BFI/Methuen, 2003.

Minney, R. J., *Puffin Asquith*, London, Leslie Frewin, 1973.

Murphy, R., *Realism and Tinsel. Cinema and Society in Britain 1939–1949*, London, Routledge, 1989.

Murphy, R., *Sixties British Cinema*, London, BFI Publishing, 1992.

Murphy, R. (ed.), *The British Cinema Book*, London, BFI Publishing, Second Edition, 2001.

Murphy, R., *British Cinema and the Second World War*, London, Continuum, 2000.

Napper, L., 'British Cinema and the Middlebrow', in J. Ashby and A. Higson (eds), *British Cinema, Past and Present*, London, Routledge, 2000, pp. 110–23.

Neale, S., 'Art Cinema as Institution', *Screen* 22:1, 1981, pp. 11–39.

Noble, P., *Anthony Asquith*, London, British Film Institute, 1951.

Panofsky, E., 'Style and Medium in the Motion Pictures', in D. Talbot (ed.), *Film. An Anthology*, Berkeley and Los Angeles, University of California Press, 1967, pp. 15–32.

Paris, M. (ed.), *The First World War and Popular Cinema. 1914 to the Present*, New Brunswick, New Jersey, Rutgers University Press, 2000.

Pascal, V., *The Disciple and His Devil*, London, Michael Joseph, 1970.

PEP (Political and Economic Planning), *The British Film Industry*, London, PEP, 1952.

Perkins, V. F., *Film as Film*, London: Penguin Books, 1972.

Pronay, N., 'The British Post-bellum Cinema: A Survey of the Films Relating to World War II Made in Britain Between 1945 and 1960', *Historical Journal of Film, Radio and Television* 8:1, 1988, pp. 39–54.

Pudney, J., *Home and Away. An Autobiographical Gambit*, London, Michael Joseph, 1960.

Pudney, J., *Thank Goodness for Cake*, London, Michael Joseph, 1978.

Rattigan, N., *This is England. British Film and the People's War, 1939–1945*, Madison, Teaneck, Fairleigh Dickinson University Press, 2001.

Rattigan, T., 'Preface', in *The Collected Plays of Terence Rattigan*. Volume 1, London, Hamish Hamilton, 1953.

Rattigan, T., *The Browning Version*, London, Nick Hern Books, 1994.

Rattigan, T., *The Winslow Boy*, London, Nick Hern Books, 1994.

Rattigan, T., *French Without Tears*, London, Nick Hern Books, 1995.

Richards, J., *Visions of Yesterday*, London, Routledge & Kegan Paul, 1973.

Richards, J., *The Age of the Dream Palace. Cinema and Society in Britain 1930–1939*, London, Routledge and Kegan Paul, 1984.

Richards, J. and Sheridan, D. (eds), *Mass Observation at the Movies*, London, Routledge and Kegan Paul, 1987.

Richards, J., *Films and British National Identity. From Dickens to Dad's Army*, Manchester, Manchester University Press, 1997.

Rotha, P., *Celluloid. The Film Today*, London, Longman's Green, 1931.

Rotha, P., *The Film Till Now*, Middlesex, Spring Books, 1967.

Sanders, A., *The Short Oxford History of English Literature*, Oxford, Oxford University Press, 1994.

Shafer, S., *British Popular Films 1929–1939. The Cinema of Reassurance*, London, Routledge, 1997.

Slide, A., *'Banned in the USA'. British Films in the United States and their Censorship, 1933–1960*, London, I. B. Tauris, 1998.

Smith, M., 'Technological Determination, Aesthetic Resistance or A Cottage on Dartmoor. Goat-Gland Talkie or Masterpiece', *Wide Angle* 2:3, 1990, pp. 80–97.

Sontag, S., 'Theatre and Film', in *Styles of Radical Will*, New York, Delta Publishing Inc., 1970.

Thomas, N., 'Asquith', in *International Dictionary of Films and Film Makers* 2, Second Edition, London, St James Press, 1991, pp. 32–4.

Thomson, D., *The New Biographical Dictionary of Cinema*, Fourth Edition, London, Little, Brown, 2003.

Turim, M., *Flashbacks in Film*, New York and London, Routledge, 1989.

Vargas, A. L., 'British Films and their Audience', *Penguin Film Review* 8, 1949.

Wansell, G., *Terence Rattigan. A Biography*, London: Fourth Estate, 1996.

Index

Lightning Source UK Ltd.
Milton Keynes UK
UKOW06f0133301217
315174UK00011B/237/P